My Generation of Achievers

Their Social History

Stacy Diacou

iUniverse LLC
Bloomington

MY GENERATION OF ACHIEVERS
THEIR SOCIAL HISTORY

iUniverse books may be ordered through booksellers or by contacting:

iUniverse
1663 Liberty Drive
Bloomington, IN 47403
www.iuniverse.com
1-800-Authors (1-800-288-4677)

ISBN: 978-1-4759-8154-4 (sc)
ISBN: 978-1-4759-8155-1 (hc)
ISBN: 978-1-4759-8156-8 (e)

Printed in the United States of America.

iUniverse rev. date: 08/02/13

CONTENTS

Dedication vii

Acknowledgements ix

Introduction 1

Columns

- 1969 7
- 1970-79 21
- Photos 162
- 1980-89 243
- 1990-96 307

Index 349

DEDICATION

I dedicate this book to Aris and Helen Angelopoulos, publishers of the *Greek Press* for many years. Though Aris left us back in 1996, I cannot forget the vital role they both played in all of our lives by being "Johnnie on the Spot" for any and all events that traveled from the news room into our homes. We were never without the knowledge of happenings abroad and in our back yard. Aris and Helen were both committed individuals who touched our lives by sharing and publishing information on what was going on in the Greek-American scene. We give them a standing ovation.

ACKNOWLEDGEMENTS

Before I begin to acknowledge those bright and selfless individuals who have worked arduously with me to make this book a reality, I would like to take a moment to point with pride to all of the achievers in our Greek-American community that, in some cases, space did not permit me to acknowledge and, in other cases, I never had the pleasure of meeting. We are all in a sense achievers: a mother who raised her children despite obstacles she might have faced; a teacher who instilled her students with not only knowledge, but the principles of right and wrong; a man who has struggled to support his family. And let us remember our parents, who were the greatest achievers of all. I sincerely hope that the next generation studies what the achievers in this generation have accomplished and follows in their footsteps.

Each year, the achievers of my generation have grown in significance with all of their accomplishments. I have always been aware of these accomplishments, as were others in my generation, but I felt that they had to be recorded, otherwise the pause that existed between the immigration movement and what followed would be lost forever. With the publication of this book, I hope to erase that gap and that all Greek-Americans in this great city will become aware of the achievements of this generation. Their success stories will no longer dwell in the shadows but will shine like a beacon.

To Martha Russis O'Connell, thank you so much for making the technicalities of publishing this book informative, fun and a great learning experience. It was a great joy to have someone sit patiently by my side at the computer for many hours, challenging me to do my best. To another supportive friend, Michael Davros, you too have been the engine of this book, and I consider it an honor and a privilege to have worked with both of you. I am proud to say that you are the achievers of your generation. And what can I say about a best and trusted friend of many years standing, Anastasia Graven, whose intelligence, kindness and consideration were always there for me. If I did not have the answers, Anastasia did.

Please enjoy some of the remnants of my columns. I wrote in the *Greek Press* for more than 20 years, and it was a great deal of fun. I made friends with so many of you and that was indeed a plus. Your social activities were recorded and if you forgot some of the facts, have fun reminiscing.

If you turn to the back of this book, you will see pictures of some members of my family. My lovely and unforgettable sister, Irene, who was a pianist; my beautiful cousin, Euthemia Matsoukas Karkazis, who, as you can see, was crowned Hellenic Queen; and members of the James Russis family posed in hilarious fashion at the wedding of Diana Heard, daughter of Katherine Russis Heard and granddaughter of William J. and Martha Russis. I could not resist sharing these with you.

INTRODUCTION

"But at my back I always hear
Time's winged chariot hurrying near."
Andrew Marvell's *To His Coy Mistress*

"I have measured out my life with coffee spoons."
T.S. Eliot's *The Love Song of J. Alfred Prufrock*

"History is a cyclic poem written by Time upon the memories of man."
Percy Bysshe Shelley

We live in an age that often disregards the historical record in favor of ephemeral moment-to-moment contact, and we so little regard the person next to us who may have made history in Chicago not so very long ago. It's easy to offend. With the recent passing of James Mezilson, Greek Chicagoans are again reminded of the passing of history and of the urgency to get it recorded. Stacy Diacou is one of those persons who did not neglect the realization that the person next to her may in fact have made history, and so her columns faithfully, gently, engagingly record many moments that need not be lost.

In preparation for a book, later to be titled *My Generation of Achievers,* Stacy Diacou, Martha Russis O'Connell, and I visited The Center for Research Libraries near the University of Chicago campus several times before we had what we considered a comprehensive yet select set of representative columns from Stacy's work with *The Greek Press.* I was astonished to find a new world that had escaped my gaze, that I had even dismissed. Romantic poet, Percy Bysshe Shelley told us, "We are all Greeks under the skin," but give the children of Greek immigrants a few generations, and the most loyal will begin to forget their roots. So scholars like Werner Sollors tell us the familiar pattern in ethnic communities and in ethnic assimilation in the United States. Stacy put me back in contact with my roots and reminded me of the two homelands that claim those of us who are the product of immigrant parents. That's the value of this current book. I wish that it were longer, to encompass all of Stacy's columns, but alas, Stacy fought Martha and me to glean only those that specifically related to a more general nature of the Greek-American experience in Chicago.

I am reminded that what I also discovered when working with Stacy and Martha, is that we all have a history. Who will remain to write our lived histories? For the time being, sturdy souls working both literally and figuratively in the vineyards of daily life compose their own histories, every moment precious and enduring. Stacy Diacou recorded our daily lives, and herself has become a part of history. I think people don't realize that they are historical beings even when they are writing or creating history. It's nice to catch Stacy off guard that way.

When Stacy was writing her columns, what was happening in the world? What are the historical contexts? When Stacy first began to compose her column in October of 1969, the Greek junta had been in place in Greece for two years and would remain for another five. President Nixon was not yet in office with the then hope and pride of Greek political life, Governor Spiro T. Agnew. The Vietnam War, a scar on the national conscience, continued to rage, almost a year after the Tet offensive. At the Center for Research Libraries in the fall of 2012, as we cleaned our ink-stained fingers, I had the opportunity to survey the few years after Stacy began to write her column. What did I find? Turkey had not yet invaded the island of Cyprus. That happened in 1974. When that cataclysm happened, *The Greek Press* documented the initial American denunciation, and then as years passed also announced in banner headlines the feeling among American Greeks that President Carter had been duplicitous in finally dropping support of the Greek-Cypriot cause. Stacy's last column concludes in the middle 1990s, before the current economic crises in Greece, after the conclusion of the first Gulf War, before President Bill Clinton scandalized himself, before our American national tragedy of 9/11.

Within the time frame 1969-c.1994, a lot happened in the world, but a lot happened in Chicago. Mayor Daley—Richard J. Daley—had been in office fourteen years, and he would die in office in 1976. The year before Stacy's columns began, Chicago made the national news as a result of the 1968 Democratic National Convention debacle. Another Daley, Richard M., would be in office at the conclusion of Stacy's columns. Under the first Mayor Daley, the city of broad shoulders experienced a downtown building boom with the John Hancock Tower quickly dwarfed by the Sears Tower, and Lake Shore Drive became the showcase for the city. The Second City was popularized in the media and in entertainment.

One additional way to contextualize Stacy's columns is to look at her work in a literary historical context. Stacy's work is not the scandalous realism characterized by turn of the 20th century writers such as Theodore Dreiser, but she does take a Henry Jamesian turn as she focuses on the details of the days of our lives. She captures the fleeting moments of our lives, a momentary pause to look not at the bride's entire dress, but to capture the moment as she turns, when the whiteness of the dress sparkles with tulle and pearls. Stacy's Jamesian moments come at that moment when the bride turns in the dance, and Stacy's snapshot images stand as *tableau vivant.* As readers, we pause to marvel at the scene, to wonder, perhaps out loud, "What is really happening?" and we await Stacy's insight. As Studs Terkel emerged on the Chicago scene, Stacy brought us closer to seeing yet again, the days of our lives, not in street scene or oral testimony but in scenes of family life; we see Chicago's captains of industry, leaders of the church, political participants at all levels, and artistic and cultural creators. Harry Mark Petrakis can be found in Stacy's columns, and he would feel very much at home there as a chronicler of the Greek-American experience in Chicago. I think one additional way to consider her work is to place it in the context of newspaper journalism. I'm reminded of the early London press, with Addison and Steele's *Tattler* and *Spectator* newspaper reporting on the events of the day, episodic and at times too local, too specific for a 20th century mentality impatient with footnotes. However, Stacy's work stands as more than a footnote; her work records a history at ground level. Let's remember, Stacy Diacou is writing sans National Hellenic Museum or other easy sources and resources. In fact, museums will now feature the work of people like Stacy Diacou as witnesses to the events of the 20th century, as witnesses to the history of a people.

She takes as her subjects the lives of Greeks of Chicago, noting the events of The Greek Women's University Club, Philoptochos Societies, Orthodox churches, the Annual Debutante Cotillion, the Hellenic Bar Association, the Hellenic Professional Society, the Republican and Democratic Party organizations, AHEPA, United Hellenic American Congress (UHAC), numerous scholarship and welfare organizations. This is only a very short breath-taking list. Who are the people and families who populate these pages? Again, a short list of names suggests the scope of the Chicago scene: Petrakis, DeMets, Gianaras, Tzakis, Carvel, Basil E. Stevens, Andrew A. Athens, Gouletas, Nicholas J. Melas, Andrew T. Kopan. Readers will touch upon prominent names, and the work, if done by a layman, becomes exhaustive. Yet Stacy's columns are controlled by grace and equanimity, the signs of the consummate professional. Her mention of any public figure is guided by a sense of generosity and fair play. This is the work of the journalist, both as recorder of events, and as witness. Although Stacy Diacou was often a participant in the events recorded, she remained in the background. Young Greek children and their second and third generation parents would do well to read this book to gauge a sense of the breadth of history and to be reminded of what Stacy's generation achieved in the public, political, charitable, cultural, and religious spheres.

Any discussion of Stacy Diacou's contribution to the culture of Chicago would be incomplete without reference to *Hellenism in Chicago*. Sponsored by United Hellenic American Congress (UHAC), Stacy's landmark 1982 book is dedicated to the "Chicago Greek-American immigrant [who] was a noble human being whose love embraced us, whose words taught us, whose ambition inspired us, whose faith in the future uplifted us. He was a pioneer who dared to succeed over adversity. Like an iron peg, hammered into the frozen ground, immovable, he ignored the obstacles at his feet and kept his eyes on the goals above, knowing full well that where dry desert ends, green grass grows. He came for a visit, stayed for a lifetime, and conquered the heart of a city."

Like *Hellenism in Chicago*, Stacy's latest venture, *My Generation of Achievers* embraces us, teaches us, and inspires us, but most of all, she invites us to understand what it meant for her generation to have achieved the foundations for prosperity and success that we currently take for granted in our ethnic group. Like *Hellenism in Chicago, My Generation of Achievers* is a reminder of the prominence and interactions of Greeks on the national scene, in the arts, in politics, and in all areas of public presence. Stacy's columns remind us that our rich national and historical heritages function not as cultural tourism but as cultural imperatives to meet today's challenges and to be worthy of the best that is in our character.

Michael G. Davros
Northeastern Illinois University
January 2013

1969

GRECIAN SOCIETY WHIRL

By STACY DIACOU

As I begin my liftoff through space in the columns of the "Greek Press," launching on a great editorial adventure, I extend my thanks to the publishers of this earthbound craft for giving me the opportunity to report the newest and most exciting happenings on the Greek social scene in Chicago. This column of "White Space" will be targeted weekly with black type. We welcome from you, our distinguished readers, an opportunity to participate in this weekly lunar trip by climbing aboard our "White Space" capsule and sending all your news rays to this columnist at her lunar pad: "Greek Press," 509 North LaSalle Street, Chicago, Ill. 60610.

MINK AND PEARLS . . . is the theme of the forthcoming luncheon fashion show to be held by the St. Andew's Women's Club on Saturday, October 18th, at the Guildhall of the Ambassador West Hotel. According to Mrs. **Stuart Polydoris**, chairman of the event, some of the nation's top models will be flown in to Chicago to pirouette the latest designs of such top couturier's as **Bill Blass, Oscar De La Renta, Geoffrey Beene, Trigere, Dior,** etc. Reservations may be made by contacting: **Miss Irene Diacou,** reservations chairman, 7440 N. Artesian, Chicago; or **Mrs. James Poulos,** co-chairman, 1601 Ashland Avenue, Wilmette.

o—o

CONDOLENCES TO . . . Mr. and Mrs. Sam Tzakis and **Mrs. Tom Lelon** on the death of their mother, **Mrs. Mary Michale**. Ditto to **Florence, Chuck** and **Mrs. Dasaky** on the death of their father and husband, respectively, **John Dasaky.**

o—o

KINDNESS AND GENTILITY . . . were recently honored in the person of **Stella Petrakis,** wife of the late **Father Mark Petrakis,** when the Second District of the Philoptohos paid homage to this selfless lady who has unflinchingly given to the community for ever so long. She is the mother of the distinguished and celebrated novelist, **Harry Mark Petrakis,** and of the charming **Mrs. John Manta.**

o—o

COMPETING FOR . . . the scholarship offered by **Vice-president Spiro T. Agnew** are the following four finalists: **Antigoni Georgopoulou, Ekaterini Goudouveli, Sotirios Grigoropoulos** and **Eugenia Koulafeti.** All four teenagers hail from Gargaliani, Greece, birthplace of the Vice-president's father and grandfather. The $1,600 scholarship was announced by Vice-president Agnew at the dinner held in his honor last February by the Gargalianon Society of Chicago. The winner shall attend the University of Athens.

o—o

POST CARD PENNINGS . . . from Nick and **Aggie Kafkis** revealed a driving trip in which 11 states were covered in 10 days. Well-known former Chicagoans who were visited by the Kafkis' were the **Ioakimidis** brothers (**Midas**) and their wives. **Tony** and **Joan** now reside in Montclair, New Jersey; **Dr. Panos** and **Voula** in Richmond, Virginia. The Kafkis' were also hosted by **Tom** and **Sophie Ross** of Richmond.

Other recent travelers include: **Fran Mavrogen Zettos,** San Francisco; **Daisy** and **Peter Farmakis, Dr. Jim Nicklas** and **Leon Marinakos,** Greece.

o—o

TURNING THE COIN . . . on the other side, **Mrs. John Kambilis,** wife of **Dr. John Kambilis** of Greece, and their daughter, **Yetta,** a law student at the University of Athens, spent two weeks in Chicago renewing friendships. House guests of **Mrs. Toula Fotoplay,** they were feted by **Mrs. Fofo Pappas** and **Mrs. Robert Smenos; Mr. and Mrs. George Manus** and their daughter, **Irene; Mrs. Angela Anthony, Alice** and **Helen,** and other well known Chicagoans.

Another recent visitor to Chicago was **Euthemia Matsoukas,** daughter of **Nick** and **Francis Matsoukas** of Mamaroneck, Long Island, New York. She was the house guest of her aunt and uncle, **Mr.** and **Mrs. William Russis.**

o—o

QUOTE OF THE WEEK . . . "The difficulty is not so great to die for a friend, as to find a friend worth dying for."—**Home.**

As I begin my liftoff through space in the columns of *The Greek Press*, launching on a great editorial adventure, I extend my thanks to the publishers of this earthbound craft for giving me the opportunity to report the newest and most exciting happenings on the Greek social scene in Chicago. This column of "White Space" will be targeted weekly with black type. We welcome from you, our distinguished readers, an opportunity to participate in this weekly lunar trip by climbing aboard our "White Space" capsule and sending all your news rays to this columnist at her lunar pad: The Greek Press, 509 North Lasalle Street, Chicago.

MINK AND PEARLS.......is the theme of the forthcoming luncheon fashion show to be held by the St. Andrew's Women's Club on Saturday, October 18th at the Guildhall of the Ambassador Hotel. According to Mrs. Stuart Polydoris, chairman, some of the nation's top models will be flown into Chicago to pirouette the latest designs of such top couturiers as Bill Blass, Oscar De La Renta, Geoffrey Beene, Trigere, Dior, etc. Reservations may be made by contacting Irene Diacou, reservations chairman, or Mrs. James Poulos, co-chairman.

CONDOLENCES TO.....Mr. and Mrs. Sam Tzakis and Mr. and Mrs. Tom Lelon on the death of their mother, Mrs. Mary Michale. Ditto to Florence, Chuck and Mrs. Dasaky on the death of their father and husband, respectively, John Dasaky.

KINDNESS AND GENTILITY......were recently honored in the person of Stella Petrakis, wife of the late Father Mark Petrakis, when the Second District of the Philoptochos paid homage to this selfless lady who has unflinchingly given to the community for ever so long. She is the mother of the distinguished and celebrated novelist, Harry Mark Petrakis, and of the charming Mrs. John Manta.

POST CARD PENNINGS……from Nick and Aggie Kafkis revealed a driving trip in which 11 states were covered in 10 days. Well-known former Chicagoans who were visited by the Kafkis' were the Ioakimidis brothers (Midas) and their wives. Tony and Joan now reside in Montclair, New Jersey; Dr. Panos and Voula in Richmond, Virginia. Other recent travelers include: Fran Mavrogen Zettos, San Francisco; Daisy and Peter Farmakis, Dr. Jim Nicklas and Leon Marinakos, Greece.

TURNING THE COIN ……on the other side, Mrs. John Kambilis, wife of Dr. John Kambilis of Athens, Greece, and their daughter, Yetta, a law student at the University of Athens, spent two weeks in Chicago renewing friendships. House guests of Mrs. Toula Fotoplay, they were feted by Mrs. Fofo Pappas, Mrs. Robert Smenos, Mr.and Mrs. George Manus and their daughter, Irene; Mrs. Angela Anthony and her daughters, Alice and Helen.

QUOTE OF THE WEEK: "The difficulty is not so great to die for a friend, as to find a friend worth dying for." – Harris

MISS TEEN-AGE TALENT……USA OF 1968, Debbie Gianopoulos of Oklahoma City, Oklahoma, will be the featured attraction at the forthcoming dinner-dance, "Aegean Splendor," to be sponsored by St. John's Greek Orthodox Church in Des Plaines. The dinner dance will be held at the Marriott Motor Inn on Sunday, November 2nd. The talented 17-year-old-beauty, who has appeared on television, plays the bouzouki and sings. She will be flown in for two evening performances. Mr. and Mrs. Leo Vasil are chairmen of the event.

AN INNOVATION....on the usual luncheon fashion show idea has been announced by the ladies of the Holy Apostle Philoptochos Society. According to Mrs Andrew Kanton, chairman, the society will hold a dinner fashion show on Wednesday, October 29th at the Holy Apostle Community Center, turning away from the traditional luncheon fashion show theme. Mrs. G. Gordon, president, has announced that the grand prize will be a cruise to Bermuda for two.

LAST MINUTE CALL....to the showing of beautiful couturier clothes by high fashion models. The almost filled to capacity luncheon fashion show, to be held by the St. Andrew's Women's Club on Saturday, October 18th at the Guildhall of the Ambassador West Hotel, promises to be even better than the memorable and recent St. Luke's-Presbyterian fashion show. Mrs. Andrew Tzakis, president of the St. Andrew's Women's Club, is keeping the exquisite raffle prizes a secret.

PERSONALITIES IN THE NEWS: Milt Pappas of the Atlanta Braves has been frequenting the Atlanta Playboy Hutch, undoubtedly bunny watching to see who, in his opinion, deserves the coveted cotton tail of the year beauty contest award currently underway.

Stanley A. Perry recently became the godfather of the Thomas Poulakidas' infant.

Reports are that Dr. Lou Paulos was recently seen discotequing in San Francisco.

To the sound of voluminous applause, Gigi Childs, 13-year old daughter of Peter and Helen Childs, modeled a swinging long, white, wet-look maxi coat at the recent "Charisma" luncheon fashion show sponsored by the Women's Club of Sts. Peter and Paul at the Hyatt House. In this great new age of the maxi, Gigi's coat, rippling wide about the ankles, allowed for a spirited and dashing stride.

STIMULATING LECTURE......that everyone should attend will be presented by the Hellenic Professional Society of Illinois on Sunday, October 26th at 3 p.m. at the Sheraton Chicago Hotel when Elroy Sandquist, Jr., a senior partner in a Chicago law firm and former head of the Civil Division of the Cook County State's Attorney Office, will address the group on "The Illinois Constitutional Convention – What It Means To You." This extremely important topic affects every citizen of Illinois for the Constitutional Convention will convene on December 8th to consider changes in the Illinois Constitution written in 1870.

QUOTE OF THE WEEK: "Both the ignorant man and the educated man are satisfied with themselves; the ignorant man calls his ignorance 'common sense,' and the educated man calls his information 'knowledge'; it is only the wise man who knows how little knowledge he has and how useless is his common sense for solving uncommon problems." - Harris

FRENCH EDUCATOR......Simon Boucheau advises parents to please teach their children all the rules, every one of them, so that they will know how to break them.

CHIC AND ERUDITE.....Greta Wylie of book review prominence, charmed her audience with her sparkling wit at the recent book review and membership tea given by The Greek Women's University Club and held at the Sheraton-Chicago Hotel on October 11th. Skilled in the art of reviewing, Ms. Wylie briefly discussed the overly discussed Mary Borelli Gallagher's, "My Life with Jacqueline Kennedy," and then gracefully entered into a review of "The Royal Family," by Ralph White, friend of the royal family since the romper days of Queen Elizabeth. Having the distinction of being written up in, "Who's Who in American Women," the delightful Ms. Wylie, with tongue-in-cheek, drew somewhat of a saucy comparison between the two international figures – the regal Queen Elizabeth and the jet setter - Jacqueline Kennedy Onassis. Special people who made this a special happening are Mrs. John Secaras and Mrs. Ernie Nassos.

SINGULAR HONOR.......was recently bestowed on Cleopatra Bugelas, currently a senior at Carleton College in Northfield, Minnesota, and daughter of George and Kathryn Bugelas of Evanston. When the president of Carleton announced his retirement plans, the progressive trustees of Carleton selected representatives from the student body to aid in the selection of the new president. Cleopatra was one of those picked for this task.

HEADING THE....youth group at Sts. Peter and Paul, Glenview, Illinois, are Perry and Connie Fotos. Already bursting at the seams with enthusiastic ideas, this energetic twosome put the youth group in high gear with a spaghetti dinner held at the church hall on October 18th. The social generation gap was bridged by the Fotos' who are now officially the leaders of the 13-17 suburbanite youth group.

SCHEDULED FOR.......December 17th publication is, "Greece: The Unclouded Eye," by Colin Simpson, whose books have glamourized vacation spots all over the world. Now this prolific author has added Greece to his list. Mr. Simpson's tour gives his readers an insight into the central and lesser cities of Greece.

PERSONALITIES IN THE NEWS: Tom and Helen Mantice of Glenview recently became the godparents of Byron Sakoulas, son of George and Goldie of Kansas City, Missouri.

All set to middle-aisle it are two gems from The Greek Women's University Club set: Madeline Demopoulos, who will wed John Samaras of Boston, Massachusetts on November 22nd and ditto for Eugenia Petropoulos who will tie the knot with Chris Koudounis on December 7th.

A real first is the promotion of Andrew Petrakis from captain to battalion chief of the Fire Department.

Condolences to Art Soter and to the members of his family on the recent death of his beloved mother, Tina.

QUOTE OF THE WEEK: "If a good face is a letter of recommendation, a good heart is a letter of credit."- Bulwer

WEST COAST...visitor, Natasha Pogrebin, head of the Fruit Pickers Association, says that California is a fine place to live – if you happen to be an orange.

A HIGH PRICED....couturier spread was offered at the recent St. Andrew's luncheon and fashion show which took place at the Guildhall of the Ambassador West Hotel. The designers' collection from Saks Fifth Avenue presented an unprecedented collection of high fashion clothes ranging from a trendy fox-cuffed pant suit to a gilded gold brocade floor length Geoffrey Beene gown slashed to the waist and enriched with a massive border of jewels that hugged both the neck and the hemline.

The collection swung with the times introducing mini, midi, and maxi down-to-the-ground coats in a fashion season in which anything goes. Tremendous shawls were worn–some dipping dramatically to one side and others tossed carelessly over the shoulder. In a season of exotic furs, Revillon's were the most exciting yet to be seen. While this firm previews its sleek and expensive wares monthly in *Harper's Bazaar* and *Vogue*, this time it took the Cadillac of the fur industry–mink–and showed it off in all its glory–in huge muffs, jackets that barely skimmed the waist, and coats that casually patted the thigh.

One of the really spectaculars was an Oscar De La Renta original maxi wool checked coat of red, green, black and white, which was adorned with a voluminous fringed scarf nonchalantly brushing the floor. The just a little above the knee dress, which accessorized the dramatic coat, featured a plaid skirt of the same material with a flaming red bodice.

Fashions from Adolfo, Brooks, Cashin, Feraud, Dior, etc, not only graced the models, but also the guests – for some of the beautiful people who paid to attend this outstanding collection were every bit as chic as the models.

Sables to Mrs. Andrew Tzakis, president, who had the foresight to awaken the dormant St. Andrew's fashion show luncheon; ditto to Mrs. Stuart Polydoris, chairman, whose leadership made this show an Oscar winning event.

THE ORPHANAGE.......of St. Basil's will receive the financial benefits accrued from the forthcoming dinner theater party to be given by the Assumption Women's Club on November 23rd at the Ivanhoe Theater and Restaurant, 3000 N Clark St., Chicago. For further information contact Mrs. George Stamas, publicity chairman.

IN THE USUAL.....gracious and traditional fashion, The Greek Women's University Club will host its annual winter cocktail dance on Saturday, November 29th in the King Arthur Room of the Sheraton Chicago Hotel. Two pretty misses will head this affair, Georgia Anargyros and Phyllis Pergakes.

QUOTE OF THE WEEK: "Misery is when a black boy starts to help an old lady across the street and she thinks he is trying to snatch her purse." – Langston Hughes

THREE OSCARS......to the members of The Greek Women's University Club. Oscar number one: For the delightful and festive: "Night in Camelot" winter cocktail dance they sponsored last Saturday at the Sheraton-Chicago Hotel. The holiday season took its first gasp of festive air during the long Thanksgiving weekend at this major bash.

Oscar number two: The GWUC has adopted a foster child –a 10 year old girl from Northern Grevana, Greece. The organization will send her support money every month through the Foster Parent Plan Inc.

Oscar number three: For the GWUC's recent financial contribution to the 100 starving children at the mud hospital near Umuahia in Biafra, all under the age of six. Incidentally, there are many hundreds of cases containing desperately needed food, concentrates and medical supplies, which could help save the lives of the children of Biafra reported to be dying at the rate of 1,000 each day. Unfortunately, however, the supplies are piled up in Chicago because of lack of money to fly them to that beleagured area. Anyone wishing to make a donation, which is tax deductible, should send it to: Biafra Relief Services Foundation, 28 E. Jackson Blvd., Chicago, Illinois 60604.

CONDOLENCES TO....Appelate Court Judge John J. Stamos, Mrs. Zoe Rummel, Sam Stamos, Mrs. Sophie Carres and Mrs. Christine Gehopolos on the death of their 82-year- old mother, Mrs. Katherine Stamos.

PERSONALITIES IN THE NEWS: Wearing their hearts at half-mast are the lovely Persey Betzelos and her Jim on the death of her father, beloved Peter Tompary. Ditto for charming Regina Skuteris of Oak Park whose father succumbed recently.

Dear friend, Harriet Lamperis Andrews and her Peter drove to our town from St. Paul, Minnesota, to spend ten days with family and friends. They were feted by many Chicagoans most of whom they entertained during the Minneapolis Ahepa convention.

Jean Pavlakos of Elmhurst hosted a big pow-wow for hubby Dino's 40th birthday at the Black Steer on Saturday, November 29th. It was a complete surprise for Dino, and oodles of fun for his many well-wishing friends who attended.

Lucille Powers and sis, Irene, are on their merry way to fun-filled Acapulco, Mexico, to bask in the sun for 10 days, then on to Mexico City to spectate at the bull fights.

Scorpios who recently celebrated their birthdays together include: Daisy Farmakis, Jim Corolis and yours truly (all born on November 18th); Helen Anthony, John Graven, Nicholas Jannes and Bill Kagianas were not born on the 18th, but they are all Scorpios.

WE TIP......our hat to William Deree, financier and philanthropist, for this noble gesture: It seems that two of the four children competing for the scholarship offered by Vice-President Spiro T. Agnew passed the examinations conducted at the University of Athens. Sotirios Grigoropoulos, first winner, was presented his scholarship by the vice-president. Mr. Deree stepped in and presented the second winner, Eugenia Koulaeti, with another scholarship.

QUOTE OF THE WEEK: "To marry without physical attraction is a crime against the body; to marry for physical attraction alone is a crime against the spirit; and both crimes eventually exact heavy punishments of different sorts." - Harris

"Remember that you are only an actor in a play which the manager directs." Epictetus

PRIVATE PREVIEW…of Harry Mark Petrakis' "A Dream of Kings" will be held on January 14th at 8:30 pm at the Roosevelt Theatre. This Chicago first, a one-night benefit showing for Ahepa charities, will be sponsored by Ahepa's Blue Ribbon District 13. Co-chairmen are Thomas Gianes and Peter Boznos.

NAMED AS….the Democratic state ticket's candidate for state superintendent of schools is 31-year-old Dr. Michael Bakalis, assistant dean of the college of liberal arts and sciences at Northern Illinois University, DeKalb. Dr. Bakalis won the Democratic nomination after vying for the position against two strong contenders, Brandt Crocker of Quincy and Melvin Kahn of Southern Illinois University. He will vie for the position in March when primary elections for various posts will be held. Dr. Bakalis will oppose incumbent Ray Page for the post. At a recent Morton Scholarship League Dinner, the outstanding educator predicted that "campus disorders and turmoil will continue to plague the nation for five to ten more years." He also predicted that by the end of the decade the number of students who will have attended college will equal the total number of all students who have attended since the beginning of the 17th century.

DELIGHTFUL LUNCHEON......honoring the immediate retiring officers and introducing the newly elected officers of the Saint Helen Women's Club was recently held at the South Shore Country Club. Mrs. Harriet Patras, two-term retiring president, gave a brief historical account of the club's 45 years of service to the community. She was lauded by the Rev. Byron Papanikolaou, pastor of St. Constantine's Greek Orthodox Church, and by Pierre DeMets, president of the board of trustees. The response was given by Mrs. Thomas Lelon, newly elected president. Chairman of the luncheon was Mrs. John Pakis.

SPECIAL CONDOLENCES.....to Nicholas and Kay Manos of Riverside, on the death of her brother, James N. Gianacakos, late of Cicero.

RECENT ISSUE....of *The Greek Sunday News*, featured an item in which George Alevizos of Dorchester, Massachusetts, was lauded on the work he has done for the blind. Mr. Alevizos will provide work throughout Greece to numerous blind girls manufacturing pillow cases, sheets and towels for wholesale marketing at hotels, hospitals and state institutions. A large number of sewing machines are needed for this massive production. If anyone would like to donate a sewing machine to a blind girl in Greece, it will help her earn three to four dollars a day at home. Each donor's name will be inscribed on the sewing machine and a picture of the blind girl and purchasing statement will be forwarded to each donor. The sewing machines will be purchased in Greece at the low cost of $88. With an addition of $37, the same machine will later be converted to local electric current. Anyone wishing to donate to this worthwhile cause can do so by sending a check to Workshop for Blind Girls in Greece or to Hellenic American Society for the Blind Inc., 100 SW 26th Road, Miami, Florida 33129.

QUOTE OF THE WEEK: "The men who crack most easily are those who are afraid to expose what they consider a weakness, who feel they must always seem strong and decisive and self-assured, even when the occasion calls for doubt and deliberation. To be really strong means having the surplus strength to admit a weakness – just as the truly brave man frankly confronts his fear." -Harris

1970-79

From Coast to Coast – A Yuletide Toast

The month of December is the time,
To turn this column into rhyme.
And in the Christmas-New Year season,
I will pause for just one reason.
To greet my readers coast to coast,
And to them all to drink a toast.

To all the friends who send me news,
I drink a hearty glass of booze,
To those contributors I hold so dear,
I sip a tall stemmed glass of cheer,
A tribute to publisher, Aris, too,
And his, Helen, to name a few.

To the mothers laboring every day,
With projects like the PTA,
To good old dad – the busiest chap,
Who gets the bills thrown in his lap,
A magnum of champagne we drain,
In lasting tribute once again.

To Fathers Hondras and Latto, too,
And all the other clergy who,
Work so hard to set us straight,
So we'll get through that pearly gate,
May happiness, good health and cheer,
Be theirs throughout the coming year.

And now we pray to the good Lord,
That those who serve on a church board,
Make wise investments every day,
So that they will be able to pay,
For raffle tickets, donations and such,
God, bless them with the Midas Touch.

And let a yuletide carol be,
Sung to the ladies able to see,
That when their skirts were worn up high,
Some showed nothing but a bulging thigh.
Other legs did not look good,
They were as skinny as a piece of wood.

Now let us strike a mellow chord,
To those on the Welfare Foundation Board,
We wish them growth and harmony,
And add a note of conviviality.

Since we have the space before us,
How about a special chorus,
To the GWUC who are my friends
of old, They are more precious than a
piece of gold.

A hearty toast is also due,
To the HPSI and the GOYA groups, too.
Let there be mistletoe and holly,
And many days which make them jolly.

We trowl the bowl and dance a jig,
And hope next year you make it big.
We hope the employer who pays you money,
Will make your life both rich and sunny.

To all my readers, once again,
From sunny Cal to rocky Maine,
Prosperity and season's cheer,
Be yours throughout the coming year,
May health and happiness abide,
With all of you at this yuletide.

"Millions who long for immortality do not know what to do with themselves on a rainy Sunday afternoon."

CHRISTMAS CARDS.....in all sizes, shapes, colors, textures and designs, bearing tidings of good will, friendship, love, faith and hope bombarded households last week as one human being communicated with another in the spirit of the holiday season. Cards received from those near and dear were warmly read; cards from those dear but not so near were even more avidly devoured. Our household was so very happy to receive greetings from many former Chicagoans who now seem to have congregated on the west coast.

A beautiful etching of "Virgin and Child," by Stefano della Bella, The Metropolitan Museum of Art, was received by Mike and Kay Johnson of Littleton, Colorado (the former Kay Karras of Skokie). From George and Helen Trapalis of Dallas (the former Helen Sellas of Chicago) an exquisite gold and green leafed card of "Madonna and Child" from the Pilot School for the Deaf. Especially well received was a card from Luke and Bess Michas of San Diego (former Bess Maheras of Chicago) with photos of their two pretty moppets, Mariana and Anthea. Also from San Diego, a card from Nick and Mimi Koukis (former Mimi Childs of Chicago). A newsletter accompanying their Christmas greeting was sent by George and Cleo Andrews of Los Angeles (former Cleo Apostle of Chicago).

One of the warmest Christmas gestures received, however, came from D. Michael Jeane of the Pick Congress Hotel whose card read, "in keeping with the Christmas spirit of love and giving, we of Albert Pick Hotels have made a donation in your name to the children of La Rabida Children's Hospital and Research Center, Chicago." Thank you, Michael Jeane.

ALL OF........New York's beautiful people attended the recent private preview of the movie version of the smash Broadway hit "Cactus Flower" held at the Astor Theater. With jet setter, Mrs. Charlotte Niarchos at the helm and Mrs. John Moscahlaidis as chairman, assisted by Mrs. Paul Sapounakis, the event was a real smash.

WEARING THEIR.....hearts at half mast over the death of their beloved father, George A. Tarachas of LaGrange Park, are his widow and three daughters: Mrs. Effie Karrys, Mrs. Lorraine Christy and Mrs. Diana Spyros.

ONE OF......our town's really beautiful persons was awarded the Rotary Good Neighbor Award for her benevolent deeds of the past. Based on helpful deeds to friends and neighbors, Mrs. Paul (Angie) Lolakos of Berwyn was selected from 35 men and women. She was presented with a trophy and a one hundred dollar bond. Congratulations to a really selfless individual.

IN NORTH......side suburbia Niles Mayor Nicholas Blase trimmed away at ribbon cutting ceremonies heralding the opening of the Golf Mill 2 Theater.

QUOTE Of THE WEEK: "The proud never have friends, not in prosperity, for then they know nobody and not in adversity, for then nobody knows them." - Harris

"When a man dies, the last thing that moves is his heart, in a woman, her tongue."

THE GREEK.....Women's University Club is seeking men and women of Hellenic descent who are artistically inclined to exhibit their paintings, sculptures, crafts, etc. at an art show and lecture to be held on April 12th at 4 p.m. at the Allerton Hotel. Interested parties should phone Maria Pappas (NE 1-6719) or Jeanette Nassos (724-7881) to obtain additional information.

KATHRYN AND...George Bugelas of Evanston, and their three lovely daughters, entertained at one of the most delightful post-holiday dinner parties of the season. The event was in honor of newlyweds Eugenia and Chris Koudounis. Flanked by their handsome husband and father, respectively, the quartet of lovelies were the epitome of graciousness. Champagne and conversation flowed endlessly making a most enjoyable evening go by much too quickly.

IT HAS OFTEN…been said,"Tell me your favorite color, and I'll tell you something about your personality." This statement was recently enforced in an article on color and personality written by Jane G. Wheeler, O.T.R. So this week, the name of the game is COLOR. What shall we color you? Don't cheat and look below. Pick a color and read on.

Did you say, "yellow?" You are full of sunlight and laughter, energy and verve. You attract attention with your happy attitude. You will always be young at heart.

Color you red? You are strong, passionate, angry and intense. Trouble to you is like a red flag to a bull. Hot, vivid and restless, you cannot keep your cool. Possessiveness and jealousy are a natural part of your makeup.

If your preference is clear, bright blue – you are content; pastel baby blue – delicate and sweet. Generally speaking, blue types are cool, calm and dignified. They are harbingers of truth.

Green people symbolize nature and, therefore, new life, which reflects innocence. If you prefer darker hues of green, you are cool and mysterious: lighter shades, warm and active.

Purple people are regal and majestic personalities who command reverence and respect. They are people of splendor, mystery and passion, coupled with awesome authority.

You like orange? You are a loner. Healthy, vigorous, courageous and expansive, you are an adventuresome type who does not really need people.

If brown is your thing, you are mother earth at its best. Healthy and vital, you are a fertile, outdoor type, rugged in build and earthy in personality – an Arizona ranch type.

Is gray your bag? If so, you had better change color for you are rather dull and quiet with no personality of your own. You are a conformist and are noted for your conservatism.

Black personalities are mysterious and somber; dignified and severe – but, oh, so depressing. You symbolize sadness, loss, tragedy. Your ominous qualities create a moody personality.

You in the white category depict innocence, purity, holiness and peaceful living. A white personality needs more backbone. You are sort of like unsalted hospital food – tasteless.

QUOTE OF THE WEEK: "If you forgive people enough you belong to them, and they to you, whether either person likes it or not – squatter's rights of the heart." - Harris

SERBIAN HUMORIST….Amar Hazos defines a fungus personality as "one who grows on you."

ILLINOIS REPUBLICANS…will be among the first in the nation to hear Vice-President Agnew report on his Asian tour for he will be the featured speaker at a fundraising reception and dinner scheduled to take place at the Conrad Hilton Hotel on February 12th. The occasion is the annual Lincoln Day celebration, traditionally a big night for Republican fundraisers.

Sponsored by the United Republican Fund of Illinois, the event is being chaired by Joseph Lanterman, chairman of the board of Amstad Industries. Pericles P. Stathas heads the sub-committee entitled, "The American Hellenic Committee for Lincoln's Birthday Dinner." In his new role as President Nixon's trouble-shooter, Vice-President Agnew is expected to attract 2,000 to the $100 a plate dinner.

NO REST…..is in sight for the hard-working officers of St. Andrew's church board. Without a ripple in the tide, they were all re-elected to serve for another term of office. The high-spirited, organizationally attuned officers include the following: Michael Cantonis,, president; George Annes, vice-president; Christ Karafotias, vice-president:

Theodore J.Theodore, treasurer; Nick Kanellos, assistant treasurer; Phillip Georgouses, assistant treasurer; Thomas Poulakidas, secretary; Evan Papageorge, assistant secretary; George Karafotias, assistant secretary.

WEDDING BELLS.....merrily chimed recently for Madeline Demopulos of Chicago, formerly of Biloxi, Mississippi, and John Michael Samaras of Lowell, Massachusetts, at the first Greek Orthodox ceremony in the south to be celebrated in a Roman Catholic Church in Biloxi. The bride is a graduate of the University of Alabama; the groom attended Lowell Institute of Technology and Bentley College in Boston.

GRIEF HAS.....has clutched the hearts of all those who knew young, talented, and soft-spoken Tom Bacouris who recently met his death in a fatal three-car accident on Chicago's Skyway. The only son of Christine and the late John Bacouris, the 30-year old southsider was an architect. Beloved by all of us who knew him, the violent and repugnant way in which he met his death should make us more vigilant than ever to the hazards involved in even casual daytime driving. This is the second time in two months that the bell has tolled for a Greek youth. Michael Heropoulos of Evanston was the first. Condolences to Mrs. Bacouris and to Alex and Glykeria Lamperis; Harriet and Peter Andrews of St. Paul, Minnesota and Magdaline and James Alexander.

BOOK BEAT: Three plays written by the late Nikos Kazantzakis entitled, "Christopher Columbus," "Melissa," and "Kouros," have recently been published. However, the late Greek novelist falls short of the level of his novels in these turgid declamatory dramas. Even, allowing for the differences in theatrical tradition between the Greek and Anglo-American stages, for all their sincerity, they are heavy breathing. "Melissa" and "Kouros "go back to Greek myths, dealing, in the former, with the disintegration of a royal family and, in the latter, with the spiritual rebirth of a god through the death of a minotaur. "Christopher Columbus" is overly long and wallows in mysticism and mock-heroics as it explores the mystical obsession of a Columbus driven to offer new lands to his Christ.

QUOTE OF THE WEEK: "Ninety percent of what passes for conversation is not communication as much as medication – it is used to make the speaker feel better, either by depreciating others or by inflating oneself." - Harris

"Chivalry," said a school boy, "is going around releasing beautiful maidens from other men's castles, and taking them to your own castle."

UNPRECEDENTED WILL.....be the appearance of two Illinois Senators at the dinner-dance of the Hellenic Bar Association scheduled to take place on February 7th ar the Guildhall, Ambassador West Hotel. The two distinguished guests are Senator Charles A. Percy, main speaker of the evening, and Senator Ralph Tyler Smith, who will extend a few remarks to those attending this posh event. Nicholas G. Manos, currently president of the Federal Bar Association, will be installed as president of the Hellenic Bar Association. Reservations chairman to this black tie event is Michael Stathos of River Forest.

THE WORLD....is a lot sadder and poorer since the demise of sprightly and energetic Mrs. Angeline Anthony, mother of Helen and Alice Anthony, who succumbed suddenly on January 20th making a dent in the hearts of both kin and friends alike. The beloved Mrs. Anthony was a most selfless human being whose buoyant energy gave much to those of us who were fortunate enough to know her. May the drops of spiritual sunshine she sprinkled in her lifetime stay with us long after her departure from this world. Condolences to her two devoted daughters, Helen and Alice.

SPECIAL RECOGNITION....was recently given to an architectural plum, the summer home of William Kagianis, DDS, by the Metropolitan Museum of Art. The museum has requested permission to photograph the beautiful Frank Lloyd Wright home located in Grand Beach,

Michigan, so that the pictures can be displayed in the American Wing of the Museum under the title, "19th Century America." The photos will be on display at the Metropolitan Museum of Art from April through September.

PERSONALITIES IN THE NEWS: A sophisticated collection of swingers gathered together at the home of Nicholas and Aggie Kafkis last week when they hosted a smashing cocktail party. As icicled people slipped out of their wet coats and into their dry martinis – temperatures rose matching the warm spirits of the charming host and hostess.

Foreign stickers are plastered all over the luggage of John and Ann Karambelas of Oakbrook who just returned from a well-earned jaunt to Europe. A few of their stops were Istanbul, Rome and Greece. They paused in Oakbrook just long enough to catch their breath. Now they're bathing in the sun-drenched gambler's paradise–Las Vegas.

Condolences to the Bartholomew clan on the death of their beloved mother, Mary. She is survived by her children: Irene (Andrew) Tzakis; James (Patricia) Bartholomew, and John (Theo) Barthlomew, a sister, four brothers and eight grandchildren.

A SPRING.....bouquet of designer's fashions will be unfolded at the annual fashion luncheon show to be sponsored by the Philoptochos Society of St. John's Greek Orthodox Church in Des Plaines. Aptly entitled, "Fashions on Canvas," this colorful spring fashion splash has been scheduled to take place on Saturday, February 21st at the Marriott. Fashions will be coordinated by Bonwit Teller.

QUOTE OF THE WEEK: "There are three wedges to a man's character: what he believes, what he does, and how he reconciles what he does with what he believes. It is in the last operation that the ultimate assessment of character must be made." Harris

"When a child complains that there is 'nothing to do,' he is not bored with his environment, but with himself; and his education in resourcefulness has been defective, no matter how well he does at school." – Harris

BLASTING OFF FOR.....a super splashdown is the St. Helen's Annual Debutante Cotillion scheduled to take place on May 9th at the Conrad Hilton Hotel. The event will be headed by Mrs. Thomas Lelon, president of the St. Helen's Women's Club and Mrs. George Gatsis, cotillion chairman. Presented for the first time in May 1965, under the auspices of the St. Helen Women's Club, the cotillion is a source of benefit for the church. Debutantes to be presented must be between the ages of 17 to 21, they must be graduating from high school, entering or attending college, and, of course, be of the Orthodox faith. The debs have the privilege of submitting the names of young men as prospective escorts. The escorts must be attending or must have graduated from a college or university and they must be of the Orthodox faith. All names are submitted to the escort committee which makes the final selection. The presentation tea will be held on March 7th at the Sheraton Blackstone Hotel.

YOUNG IS BEAUTIFUL.....and Maria Papas of Wilmette depicted shiny, radiant beauty at the recent black tie dinner party at which her engagement was announced to John Gleason, Jr. Daughter of Dina and the late and beloved, Spiro J. Papas, the dinner party at which Maria's engagement was announced was hosted by her mother in honor of the tenth wedding anniversary of her sister and brother-in-law, Aliki and William Bryant of Washington, DC. The surprise dual celebration, which took place in the Crystal Ballroom of the Sheraton-Blackstone Hotel, put a sparkle in the eyes of the 200 family friends and relatives who had congregated to wish Bill and Aliki a happy anniversary.

Maria is the granddaughter of Mr. and Mrs. S.J .Gregory of Wilmette and Mrs. John Papas of Lake Shore Drive. A graduate of Northwestern University, she was president of her sorority, Kappa Alpha Theta, and business manager of Northwestern's Wau Mu show. Of late, she had been working in the Washington, DC office of Senator Ralph Tyler Smith of Illinois.

The handsome brown-haired blue-eyed John is also a Northwestern graduate. A member of Delta Upsilon fraternity, he is currently affiliated with Inland Steel. The couple plans a May wedding at St. Andrew's Greek Orthodox Church.

TAKE YOUR HEART.....to the St. Demetrios Cultural Center on Valentine's Day to participate in the "Have a Heart for the Mother Church" Greek night dance. John Secaras, president of the Annunciation and St. Demetrios Churches, has announced that proceeds of this event will go to the Annunciation Cathedral Fund.

QUOTE OF THE WEEK: "The shrewd man looks ahead; the simple man looks around, the resigned man looks down; the frightened man looks behind, only the wise man looks within."-Harris

"A fanatic is one who believes that man's best friend is his dogma."

SPECIAL TREAT.....for some of us was attending the 1970 Lincoln Day Dinner sponsored by the United Republican Fund of Illinois at which our beloved Vice-President Spiro T. Agnew addressed a crowd of 2,500 persons at a dinner which took place at the Conrad Hilton. Vice-President Agnew, who "speaks softly and carries a big stick," jokingly accepted jabs from Senator Charles Percy about his "great golf game" regaling the audience with his sharp wit. He gracefully acknowledged all of the Greek-Americans in the audience prior to beginning his actual address in which he blasted racial quotas on college admissions as "some strange madness." Prolonged applause greeted his outspoken criticism of the recent policies of some colleges and universities to accept students and instructors on the basis of ethnic and racial considerations. His Abraham Lincoln Day dinner speech was tied to pronouncements of the Civil War President.

A SOPHISTICATED......and gay spirited collection of beautiful people gathered together at the Guildhall of the Ambassador West Hotel on February 7th to attend the gala black tie 20th annual installation dinner-dance of the Hellenic Bar Association at which erudite and charming Nicholas G. Manos was installed as president. The head table was studded with personalities high up in the local and national political arena, and the dignified humor with which the introduction of these honored guests was facilitated by John Secaras, toastmaster, made the event both entertaining and memorable. Between handsome and polished United States Senator Charles Percy (who certainly gets around in Greek circles) and deep and resonant voiced United States Senator Ralph Tyler Smith, boy watching was at a premium for female guests. The chicness of female guests also rated high, however, giving the girl oglers in the crowd something to feast their eyes on. A fashion Oscar to Dina (Ted) Anastos for her sensational peek-a-boo mid-riffed white filmy gown, splashed with crystals throughout. Fashion runner-up included Kay Manos, wife of newly elected president, Nick, who moved gracefully in a Grecian white chiffon floor length gown adorned with opulent stones of turquoise, coral, gold and white. Another scene stealer was Georgia (James) Regas in a magnificent black crepe tunic pant outfit trimmed with rhinestones. With a sunburst of smiles on her face, Martha (Leon) Scan, a delight in a gold brocade patterned mandarin type cocktail gown, could easily have won the coveted "Miss Congeniality" award. All in all, it was a refreshing evening.

VIEWS ON LAW......and order will be exchanged by those in the "know" at the panel discussion to be sponsored by The Hellenic Professional Society of Illinois scheduled to take place in the East Room of the Sheraton Chicago Hotel on Sunday afternoon, February 22nd. Participating panel members will include: Honorable Joseph Woods, sheriff of Cook County; Jay A. Miller, executive director of the American Civil Liberties Union; James Thompson, assistant attorney general and chief of the Department of Law Enforcement and Public Protection and George Cotsirilos, prominent Chicago attorney. Moderator will be society member and officer, George Karcazes.

QUOTE OF THE WEEK: "Silence and egotism go together more commonly than we suspect; the chatterbox merely hopes to be liked for what he expresses; the taciturn demands to be respected for what he contains." - Harris

Hadji Sessur says, "A cynic is one who is prematurely disappointed in the future."

PURE, BLOODY-MINDED……egotism has always made the Greek people brag about their way of life, their conquests, and achievements: it is the kind of chauvinism that they used to transfer to the culture and antiquity of the land. But whatever it is or was – no one Greek-American writer in our generation has been able to capture this pulse beat of the Greek ego as well as our own Harry Mark Petrakis, who has so graciously accepted an invitation extended by the St. Andrew's Women's Club to present a lecture reading on March 6th at 8 pm. The event promises to thoroughly satiate the minds of those attending.

Essentially, the nationally acclaimed Harry Mark Petrakis' scene is the Greeks, and his analysis of the Greek character began back in 1959 with the publication of his first novel, "Lion At My Heart." This was followed with the 1963 publication of "The Odyssey of Kostas Volakis." Two years later, his prolific pen came up with a first collection of short stories, "Pericles on 31st Street." Both this collection and a third novel, "A Dream of Kings," published in 1966, were nominated for the National Book Award in the category of fiction. A second collection of short stories, "The Waves of Night," was published in 1969. "Stelmark - A Family Recollection," a compilation of autobiographical fragments, will be published by David MacKay in June 1970.

SHOWCASE FOR CELEBRITIES…the Johnny Carson Show, featured a well-known friend of many Chicagoans, Nick John Matsoukas of New York City, who made a spectacular guest appearance on the Carson show on spooks day, Friday, February 13th. Recently appointed coordinator of special events and community relations of Loews' Theater in New York City, Nick added a delightful zest to the nightly tube show. The name of the game was superstition, and Nick climbed under ladders and broke mirrors in a valiant attempt to prove that superstition is the bunk.

A graduate of the University of Chicago with the degree of PhD in sociology and anthropology, he has served as a reporter with the *Chicago Daily News* and as advertising and promotion director for the Cinema Art Theater in Chicago. Nick is also a veteran of the motion picture industry and is widely known for his many worthwhile projects for the benefit of the Greek-American community. A brother of Martha Russis of Chicago, he formerly worked for the Skouras Corporation.

PERSONALITIES IN THE NEWS: A zingy time recently was had by Chris and Elayne Pappas of Elgin and their cohorts, Ann and Steve Stevens, when the two couples flew the friendly skies to Santa Domingo in the Dominican Republic.

To the beat, beat, beat of the tom toms, Theodora Kanellos, who spent last summer in Africa, presented members of The Greek Women's University Club with a short film on Africa relating some fascinating experiences.

QUOTE OF THE WEEK: "It is weak men, not strong men, who are cruel – for cruelty is almost always an admission of failure of character in the past, and a desperate effort to rectify by pain what should have been prevented by firmness."

"It is fruitless to look back upon our parents and grandparents and exclaim that they got along better in marriage than the majority of people do today. They got along better because they expected less, and we, unfortunately, live in an era of rising expectations, not only economically, but emotionally as well."

REMEMBER THE.......crowds and the hoop te do when the astronauts paraded down State Street? Well – that was nothing in comparison to the hoop te do that accompanied this year's fabulous 15th Annual Greek Independence Day Parade. The Greek heart was bursting with pride at this heritage – for it really was a sight to behold. But, of course, we knew it would be with one of our town's most adored citizens, soft-spoken Chris Pappageorge at the helm. Chris worked feverishly to coordinate all the Greek Heritage '81 events – and he certainly succeeded.

While congratulations are due to such Greek Heritage '81 luminaries as our beloved Andrew Athens, Jim Peponis, Leon Marinakos, Nicholas Manos, Anthony Nichols, Mike Svourakis, Peter Cappas, Kathy Adinamis, Annette Kouimelis, Theano Rexinis, Dr. Nicholas G. Mitchell – to name a few – I tip my beige straw fedora to float chairman, Stanley A. Kakis – for doing such a super job year after year.

Most delightful touch at the parade? Fabulous Petros of Diana's Opa fame – dramatically tossing flowers at parade watchers from his white limo. Loved his style.

WE POINT.....with pride to our very own native Chicagoan, Billy Dare Sedaras, international cabaret entertainer, singer-comedian, now starting his sixth month at Chicago's ultra elegant Lake Point Tower Club, Billy was given a star-studded write-up in famed columnist Mark Tan's "Celebrity File" in the *Los Angeles Herald Examiner*. The best in the world of entertainment, Billy has played Tel Aviv, Athens, Munich, Corfu, Honolulu and Hollywood – to name a few.

ONE OF.......our town's most outstanding attorneys, John H. Secaras, was recently installed as president of the Chicago Chapter of the Federal Bar Association. Deputy regional solicitor of the U.S. Department of Labor, John has been a member of the Federal Bar Association for over 20 years and was awarded the first Milton Gordon Award for Outstanding Government Service by the Chicago Chapter in 1969. He has been with the U.S. Labor Department for over 25 years and has received numerous awards for his outstanding government service, including the department's highest award, "Distinguished Career Service Award." A

Kenilworth resident, John and his lovely wife, Mary, have three children – Harry, Katina and Evangeline.

AND PRETTY.......and talented Elaine Markoutsas, she of the prolific pen, is not only writing for the *Chicago Tribune* – but for *Good Housekeeping* and *Reader's Digest*. An article written by Elaine on surrogate mothers appeared in the April issue of *Good Housekeeping* and was picked up by *Reader's Digest*. It will be reprinted in the August issue of that magazine. Elaine has also written an article on courageous Georgia Karafotas—a 38-year-old beauty with lymphoma, whose use of interferon has come to fore—giving all cancer victims a ray of hope.

QUOTE OF THE WEEK: "Human nature, as a whole, is somewhat manic-depressive, for things are never quite as good nor quite as bad as we think they are."

"Unreciprocated love is a meaningless phrase; it is as impossible as clapping with one hand."

SHOWCASE FOR.....the new breed of big beautiful dolls with freshly laundered hair and shining eyes, who will make their debut at the forthcoming St. Helen's Annual Debutante Cotillion, was the recent presentation tea given under the auspices of the St. Helen Women's Club in the elegant Mayfair Room of the Sheraton-Blackstone Hotel. Over 300 ladies of assorted sizes and shapes came to sip tea and nibble on fingertip tidbits and delightful French pastries while sneaking peaks at the new crop of pretties who will be presented in May.

Snowballing into action officially will be: Maria Magdaline Bymakos, daughter of Mr. and Mrs. Nicholas Bymakos of Akron, Ohio: Pamela Chimoures, daughter of Mr.and Mrs.Peter Chimoures of Winnetka; Karen Katsenes, daughter of Mr. and Mrs. Nicholas Katsenes of Oak Lawn; Pamela Koconis, daughter of Mr. and Mrs. Peter Koconis of Lake

Forest; Deborah Marie Kouchoukos, daughter of Mr. and Mrs. James Kouchoukos of Chicago; Virginia Suzan Mammas, daughter of Mr. and Mrs. Steven Mammas of Chicago; Pamela Gail Papas, daughter of Mr. and Mrs. George Papas of Caracas, Venezuela, South America; Alexandra Maria Politis, daughter of Dr. and Mrs. Lucas Politis of River Forest; Elaine Sampalis, daughter of Mr. and Mrs Nicholas Sampalis of Oak Lawn; Alexandra Tripodis, daughter of Mr. and Mrs. Marinos Tripodis of Chicago.

Accolades to Mrs. Thomas Lelon of Evergreen Park; Mrs. George Gatsis of Des Plaines; Mrs. Sam Tzakis of Lake Forest; Mrs. Frank J. Manta of Olympia Fields; Mrs. James Papas of Palos Park; and Mrs. Gust Vallas of Palos Heights.

Frosting on this afternoon tea cake was the bevy of lovely post-debs who pirouetted across the room displaying a beautiful collection of sensational white floor length gowns from Saks Fifth Avenue, thus pulling down the curtain of the first act in the St. Helen's Annual Debutante Cotillion.

FORMER CHICAGO ....priest, beloved by his flock, the Reverend Basil S. Gregory, who now resides in New York, has been appointed director of the Division of Public Affairs (press information, mass media and public relations). The appointment was announced by His Eminence Archbishop Iakovos, Primate of the Greek Orthodox Church of North and South America. All correspondence and inquiries should be directed to his attention at The Greek Orthodox Archdiocese of North and South America, 10 East 79th Street, New York 10027.

BOOK BEAT: "House Arrest," by Helen Vlachos. The indomitable Greek newspaper publisher's eloquent story of her arrest by the junta of colonels gives a candid look at Greek people, politics and press.

QUOTE OF THE WEEK: "Marriage has been called a 'tie,' but it is more like a belt, which cannot be too tight (or it binds) and cannot be too loose (or it falls): and marriages that fail are those which have only one notch in the belt so that it cannot be loosened or tightened to adjust to the changing weights and pressures of the relationship." - Harris

"Children play at being soldiers: the ones who never grow up tend to become generals."

VICTORIOUS IN……his bid for re-election as Maine Township Democratic committeeman was Nicholas B. Blase of Niles, Illinois. In his frequent television appearances prior to his re-election to this post, Mayor Blase struck out on his own in a mini-rebellion against Chicago's City Hall. What Blase actually wants is to make the Cook County Democratic party more suburban oriented - up to now a "no-no" for Chicago's big boss, Mayor Richard Daley.

Residents of Niles recently paid homage to their Mayor by attending the annual dinner-dance sponsored by the Regular Democratic Maine Township Organization on March 14th at the Sheraton-O'Hare Inn. In his address before the group, the down-to-earth Mayor Blase who has been top banana of Niles since 1961, winning a number of coveted awards for his performance as Mayor, explained to those attending the importance of voting in primaries – regardless of party affiliation.

During the jam-packed dinner, Toastmaster Angelo Geocaris, who handled the program deftly, introduced many distinguished personalities in the audience – as well as the speakers who graced the podium. Some of them included: Lt. Gov. Paul Simon, Adlai Stevenson III, unopposed democratic candidate for U.S. Senator, and Michael Bakalis, assistant dean of the College of Liberal Arts and Sciences at Northern Illinois University, DeKalb, Democratic candidate for superintendent of public instruction.

GUEST OF HONOR…..at a dinner-party scheduled to take place on April 10th will be Dr. Nicholas T. Mannos, principal of Niles West High School. Marking the 10th anniversary of the educator's appointment as principal of Niles West, the dinner will be held at the Morton Grove Moose Lodge 376. Reservations to the dinner, limited to a first- come-first served basis, can be made through the office of Thomas Schynepper, assistant principal.

CONDOLENCES TO.......Gus and Tula Mazarakis of Skokie, Illinois, and to Thomas Mazarakis, also of Skokie, on the death of their mother and wife, respectively.

CONGRATULATIONS TO........Chuck and Katherine (Russis) Heard of Mount Prospect, on the birth of their first son, third child, Charles William, born at Lutheran General Hospital on March 15th. Their two daughters are Diana and Carla.

BOOK BEAT: "The Heroes," Greek Fairy Tales by Charles Kingsley, illustrated by M.H. Squire and E. Mars. The stories of Perseus, Jason and Theseus are among the Greek legends in this book.

QUOTE OF THE WEEK: "The deepest and rarest kind of courage has nothing to do with feats or obstacles in the outside world; and, indeed, has nothing to do with the outside world – it is the courage to be who you are." - Harris

"People who are inordinately proud of their 'common sense' usually have little else to be proud of."

SPARKS THAT.....will ignite the Rembrandt in your soul will burst forth on Sunday afternoon, April 12th, when The Greek Women's University Club will adorn the walls of the Tip Top Tap and the Cloud Rooms of the Allerton Hotel. Capturing your artistic soul with their dabbles of originality will be the following artists:

James Georgantas, Dee Tzakis, Helen Brahos, Alexandria Kotsakis, Chris Poulos, Elaine Markoutsas, Mrs. George Markoutsas, Connie Pandas, Joanne Basil, Solon Banas, Mrs. George Kalevas, Dawn Kalevas, Mrs. George Demes, Antonia Deligiannis, Mrs. Constantine Paulos, Mrs. Denny Laskaris, Mrs. Ivan Tschilds, Dorothea Bilder, the late Dennis Kokoshis, Mrs. Nicholas Scholomiti, Mrs. Andrew

Cuser, Nicholas Nikolaidis, Nina Andoniadis, Nicholas Emanuel and Dimmy Andoniadis, Shirley Kontos, Ioannis Terzis, Sophie Pichinos, Nikki Pichinos, Stanley Anast, Gust Anast, Margaret Safrithis, Thomas Pecharis, Mrs. Joeffrey Jones, Kathryn Mandis, Linda Katagis, Anastasios Vasilatos, Elizabeth Kariotis, Christ Contoguris, George Economou, Kathy Adinamis and George Tsenes.

While focusing in on the accomplishments of these painters and sculptors, who will exhibit their imaginative wares, you will also be able to cut your mental teeth on the storehouse of information that will be disseminated by lecturer, J. Dimitri Liakos, professor of art history at Northern Illinois in DeKalb, who will speak on, "Byzantine Art, A European Art."

AND WHILE....we're on the subject of The Greek Women's University Club, Presvytera Theano Rexinis recently chaired a tea sponsored by this organization. Held in the Social Room # 3 of Winston Towers, members and their guests had the delightful pleasure of hearing a lecture by the distinguished prose-writer, Mrs. Theano Papazoglou Margaris. The only member of the National Association of Greek Literati living in America. Mrs. Margaris is listed in the Greek "Who's Who" as the promoter of Greek Letters, living in the United States. A regular columnist for *The Greek Press*, the *Greek Star* and *National Herald*, Mrs. Margaris has written such books as: "Happiness and other Short Stories," "A Tear for Uncle Jim," and her prize winning book, "Chronicles of Halsted Street." In 1963, through the Department of Education, Greece awarded Mrs. Margaris second prize in its national literary contest.

BOOK BEAT: "Those Fabulous Greeks: Onassis, Niarchos and Livanos" by Doris Lilly is a spicy saga of three shipping billionaires, Stavros Niarchos, Aristotle Onassis and Stavros Livanos, by the author of "How to Marry a Millionaire," and "How To Make Love in Five Languages." Their incredible lives are inexorably intertwined by the fact that Niarchos and Onassis each married, and later divorced, one of Livanos' daughters. Both men started their dazzling careers in the shipping room of their powerful father-in-law, and their bitter rivalry has been legend.

QUOTE OF THE WEEK: "The alcoholism of the rich consists in compulsive traveling; the poor man can alter his environment only internally, by narcotizing himself through liquor; while the more affluent are able to alter their environment externally, by constantly traveling for no purpose except release from reality."

"Few things are more disconcerting than being utterly agreed with by a person whose general views you find revolting."

A TEXAN.....owned a small farm near the outskirts of Dallas, and a handful of sheep represented his entire stock. One day his wife, while dyeing some bedspreads blue, saw one of the lambs tip over the bucket of dye. A passing motorist spotted the lamb with the blue fleece, stopped and offered the Texan $75.00 for it. So the Texan figured he had stumbled onto a good thing and colored more of his lambs with blue dye – which brought him more profits. "Pretty soon," he recalled, "I was buying all the lambs I could get my hands on and coloring them blue, green, yellow, lavender and you know-now I'm the biggest lamb dyer in Texas!"

This amusing yarn, spun by a native Texan, was related to me during a recent jaunt to the "Big D," Dallas. Here, Texans laugh over the fact that people in other states think they are rich; they laugh because they know that any number of them are so poor they have to wash their own Cadillacs. But being in Texas was an unforgettable experience for it gave me the opportunity to spend some time with some very special people. Gus and Katie Xeros (the former Katie Lithas) and their two children – pretty teenager Julie and flaming red-haired Peter; George and Helen Trapalis (the former Helen Sellas) and their brainy six-year old, Mary Ann, and tender-hearted senior citizens, George and Julia Stratigos and Helen Lithas. My thanks to all of them for helping me capture the pulse beat that is Texas.

Special "Big D" eye-openers included Southern Methodist University, whose Owen Arts Center (a $9.5 million arts complex) encompasses such architectural masterpieces as the Caruth Auditorium, the Meadows Art Museum, with its collection of Spanish paintings; the Bob Hope Theater. Dallas' gift to gastronomy, the Twenty-One Turtle Club, owned by Tony Costas is frequented by the big, beautiful people of Dallas – who, incidentally, also pay court to what has to be one of the glamorous hotels in America – The Fairmont. The interior of this posh pad is a cool, dark den of splendor in which you can rest your weary bones in unfettered luxury. The twin-towered edifice stands defiantly in space breathing clean Texas air.

MEANWHILE......in my one and only true love – polluted old Chicago, a distinguished and deserving gentleman, Dr. Theodore G. Phillips, was made president of Amundson-Mayfair College at ceremonies conducted at St. James Episcopal Cathedral. The inauguration was followed by a dinner-dance at which both President and Mrs. Phillips were honored.

Mrs. Tina Zoumboulis, grand treasurer of Mantine Chapter #152, Daughters of Penelope, was honored at a luncheon given at the Flying Carpet Motor Inn. The event was chaired by Mrs. Clara Ellis.

Helen (Dean) Koretos gave a baby shower for sis Chris (Stash) Anagnostopoulos at the Brass Rail, Sheraton Motor Inn.

Another downpour of gifts went to bride-to-be, Maria Papas, at a shower given by Mrs. Alexis Relias. Other pre-nuptial parties given for Maria and fiancée, John Gleason, included a swinging cocktail and dinner party hosted by Evie and Peter Chimoures of Winnetka, and a tea party given by Kathryn (George) Bugelas of Evanston, at which 65 women honored Maria while sipping champagne and nibbling on delectable tidbits.

QUOTE OF THE WEEK: "We forget kindnesses far more easily than we forget injuries, for we unconsciously regard a kindness as something that is our due, while we regard an injury as utterly undeserved, even when it is not." - Harris

Spanish saying: "You must make up your mind what you want most out of marriage: to cherish or to conquer."

LARGE DOSES.......of great head-to-shoe looks, sprinkled with fashion forecasts of what's coming, what's going, and what's staying, will be spoon fed to the ladies who will attend the forthcoming fashion show to be presented by the St. Demetrios Philoptochos on May 2nd in the Grand Ballroom of the Marriott Motor Hotel. "Age of Aquarius in Zodiac Fashion," a sign of the times title, will cater to the totally young group – young in age, in thought, in spirit, and in movement. Reservations to this delightful happening may be made by calling Mrs. Gust Tompary at 878-3029.

FOR THOSE.....of you who are Paris bound this summer, make sure you pick up a copy of a book which is a veritable storehouse of information, describing where to eat, drink, shop and look in Gay Paree. Put yourself in the hands of Henri Gault and Christian Milau, the enthusiastic authors of the Julliard Guide to good eating places, as well as the authors of a number of holiday articles on food and drink. They have produced a little number entitled, "A Parisian's Guide to Paris," which will make the ominous threat of missing out on something in Paris fade from the horizon.

GREEK MOVIE......benefit show, sponsored by the Women's Auxiliary of the Greek Archdiocese Welfare Foundation, can be viewed at the Commodore Theater in Chicago on May 15th. The amusing technicolor film will be featured at 6:30pm and 8:30pm.

IT'S JOLLY.......fun filching facts on the femme fatales who will bow at the Deb Cotillion on May 9th at the Conrad Hilton Hotel:

One of this year's crop, Pamela Papas, who attends Miss Porter's School in Farmington, Connecticut, hails from Caracas, Venezuela, South America.

Pamela Chimoures, who attends Pine Manor Junior College, is the second member of her family to be presented at the Cotillion. Pamela's artistically inclined mom, Evie, is chairman of the Cotillion's Theme and Décor Committee.

When their daughter, Alexandra, bows at this year's event, it will be a repetitious event for Dr. and Mrs. Lucas Politis. While daughter, Alexandra, is busy planning for her debut, Tina (post deb) is making arrangements for her Lohengrin to Michael Adinamis.

Second time around for Mr. and Mrs. Nicholas Sampalis, whose daughter, Elaine, is bowing. They, too, are busy with wedding plans for their post deb daughter, Sue, who will middle-aisle it in June with George Kamberos.

While this is the first deb in their family (daughter, Virginia) the Steven Mammas' are very familiar with Cotillion procedures for Mrs. Mammas has been active on Cotillion committees for some time.

Maria Bymakos, another deb, attends the University of Akron; pretty doe-eyed Pamela Koconis is a senior at Libertyville High School; ditto for Debra Kouchoukos, another senior at Luther North High School; Karen Katsenes attends St. Xavier College; and Alexandra Tripodis, Western Illinois University.

QUOTE OF THE WEEK: "It is a mistake of immaturity to regard pain and suffering as things that 'happen in life,' like so many raisins in a cake; they are, rather, the modes in which life itself is expressed, like the flour in every cake; and a person who refuses to accept this truth may justly be called childish."

"When we no longer fear an enemy, we begin to pity him-more proof that hate is always based on some kind of fear."

DURING A RECENT.....discussion with some of the mainsprings of our community, a request was made to present a problem, in this column, which many feel exists in our community. It is a problem that apathy has allowed to remain dormant. It is a problem that, at one time or another, has vexed all organizational leaders – church board officers, heads of professional groups, fraternal groups, etc. It is one that has been a financial thorn in the side of some organizations. It is the problem of scheduling – of clearing all social events through a central body so that two major organizations do not schedule money-making projects on the same day. To the frenetic chairman of a dinner-dance or a picnic who, in all good conscience, selected a date months in advance: to the arduous committee members who have painstakingly contributed man hours, their cool, and a right hand which has grown limp from addressing envelopes, this lack of ability to clear social events through a central body has proved quite disconcerting.

When a calendar of events column made its newspaper debut some years ago, a certain semblance of order was followed – at least for a short period of time. Today, however, this is history. Organizational leaders have turned apathetic. They refuse to find the time to check, much less list, a date in a dates column. Because of this, many "foul balls" have gone to bat at a late date sometimes scoring an undeserved hit.

Consider the plight of a major professional group that recently sponsored an art show conscientiously listing its date in the calendar of events months in advance. A prominent church PTA group decided to sponsor a fashion show on the same day at the same time. Early in March of this year, a north suburban church held its annual dinner-dance. This group also had listed its date in the column months in advance. Another nearby suburban church competitively sponsored a social on the same evening.

A close inspection of these incidents uncovers irritations which, perhaps, should not be left unchallenged nor passed over lightly. Perhaps the offending culprits, who thoughtlessly planned events on the same day and at the same time, should be made to mend their ways through the interception of a central clearing board with which official registration could be made of all community sponsored events. On the other hand, perhaps they should not be given the dignity of even cursory consideration.

On the flip side, perhaps the situation should remain at a status quo thus granting latitude to all the organizations in our community.

The gnat could turn into a problem barracuda with all the red tape involved. Perhaps a board would only serve the purpose of stifling the free flow of community enterprise thereby helping us to commit organizational suicide. Perhaps well enough should be left alone and, if a conflict of dates should occur, as in the past – may the wisest reap the profits. Perhaps some of our learned and dynamic community leaders, well- versed in the psychological shenanigans that plague group activity, can come up with a solution to this problem –if they think there is a problem. We'd certainly like to hear from them.

QUOTE OF THE WEEK: "Those who make a habit of flattery lack the capacity to love; flattery is always a sign of emotional impotence, seeking to achieve the effect in words that it cannot attain in deed."

"A woman finds nothing quite so unsatisfactory as a friend without faults she can talk about."

SPIFFY NEW....eatery, brain child of Nick Demet and Curt Chioles, recently opened in Morton Grove. Named "Parfaits," the architectural delight was designed by architect Curt's up and coming firm, United Design, Inc. There are a lot of yum yums in this family type restaurant.

IT WAS.......nice to note that one of our Greek Orthodox Churches, Sts. Peter and Paul, Glenview, had a small portion of its Easter Sunday Agape services covered by CBS-TV news department.

RUMOR HAS.....it that the nimble new song and dance team, Chris and Elayne Pappas of Elgin, did their thing so well that professional offers have been pouring in from the east coast following their performance in "Much Ado in May" produced by the Elgin Junior Women's Board. Elayne, also talent chairman for the Elgin production and hubby, Chris, wiggled a few through this delightful variety show which had a two-day run at the Hemmens Auditorium, a spanking new building in Elgin. Purpose of the show was to provide dental care for underprivileged children. Rick Northcutt, well-known New York choreographer, handled the production numbers.

THE NATIONAL.......Cash Register Company has appointed the W.J. Russis and Company, Inc. the complete programming and systems development of all the NCR 500 series computers in the Chicago area. John Demos, formerly the total systems manager for the NCR Company, has joined the Russis firm as systems and programming director, along with Ronald Bowman and Louis Nagy of the Cordox Company and Dan Matsoukas of the Lincoln National Bank. This brain trust is headed by James Russis.

AND TO.......the warm, wonderful world of little people whom I have neglected of late: To my pretty moppet goddaughter, Dana Pappas, happy ninth birthday; ditto to chubby-cheeked Danny Koretzky on his third; a big hug to lovable Vance Koretos for his pluckiness following a surgical knee bout; and a thunderous ovation to my favorite 10-year-old, Bobby Kafkis, who modeled so well at a recent kiddie fashion show.

THAT LONG.......legged bird just delivered an 8 lb. 6 oz. son, Kevin, to Chris and Stash Anagnostopoulos. Another son also was delivered to James and Bonnie Jean Boosales of Wenham, Massachusetts, who are now the proud parents of their second child. James is the son of the late Sam and Connie Boosales of Skokie.

IT WAS.....certainly pleasant to see good friend, Bess Maheras Michas, back in Chicago again. Hubby, Luke, is waiting patiently back in San Diego, California, while Bess spends a bit of time with her family and friends.

AND FROM.......The Women's Auxiliary of the Greek Archdiocese Welfare Foundation – a note to the effect that its movie theater benefit, scheduled to take place on Friday evening, May 15th, has been cancelled due to the fact that the theater is no longer showing Greek films. The auxiliary is planning another movie benefit at another theater, and the date will be announced as soon as arrangements have been completed. Money will be refunded for tickets already sold.

QUOTE OF THE WEEK: "People should hang out their minds for an airing every so often, if they want their opinions to smell as fresh and sweet as their linen. The sour odor of stale convictions cling to most of us like a mist."

"The hardest way for a man to earn money is by marrying it." – West

SLATED TO....open at the Royal-George Theater, 1641 N. Halsted, for an open-ended run is the exciting play, "Steel Magnolias," a play written by Robert Harling that proved to be a smash broadway hit. The Hellenic Professional Society of Illinois has picked up on this hit. On November 12th, the HPSI has planned an exciting evening which will include attending this hit and dining at the adjacent Café Royal. The evening will include a pre-show buffet dinner at 6:30pm, a theater ticket for the 8pm show, and pastries during intermission.

AN UNUSUAL.....Memorial Day was spent by all those invited to an outing by dear friend, Sophia Koretzky. What with inclement weather – and so forth – everyone ended up in Sophia's high-rise apartment giving her an "A" for being able to handle such a big crowd on such short notice.

THIS WEEK......we point with pride to Andrew A. Athens, national chairman of United Hellenic American Congress, who was lauded in the October 10th issue of *Crain's Chicago Business.* The article on Andy, entitled, "A Quiet Man Raises Big Bucks for the Duke," pointed him out as one of the biggest fund-raisers nationally for the democratic presidential nominee reversing a democratic tradition of lagging fund-raising efforts for presidential campaigns in Illinois. Early last year, he had raised $20,000 for a George Bush fund-raiser. The article pointed out that Andy has always remained politically neutral. A Dukakis fund-raising event in Chicago late last month brought in about $2 million, far more than any democratic presidential nominee has raised in the state.

TWO OF….our town's greatest scholars, Andrew and Alice Kopan, recently had a private audience with His Holiness Patriarch Demetrios at the Ecumenical Patriarchate in Istanbul. His Holiness received Professsor and Mrs. Kopan at his office in the Phanar. The audience took place during the 14th Annual DePaul University tour to Europe.

IN CELEBRATION….of its 60th anniversary, the St. Demetrios Greek Orthodox Church of Chicago will hold its Diamond Jubilee Ball, November 5th at the O'Hare Marriott Hotel. According to Paul Stamos, Alex Kopsian and George Atsaves, co-chairmen, the ball will highlight 60 years of Christian service to the community.

QUOTE OF THE WEEK: "In times of misfortune, we are prone to reflect that we do not deserve such unhappiness, but in times of felicity, it rarely occurs to us that we are equally undeserving of such happiness."

"We truly possess only what we are able to renounce; otherwise, we are simply possessed by our possessions."

HUNDREDS…….of tender, fragrant, blushing roses, plucked at their fleeting moment of perfection, permeated the air with refreshing sweetness at the wedding of Maria Papas and John Martin Gleason,

Jr., son of Mr. and Mrs. John Martin Gleason, Sr., which took place on Sunday, May 3rd at 6pm. at St. Andrew's Greek Orthodox Church.

The bride, who is the daughter of Dina Gregory Papas and the late and beloved Spiro Papas, was given in marriage by her stately and distinguished grandfather, S.J. Gregory. The radiant bride wore a gown of candlelight ivory English tulle and re-embroidered Princess Alencon lace with accents of custom beading in seedling pearls, crystals and paillettes. The custom designed cloche of pseudo pearls, which framed Maria's beautiful face, was caught by a cathedral length mantilla of heirloom lace used by the bride's mother for her wedding. Her bouquet was a shower of white roses, lily of the valley and orange blossoms.

The bride's aunt, Mrs. William L. Bryant of McLean, Virginia, was matron of honor; her cousin, Andrea Spheeris of Milwaukee, Wisconsin, was maid of honor. Carrying garlands of roses in shades of pink, the matron and maid of honor and six candy-sweet bridesmaids were wrapped in azure blue floor length gowns of pure silk peau de soie trimmed with jewels. They included: Natalie Bryant of McLean; Mrs. Frank B. Chaunter of New York City; Letitia Parker of Boston; Margarita Stassinopoulos of Athens, Greece; Elizabeth Tubekis of Wilmette; and the bridegroom's sister, Lillian Gleason. William Bryant was best man.

Ron Amey designed the floor length gown worn by the bride's mother – an oriental flower garden brocade in multi-hued tones embellished with ties of apple green satin. The groom's mother wore a gown of azalea pink textured silk with jeweled accents.

Guests were received in the French Room of the Drake Hotel in front of a screen encircled with full bloomed roses warmed to the height of their fragrance and flanked by a pair of Byzantine topiary rose trees. The dinner tables in the Gold Coast Room were ornamented with tall Grecian columns festooned with roses and trellises of fresh strawberries.

Official toastmaster of the evening was Andrew Spheeris of Milwaukee, uncle of the bride. Armed with words of wit and enthusiasm, he introduced some of the family members who took their turn in expressing their happiness at the occasion. Adding a splash of foreign flavor to the list of speakers was handsome, Nicholas Stassinopoulos of Athens, Greece, and his vivacious wife, Jean, aunt of the bride, who flew in for the wedding with their three children and their soon-to-be son-in-law. Most sentimental speaker of the evening was the beloved patriarch of the family, S.J.Gregory, who touched the hearts of those present with his remarks.

QUOTE OF THE WEEK: "When they are young, people believe that 'speaking the truth' is the most important thing; as people grow older, if they ripen, they learn that speaking the truth lovingly is the only way to make it count – for truth without love merely cuts without curing."

"One does not fall into love; one grows into love, and love grows in him." – Karl Menninger

THE ELEGANT……doors of the Casino will swing open for The Greek Women's University Club's annual spring dance, "La Soiree de la Fleur de Lis." Nancy Chirigos, in charge of arrangements, has announced that this delightful event will take place on June 6th at 8:30 pm. The Greek Lads will supply the music.

The membership of The Greek Women's University Club and its charming president, Mary Secaras, would like to express appreciation to the many creative artists who so graciously contributed their original wares to the recent art show sponsored by the group.

REALLY TICKING…..is Chris Michas, chairman of the forthcoming Annual Presentation Dinner Dance to be sponsored by The Hellenic Professional Society of Illinois, for giving all those who attend the event a chance to hear the dignified and dynamic United States Senator Ralph Tyler Smith who has consented to be the keynote speaker of the evening. Site of this splash will be the Grand Cotillion Ballroom of the Continental Plaza Hotel on June 27th. Graduates chairmen Roula Christos and Dean Dranias would appreciate receiving the names of graduates of Hellenic descent who have graduated or are going to graduate from college or post-college levels from the period between July 1969 to June 1970, so that they can be presented at this 45th annual event. Please contact either Roula Christos or Dean Dranias. This promises to be a delicious summer frolic.

ARCHBISHOP IAKOVOS.......Primate of our Greek Orthodox Church, has been named clergyman of the year by Religious Heritage of America. According to the Rev. Dr. Herbert Richards, Minister of the First United Methodist Church of Eugene, Oregon, His Eminence was selected for his leadership in community and ecumenical activities at home and abroad.

CONDOLENCES ARE......extended to the family of Christ Andrews of St. Paul, Minnesota, who succumbed recently. The well-known Mr. Andrews was revered by many in the St. Paul-Minneapolis community. He is survived by his wife, Marika, a daughter, Theodora, and a son and daughter-in-law, Peter and Harriet Andrews.

MORE THAN.....$200,000 in contributions have been received for the new summer camp of the Greek Orthodox Archdiocese of North and South America opening in Bartholomio, Greece this summer. Archbishop Iakovos announced that this figure includes two recent gifts: $10,000 from Anthony Chandris, president of the Chandris Lines, which was presented by Basil Zaharis,, vice-president of the firm, and $1,000 from the Macedonian Federation of the U.S. presented by Constantine Papafotiou, supreme secretary, on behalf of John Juris, supreme president of the organization. Total cost of the project is estimated at $400,000.

QUOTE OF THE WEEK: "It is axiomatic that the person who is not pleased with others is never pleased with himself, no matter how egocentric he seems to be; the chronic fault finder is always projecting a profound sense of dissatisfaction with himself."

"Those who end their letters with the phrase, 'as ever,' are giving reassurance that they have not changed, to people who perhaps wish they would."

YOU'RE ON.......the right track to excitement and a week-end filled with enthusiasm and flavor if you are planning to spend some of your waking hours at O'Hare Inn, headquarters of the forthcoming Ahepa District Convention, on Memorial Day weekend. According to Dina (Ted) Anastos (he of trucking TV law fame and she the 13th district governor of the Daughters of Penelope) the scene will be one big massive dose of lively fun. The two big groovy events, at which you will be able to rap with your friends to your heart's content, will be the Greek Festival on Friday night, and the banquet and ball on Saturday night.

For the chic-conscious fashion ladies, the Daughters of Penelope have scheduled a ring-a-ding fashion luncheon show to take place on Saturday at noon. Bright and blooming clothes from Bramson's will be modeled by the members of the various chapters of the Daughters of Penelope. Mario Tonnelli, board member of the Cook County Air Pollution Bureau, will give a timely address at the Daughter's Saturday afternoon meeting. He will breathe the real story behind "Environmental Pollution Control."

LIVES OF......depressed and down hearted patients at Oak Lawn Hospital, most of whom are terminally ill, were enriched and enlivened by The Greek Women's University Club when representative members of the organization personally delivered Easter baskets to 39 Orthodox Christians at the hospital. Plaudits to Stella Mantelos and Maria Pappas for the work they did on this worthwhile project.

AND TO...supply answers to the flood of queries that have besieged Kay Phillips, general chairman of the forthcoming "Olympian Fashions" fashion show luncheon, sponsored by the Assumption Women's Society, she has offered the following information: The model representing a specific organization must be an active member of the organization and one who has not modeled professionally. The only requirement for entrance is that each participating club reserve a table of ten for the luncheon and that remittances be mailed to the society with the model's entry form. This is not to include the model for she will be the society's guest for lunch. An impartial panel of judges will select the winning models and cash prizes will be awarded to the winning organizations. The event will take place on November 7th at the Olympia Fields Country Club.

BOOK BEAT: "Man's Freedom" by Andreas G. Papandreou, Carnegie Mellon University, May publication date. There are some plain spoken charges as well as some tough-minded analyses in this slender volume based on the Benjamin Fairless Memorial Lectures (1969) delivered by the former Greek Minister of State who is now the exiled leader of the Panhellenic Liberation Movement. Papandreou is a sharp critic both of our own capitalist-managerial system and of the Soviet brand of socialism.

QUOTE OF THE WEEK: "There are some personalities that make a life-long career out of being disappointed in people. This enables them to satisfy two disparate desires at once – to feel superior, and at the same time to rationalize their continual failures in personal relationships."

"Many parents never learn the fundamental lesson that sometimes the best way to convince a child he is wrong is to let him have his own way."

MEMO TO.......Georgia Photopulos, pride of the community for the inner-outer beauty she has maintained despite ill health, who is currently convalescing from another major surgical bout: Your legion of admirers have asked me to tell you that they have thoughtfully heeded the advice of your physicians and have not barraged you with calls and visits. But let it be known that their hearts have fluttered for your well being. Each hour of each day they plant a harvest of prayers in your name. Georgia, one of the truly bright lights of this chaotic world, is the wife of handsome, Bud Photopulos, newscaster for ABC-TV.

A VERY.......hard-working and deserving lady, Mrs. Andrew (Irene) Tzakis, has once again won a vote of confidence from her membership for the great work she has done as president of the St. Andrew's Women's Club, by being re-elected into office for another two years. Those re-elected to serve with her include the following: Mrs. Alec (Vi) Gianaras, first vice-president; Mrs. Evan (Helen) Papageorge, second vice-president; Mrs. Christ (Angie) Karafotias, recording secretary; Mrs. Nicholas (Aggie) Kafkis, corresponding secretary; Mrs. James (Ann) Poulos, treasurer.

RECENT APPOINTMENT.......was received by the very capable Sam Booras of Lincolnwood. Sam was one of three specialists in air pollution control appointed by George Dunne, president of the Cook County Board of Commissions. He will serve on the newly formed advisory committee of the Cook County Air Pollution Control Bureau.

WEARING THEIR......hearts at half-mast are members of the family of D.N. Karalis of Minneapolis, Minnesota, who succumbed recently. Active in Ahepa, he was the brother of the late Fred Karalis of Chicago, beloved pie company tycoon. Mr. Karalis is survived by his wife, Pauline and two children, Elena and George. Nieces Esther Poulos of Fort Lauderdale, Florida, and Georgia Booras of Lincolnwood, trekked to Minneapolis for the burial.

ONE OF.......five religious leaders to be honored by the National Conference of Christians and Jews for "courageous leadership in inter-racial relations" will be the Rev. Leonidas Contos, president of Hellenic College in Brookline, Massachusetts. The NCCJ is praising Father Contos for his "exceptional involvement in civic and ecumenical activities in the United States and abroad," and for his "inspired dedication to young people as friend, teacher and counselor." All five of the religious leaders will receive gold medallions on June 8th at the conference's Fourth Annual Religious Leaders' Dinner in New York City.

FIFTEEN DAY.........Eastern Orthodox Pilgrimage to the Holy Land will be led by the Rev. Anthony Coniaris of Minneapolis. The pilgrimage will leave New York City on July 20th. The total cost is $699 and covers first class hotels, three meals a day, all tours and tips.

QUOTE OF THE WEEK: "Apart from all other considerations, the deep psychological reason that we need someone to love us is that we can freely confess our faults and defects only to someone who acknowledges our lovability."

"Last year they went to the moon during our picnic. Come and see what they do this year." - Sts. Peter and Paul Committee

WHEN the.....world comes alive on a hot, sweltering summer day and breezes blow caressingly ruffling blades of grass on stretches of green velvet lawn, Greek people traditionally get together at church sponsored carnivals, or picnics and eat, drink, dance, gossip and eyeball each other on one to three-day binges. Some groan and grunt pretending they hate the stuff: they spend days in anguished indecision as to whether or not to attend. They are usually the first ones there. Some phase out with dignity, picnics not being their bag; older eyes grow misty while older speech waxes philosophically at the thought of not attending. Each church group discusses as mystique the idea that any picnic could be better than its very own picnic. It is "our picnic" versus "their picnic." The wise ones smile through the skirmish and attend them all. They become "picnic happy" and by the end of the summer they have had a bellyful of souvlakia, feta cheese, loukoumades dripping with honey, and other traditional Greek goodies. Until next year, that is.

Well, the picnic season is almost upon us and one of the nicest one-day binges you can attend has been scheduled to take place on Sunday, July 12th. This is the 9th Annual St. Andrew's Greek Orthodox Church picnic at which festivities begin on the church grounds immediately following church services. This year exciting raffle prizes will be offered by the W. Clement Stone's of the Greek community. Grand prize is a two-door Buick Skylark; second prize, a 20" color television set; third prize, a 19" portable television set; fourth prize, a stereo AM/FM console; fifth prize, an 8mm movie camera.

I have a sneaking suspicion that this year, like last year, some of our picnics just might be invaded by a lot of the cute little kids who pop out of high-rise buildings and clipped hedges of suburbia. You know the ones I mean. They dress like kooks, don't wash, braid daisies, eat LSD, smoke pot, and sit on cold, concrete curbstones. Most of them are flat broke and rely on pop to foot the bill that will put power into the guitar industry and rebuild the little old chemistry lab that was accidentally burned down last week.

Well, if some of the disillusioned and dismayed hippies pay the tab of admission to breathe in a stable old-fashioned, non-polluted family type atmosphere, let's show them all – the drop-out young, the drop-in young, the sit-in young, and the sit-out young; the sit-down young, and the stand-up young; the march-up and down young, the rebellious young, and the young-young – how much fun being young really can be. Let's show them that being young doesn't have to be such an awesome business. It doesn't mean you have to work so hard at it.

It doesn't have to mean spinning around in the swivel chairs of university presidents. It doesn't have to mean shouldering so much responsibility. It doesn't have to mean creating so much clamor and controversy, so much turmoil and concern. It can mean being loved. It can mean being heard. It can mean being understood. It can mean communicating without violence. It can be a positive fun-filled adventure – not the flaky heap it has become of late.

FASCINATING RAGS…..to riches Horatio Alger story appears in the May 1970 issue of *Signature* magazine. It tells about Tom Carvel, Ice

Cream King of the East. Born in Athens, Greece, 63 years ago, Carvel came to the U.S. at the age of 5 and worked as a shoe shine boy, farm hand, vaudeville hoofer, etc., before going into business for himself peddling ice cream from the back of a small house trailer in Hartsdale, New York. Today he lives in a $200,000 home nestled on a 13-acre wooded estate in Westchester County.

QUOTE OF THE WEEK: "Ten out of ten Greeks expect their daughters to marry Greeks. Our picnic is your chance to get things rolling." Sts. Peter & Paul Picnic Committee

"Our picnic is brought to you by the same people that gave you democracy, the Olympics, feta cheese and Spiro Agnew." –Sts. Peter and Paul Picnic Committee

NEW SETTINGS.....for "Old Country Weddings" is the title of a delightful and informative 8-page spread which appears in the June issue of *McCall's* magazine. According to the article, many modern weddings have lost some of their traditions – but not so those imported from Italy, Greece, Poland and Denmark. The two-page color spread, devoted to the ornate ritual of a Greek Orthodox wedding, is entitled, "Zeto E Ellas." Wrapped in blue and white tradition, it tells, among other things, how the crowning of both bride and groom denotes a sharing of joy and sorrow; how Jordan almonds are thrown at the couple for fertility; silver coins and rice for prosperity: and how, to the happy sounds of the dranga-dranga-bouzouki, repeated toasts are drunk and chinaware is broken.

Diamond in the navel of this story is, and I quote from *McCall's*: "The bride's mother tells her daughter to stamp on her new husband's foot to signify that in the home she will rule the guests." Not only does this tradition sound like the basis for mother-in-law hostility jokes – it could be the basis of Jackie's blitzing Ari's Mickey Mouse bank to the tune of $19,500 a year to help keep the image intact. If you remember the United Press-Associated Press stories at the time of this moon-spoon sentiment little Lohengrin, since mama wasn't there, Jackie stomped real hard on Ari's foot with her indestructible size nines. She now rules the guests and the host proving there is a moral to this story?????

Thousands of the brightest people in the United States will attend the Sts. Peter and Paul Picnic, July 17-19.

A WHALE……of an evening was enjoyed by all those attending the recent bash given by The Greek Women's University Club which took place at The Casino on Chicago's near north side. New at the helm are the following lovely ladies: Theano Rexinis, Jeanette Nassos, Theodora Kanellos, Violet Georgopoulos, Rosemary Xenakis and Myrsini Terzis.

Come to the Sts. Peter and Paul picnic and meet your wife's old boyfriends, July 17-19.

FOR THE ……first time in Florida history, the Greek Orthodox Churches of Tarpon Springs, Tampa, St. Petersburg, Clearwater, Daytona Beach, Orlando, Jacksonville and Tallahassee all joined together in religious observance for a single cause – the building of a $200,000 St. Nicholas Educational facility. The diocesan-house fund of the bishop provided the vehicle for such united effort. The event gained an avalanche of publicity throughout Florida as a result of comprehensive coverage by the press, radio and television. The program opened with special services at St. Nicholas Greek Orthodox Church in Tarpon Springs. After the services, ground-breaking ceremonies were held. Later, a capacity crowd filled the Clearwater Municipal Auditorium for the festive celebration of the Sunday of Orthodox Unity – the Byzantine Ball.

QUOTE OF THE WEEK: "When we say that someone has 'independent means,' we usually mean precisely the opposite – that he or she has inherited or married money and is dependent upon the legacy achieved through another's efforts. Such independence most often exacts a high price." - Harris

"By the time the meek inherit the earth, it will be a liability not an asset."

HILARIOUS MAILERS.....that had my office in a tickle all morning have been created by a really bright, talented and articulate guy, George Maniates, art director of Campbell-Ewald Advertising Company, John Hancock Center, for the forthcoming picnic to be sponsored by the Sts. Peter and Paul Greek Orthodox Church in Glenview, July 17-19. While I'm probably committing a grave injustice by even attempting to describe one of his supercolossal and uproarious gems, nevertheless I have to share one of these funnies with you.

Take out a relative's old wedding picture – you know the one I mean – vintage 1920 – with all the bridesmaids, best man, bride and groom. Mount it on 18" x 18" colored paper. Place a big, black bold headline on top of it which reads; DON'T CRY, MA. Then read this copy:

"This is what you wanted for Sophie. She's happy now. And Nick is a lucky guy. They shared a seat on the ferris wheel at the Sts. Peter & Paul picnic, a year ago. Proof again that if you want your daughter to marry a Greek, our picnic is your chance to get things rolling. We've got all kinds of nice Greek boys – doctors, lawyers, professional people. A few restaurant owners left over from last year. So don't miss this year's event. Rides, games, shishkabob, loukoumades, music, dancing and refreshments. But most of all we've got people. The kind you want your daughter to meet. You might win a 21-day trip to Greece or $2,000 in cash. Some wedding present. July 17-19, Friday and Saturday night, Sunday, all day and all night on the church grounds.

You can't go wrong with this kind of talent in your ball park.

BE ON.......the lookout for three school marms who bear the mark of explosive happiness. They captured the hearts of two attorneys and another school teacher while attending meetings of the Hellenic Professional Society of Illinois. Armed with plans for summer weddings are: Attorney Arthur Perivolidis of Oak Park, president of the society, who will middle-aisle it with Phyllis Pergakes of Elmhurst, a member of the society and a teacher in Northbrook. Attorney George Karcazes of Chicago, past president of the society, will promise to love, honor and cherish Roula Christos of Winnetka, corresponding secretary of the society and a teacher in Hoffman Estates. Teacher George Geane of Arlington Heights, who will exchange wedding vows with Georgia Kariotis of Park Ridge, is a member of the society and a teacher in Hoffman Estates.

CONGRATULATIONS TO.....Gigi Childs, daughter of Peter and Helen Childs of Northfield, who graduated from Sunset Ridge Grammar School. This delightful charmer will attend New Trier West. Ditto to pretty Faye Pappageorge, daughter of Chris and Gloria Pappageorge of Glenview, who recently went through commencement high school exercises. She will be attending Cornell College in Iowa. Solon Tsaoussis, son of Themis and Frances Tsaoussis of Chicago, recently went through graduation ceremonies at Roycemore. His sister, Carrie, a valedictorian at last year's Roycemore commencement exercises, is currently attending Northwestern University.

QUOTE OF THE WEEK: "Most criticism is a form of egotism. The more different kinds of people a man does not like, the more right we have to suspect that he wholly approves only of those who are precisely like him. But the neurotic inconsistency in such a critical person is that, if we probe deeply enough, it will be found that he doesn't like himself very much at bottom."-Harris

"The most utterly lost of all days is that in which you have not once laughed." –Chamfort

PENNINGS FROM.....pretty Eva Polydoris of Glenview, who visited a delightful and quaint Greek Orthodox Church in Honolulu, Hawaii: "Everything was so very beautiful, but for me, it was something very, very special."

A short time ago, Eva and Stuart Polydoris went to Hawaii with Mr. and Mrs. Malcolm Stuart of England. On the first Sunday of their stay at the Hilton Hawaiian Village, Eva checked to see if there was a Greek Orthodox Church in Honolulu.

According to Eva: "The first view of the church, nestled high on the side of a mountain in lush green surroundings, was breathtaking; Diamond Head could clearly be seen on the opposite side of the mountain. As we alighted from our cab, we were greeted by a colorful old man with crinkly eyes, who welcomed us.

"The interior of the tiny church had a silent, moving beauty all its own.

"All 25 members of the congregation came over and introduced themselves. Coffee and sweets were served. A shy, elderly gentleman with a crooked grin, brought each of us a jar of honey to take back home with us. A ride was arranged for our departure back to the hotel.

"The parish priest, Reverend Dean Gigicos, introduced himself. With pride in his voice he explained that the church, which has no name, is quite poor. Only the strong faith of the congregation holds it together.

"I would advise anyone visiting Honolulu to attend services at this church," concluded Eva. "It is an unbelievably serene experience. This, to me, is religion at its best."

FACES AND PLACES: Nicholas Jannes, graphic designer and inventor of the pop up card, recently took his jaunty boat, the Achilles, for a cruise around the Michigan coastline. Now off to Athens, Greece, he will do some island hopping with other graphic designers.

SHEER DELIGHT......was the trip recently taken by Kay Gianaris who flipped her fandana over the social fanfare she received while visiting Hawaii, Japan and Hong Kong.

WE POINT.....with pride to Dr. James V. Apostol, son of Mr. and Mrs. S.D. Apostol of Chicago, who was recently appointed assistant professor of surgery at Northwestern University's Medical School.

WEARING THEIR......hearts at half mast are Nike Giannakis, William and Matia Cocoris, and Sophia Koretzky on the recent death of their husband and father, respectively, Dennis Giannakis. A man who loved life and who knew how to live it, he will be sorely missed by all those who knew him.

QUOTE OF THE WEEK: "Nowhere is it more important to 'hate the sin, but love the sinner' than in rebuking or punishing a child. While a child's action may be called 'bad' he, himself, must never be called 'bad' and we must enable him to distinguish between behavior and character, so that his self-confidence is not broken down."

"Hypocrisy is the homage that vice pays to virtue."

THE MOMENT......of truth for women who put a high priority on being fashionable will be on hand at the forthcoming luncheon-fashion show scheduled to take place in the Guildhall of the Ambassador Hotel on Saturday, October 17th. Ladies will not only be scrutinizing the dazzlers on the runway at this prestigious event, but each other, for this year there is the question of hemlines, and it will come to fore at this show which always draws an audience of the city's most fashionable and fashion conscious socializers. However, if the movers and shakers of fashion shows are indicative of trends, we've seen the last of milady's knees. Everything will be long and all the sad head-shaking by leg-happy gentlemen will not change what fashion dictates. The short skirt fans will simply have to live to fight another day.

Since the word has leaked out that this year's designer's collection of fashion will come out of the fabulous Elizabeth Arden Salon, where gilded, gold hairpins cost a left lung, telephones have been jangling unnerving committee members on where and how to make reservations to this super colossal splash. With invitations hot off the press, Irene Diacou, reservations chairman, has already been deluged with reservation requests. Since they will be accepted in order of receipt of checks, we suggest you send your reservations to her pronto at: 7440 N . Artesian, Chicago 60645.

The very chic Elizabeth Arden Salon is a tightly knit shop that sifts and resifts all fashion show requests giving prime time only to what is considered by those in charge to be a select clientele. Through the tireless efforts of Mrs. Andrew (Irene) Tzakis, president, and Mrs. Ted (Dina) Anastos, chairman, the St. Andrew's Women's Club made the grade – once again scoring a first for this banner group. So, ladies, pack up your minis in your old kit bag and go to the Ambassador on the 17th to view a spectacular designer's collection of fashions that will eat both your heart and your pocketbook out. Later, there will be a mini effigy.

BRIGHT AND.......articulate Dr. Bergen Evans, professor of English at Northwestern University, will be presented by The Greek Women's University Club on October 18th at the S.J. Gregory Auditorium. Penny Xenakis, chairman, and Myrsini Terzis, co-chairman, have announced Dr. Evans' title will be, "Ancient Greece: Beginning of Sanity."

The knowledgeable Dr. Evans is the author of seven books some of which have gone through six American editions in hardcover and four paperback printings. He has written more than 100 articles some of which have appeared in the *Atlantic, Harper's, New Republic, Saturday Review, Esquire, Vogue, Harper's Bazaar, Cosmopolitan, Reader's Digest, Coronet,* etc.

PERSONALITIES IN THE NEWS: What journalist recently took a two-day trek to Washington, D.C. to confer with a national political biggie on a book she is writing? While there, she was offered a national press appointment available in mid '71.

Mrs. Ted (Dina) Anastos recently hosted a tea for 150 women in her spacious Morton Grove home. It was given in honor of Congressman Philip Crane of the 13th Congressional District.

Helen Beldecos of Pennsylvania, grand president of the Daughters of Penelope, recently made the following national appointments in District 13: Mrs. Steve (Irene) Betzelos of Chicago, chairman of legislation; Vickie Katsis of Chicago, reappointed national education chairman. Mrs. James (Tina) Zoumboulis was elected grand secretary of the Daughters of Penelope.

QUOTE OF THE WEEK: "The road to hell is paved with inattentions; surely more sins are committed through neglect than through calculated purpose."

"We make positive judgments about men and negative judgments about women, in the sense that a good man is known by what he does, but a good woman is known by what she doesn't do."

IT IS….not the task of this columnist to endorse political candidates, nor is this column concerned with the exercising of political views. Nevertheless, after a great deal of deliberation, I decided that I would indeed be remiss in my job of disseminating information to the public if the readers of this column were not informed about the exceptional qualifications of a young man in our community whom the Republican Party has slated as a merit candidate for the position of judge of the Illinois Appellate Court in the November 3rd elections. The man I have in mind is Nicholas G. Manos of Riverside, Illinois, immediate past president of the Chicago Chapter of the Federal Bar Association, and currently president of the Hellenic Bar Association of Illinois.

I had the good fortune to meet Nick over two years ago when we worked together on the dinner honoring our beloved Vice-President Spiro T. Agnew. This very brilliant and dedicated young barrister served as toastmaster winning the esteem of all those present.

A short time prior to this festive occasion, Nick had been slated by the Cook County Republican Organization as a candidate for judge of the Circuit Court of Cook County. While endorsed by all four Chicago daily newspapers and the Better Government Association as an exceptional candidate highly qualified to serve as judge, Nick was defeated along with all Republican candidates. Nevertheless, at that memorable dinner, Vice-President Agnew, who was and still is aware of Nick's excellent political potential, predicted, in his after dinner speech, that Nick's defeat would be his last and urged him to once again run for office. This he is doing.

Those of us who are privileged to know him are aware of the fact that there is no better man suited for the position of judge of the Illinois Appellate Court. I urge you all to give this man your thoughtful consideration for there is no candidate as well qualified to serve the cause of justice in the state of Illinois as Nicholas G. Manos.

CLUSTERS OF.....succulent grapes, jugs of rich, red wine; slabs of crisp, crusty bread; sizzling, hot tidbits of mezethakea; and the spirited and unrestrained bouzouki rhythms of Harry Lemonopoulos of bouzouki fame, will weave an enchanting spell of magic at the forthcoming Bouzouki Festival sponsored by the Women's Club of Sts.Peter and Paul Greek Orthodox Church on October 18th at 7 pm. Mr. Lemonopoulos, who has tingled the toes of the Carnegie Hall crowd with his performance on the bouzouki, will be accompanied by a cast of high-spirited performers singing, dancing, and doing their thing to the tune of the bouzouki. Tying this ring-a-ding-thing together are Mrs. Peter Christopoulos, chairman; and Mrs. William Kouracos, co-chairman.

MEMBERS OF ....the Christ J. Dinou family are wearing their hearts at half-mast over the death of their beloved husband and father, respectively. Condolences are extended to his widow, Helen, and his children: Carol (Constantine) Pyshos, John (Marina) Dinou and Kriton Dinou.

THIRD MALE……offspring of George and Nancy Canellis, George, Jr., was recently christened by Mitzie and Ted Georgis A small dinner and patio party followed at the Oak Lawn Canellis home. A short time later, senior citizens, Mr. and Mrs. Peter Allas were invited to a party given in their honor by their children, George and Nancy Canellis, Bill and Mary Allas and Mary and Nick Kladis. The occasion was the celebration of 40 years of marital bliss.

QUOTE OF THE WEEK: "There comes a time in life when we have to retreat in order to advance; when we have to retrace part of our path in order to find the right turn we missed – and those who cannot go back are doomed to travel in circles."

"If you cannot endure to be thought in the wrong, you will begin to do terrible things to make the wrong appear right."

ON NOVEMBER……3rd all conscientious citizens will go to the polls to vote for the candidates of their choice. The candidate of my choice for judge of the Illinois Appellate Court is Nicholas G. Manos of Riverside. His name will appear on the white ticket together with the names of all judicial candidates. Today, I am reprinting a letter to the editor that he wrote. It appeared in both the *Chicago Tribune* and *The Chicago Daily News*. Its contents should bring you one step closer to putting an "x" after the name of Candidate Manos.

"Once again the Cook County electorate will be subjected to the ridiculous charade of voting for judicial candidates whose names are completely unknown to them. Depending on which political winds will favor one of the two major political parties, candidates for judge will be swept into office under a partisan label. Last minute efforts by bar associations and the news media to acquaint voters with the record and backgrounds of the candidates are ineffective and rarely influence a final result in a judicial election.

"Some of these candidates are so steeped in politics that when elevated to the bench, grave doubts are cast upon their ability to subordinate their political friendships and loyalties to the public interest.

"A judge has it within his power to affect the lives and property of thousands of citizens by his decision, and yet these very same citizens foolishly depend upon township and ward committeemen to pass upon professional qualifications of lawyers and to present a slate of candidates which, once elected, remains in office until retirement age.

"The obvious alternative for the electorate is to eliminate partisan election of judges and to support the merit selection proposed by the Constitutional Convention and to be presented as an issue in the December referendum. Merit selection is not foolproof and mistakes will probably be made in some instances. The improvement over the present system, however, can be overwhelming.

"I happen to be a judicial candidate in the November election, but win or lose, I fervently hope that this partisan election is the last one for any judicial office." –Nicholas G. Manos

THE PRESTIGIOUS…..Elizabeth Arden Salon presented a dazzling designer's collection of luxurious clothes at the recent luncheon fashion show sponsored by the St. Andrew's Women's Club at the Guildhall, Ambassador West on October 17th. The show, which drew an audience of 500, was a long story – from start to finish. The clothes were quality merchandise – elegantly presented by exquisite mannequins whose bones were sparsely covered by flesh. The undercurrent of rebellion at the new length was amusing as the mini-skirted die-hards in the enemy camp walked around glaring at those in the more fashionable length. There has not been this much controversy in the land since the feds turned off the bubbly machine.

Guaranteed to trap the most reluctant of males with its see-through midriff and jeweled belt was a siren song pants-dress of black chiffon. There were pants, pants and more pants. But the return to regality is upon us and it was presented at its very best by the regal ladies of the St. Andrew's Women's Club.

QUOTE OF THE WEEK: "For every one bad person who lies in order to cause trouble, there are a hundred weak persons who lie in order to avoid trouble, and by so doing cause more trouble than the bad persons."

"There are no true synonyms in the language. The difference between 'vision' and 'sight' is the same woman in the evening and in the morning."

INTELLECTUALS, DO-GOODERS....social lions, those with the wit of Bob Hope, the political flexibility of Billy Graham, the household name of Spiro Agnew, the drinking arm of Dean Martin, and the stamina of Vic Tanney will be attending the annual dinner-dance, "In the Mood," sponsored by Saint John the Baptist Greek Orthodox Church, Des Plaines. This event, which promises to be a smash, is scheduled to take place this Saturday, November 14th at the Sheraton O'Hare. Music will be supplied by Henry Brandon (of Edgewater Beach fame) and Markogiannakis. This northwest suburban parish breaks ground for construction of a new church building sometime in December. Proceeds from this dinner-dance will go toward the new building anticipated cost of which will be $518,000. Fastening this big pin together will be Mr. and Mrs. Charles Esposito who have done a magnificent job of heading the GOYA group at that church. Cocktails, scheduled for 6:30pm, will send you orbiting in to dinner at 8pm.

SMASH PREMIER........theater opening was held at the Avon Theater on Friday evening, October 30th, when the film, "The Isle of Aphrodite," starring Katina Paxinou, made its debut. The film, one of the most outstanding Greek movies I have ever seen, holds a dramatic peak that separates it from any other movie of its type. Nothing in it is trivial or inconsequential; there are no compromises made, no half truths. The creation is total with no frayed ends, only whole cloth. The power and depth of the great Paxinou reaches its peak in this movie for she holds her audience spellbound in a tight grip throughout the entire movie.

WHERE WILL....the action be on Sunday, November 22nd? At the S.J.Gregory Auditorium, where the ladies of the St. Andrew's PTA will hold their annual Holiday Bazaar. According to Mrs. Byron Leonard, chairman, and Mrs. Spiro Melonides, co-chairman, proceeds from this bazaar will be donated to the church for the benefit of the children. Beginning immediately following church services, the handmade delights on display will be the handiwork of the hard-working members of the PTA. Guaranteed to delight all holiday shoppers will be Christmas decorations, Christmas stocking stuffers, grab bag gifts, gifts for family and friends, Greek pastries, holiday breads, cookies, and candies, and – goody, goody, gum-drops. The ladies of the PTA were able to snatch Santa Claus for one of his first personal appearances of the season.

PERSONALITIES IN THE NEWS: Happy, happy birthday to all Scorpios throughout the land, but a special birthday hug to three very dear friends who happen to share a birthday with this columnist – Daisy Farmakis, Jim Corolis and Dee Tzakis. Happy November 18th.

The stork dropped a bundle of male joy at the home of Gus and Tula Mazarakis of Skokie, whose first little tax exemption will be named, Thomas Constantine.

The Rev. Dennis Latto of Sts. Peter and Paul Greek Orthodox Church was indeed an inspiring symbol of faith and love in the way he officiated at one of the most beautiful services ever celebrated on television's Channel 9.

QUOTE OF THE WEEK: "A well-adjusted person nowadays is one who is reconciled to his lack of adjustment to the world, and neither mourns it nor fights it; to be obviously adjusted to this world is to be insane along the same grain." -Harris

"Genuine maturity is so hard to achieve because it consists of two opposite processes: developing a sophisticated mind, while retaining a naïve heart, believing little but trusting much."

SUPERCOLOSSAL DO-GOODER.....Alec K. Gianaras, who has won the hearts of the entire Chicago community with his philanthropic deeds, is at it once again. This time, this steam roller is heading the Little City Testimonial Dinner for Bishop Timotheos, head of the Greek Orthodox Church, Second Archdiocesan District. Slated to be a huge success, the testimonial dinner will be held on Thursday, December 3rd in the Grand Ballroom of the Palmer House. The $50-a-plate will establish the Bishop Timotheos Research Complex at Little City, Palatine, Illinois, a residential community for childen with disabilities.

Jet-propelled Gianaras is a well-known business man whose interests include: president and chairman of the board of Transformer Manufacturers, Inc., Chicago; vice-president of the Seven Eagles Restaurant, Des Plaines; board member of the First National Bank of Deerfield; vice-president of Davis Electric Company, Cape Girardeau, Missouri; president of the Austin-Sherman Apartments, Inc., Chicago; president of G-2 Investment Corporation; partner, Gorra Importing Company; partner, Village Manor Apartments, Inc.; and associate, Peter M Tsolinas Architectural Firm.

The recipient of many awards for his outstanding charitable and humanitarian work, Alec's two latest honors include being selected as "Greek Man of the Year" by the Greek Independence Day Parade and being presented with honors at the recent dinner held by the Holy Trinity Socrates School Alumni.

With a master fundraiser like this at the helm, the testimonial dinner promises to be a huge success. A few tickets are still available so be sure to purchase one to this most worthwhile cause.

MANY CHICAGOANS....wore their hearts at half-mast last week when they learned of the death of Dr. Basil E. Stevens, beloved senior citizen and retired prominent medical internist. A native of Tripoli, Greece, the affable Dr. Stevens received his medical degree in Athens.

Following a five year sojourn in Paris, where he undertook further medical studies, he went to New York where he passed his board exams and began his practice of medicine. A short time later, he made a permanent move to Chicago.

Active in Greek War Relief, Dr, Stevens made several financial contributions to his hometown of Tripoli during his lifetime. A major financial contribution, in the amount of $700,000 was made by Dr. Stevens to his parish, St. Andrew's Greek Orthodox Church. To honor him, in return, the body of Dr. Stevens lay in state in the church proper until the time of his funeral service.

He is survived by his wife, the charming and gracious Julia (nee Giannopoulos) who did much to enrich his life with her warmth and understanding.

IT'S ANOTHER.....male offspring for Steve and Priscilla Poulos of Wilmette. This little bundle of joy, Todd Steven, was born on November 5th. Older brother, Craig Steven, is a cuddly bundle.

QUOTE OF THE WEEK: "Bad marriages do not collapse nearly as often as uncomfortable ones for the same reason that it is easier to stand a pain than an itch." -Harris

"Happiness is a butterfly, which, when pursued is always just beyond your grasp, but which, if you will sit down quietly, might alight upon you."

BLISSFULLY RELAXING......is the month of January following a hectic and highly exuberant month of December in which all we did was flip flap from wigwam to wigwam for holiday cheer. Opening up our season with a bang was an invitation to the grand opening of one of the most beautiful steak houses to fringe the city of Chicago. Appropriately named the "Two Knights," it is located in Itasca, and is the brain child of personable Chris W. Pappas, well-known restaurateur of Elgin, and architect George Kouros of Glen Ellyn. Done in resplendent shades of red, its luxuriously padded rug hails from merrie old England; its magnificent stained glass windows were flown in from Spain; and all the other clever little magic touches apparent immediately upon entrance place it in a unique category all its own. The menu, we're happy to add, is a superb balance of savory concoctions that would tickle any palate. My prediction is that this flawless jewel of an eatery will fast become a gathering spot for all of the northwest suburban "in" crowd.

MASTERS OF……flawless entertainment during the holiday season included John and Ann Graven, who served brunch to an intimate few in their Lake Shore Drive pad in honor of Harriet and Peter Andrews of St. Paul, Minnesota, who visited our city for a few short days during the early part of December; Peter and Daisy Farmakis, who gave a swinging cocktail party in honor of their then-engaged-now-married nephew and his bride; Jim and Percy Betzelos, who were delightful host and hostess, respectively, at a smashing sit down dinner for 70 people in their spacious home; Consul General Athanasios Petropoulos who paid homage to his fellow corps members and his close friends up in the sky at the Seventy-One Club; and Dr. Lambros and Euthemia Karkazis who, together with their many friends and relatives, greeted in the New Year at their Deerfield home.

YOU DON'T……have to live on pill hill to attend the festive occasion being planned by the stalwart members of the world of medicine. The annual scholarship dinner dance of the Hellenic Medical Society has been scheduled to take place at the Boulevard Room of the Conrad Hilton Hotel. For further information contact any of the following members of the reservations committee: Mrs. Michael Karazeris, Mrs. Stephen Kurtides, Mrs. John Panton, Mrs. George Poulos. The event will take place on Saturday, January 23rd.

ANOTHER WING-DING……is being offered on the same night – but not by the stethoscope crowd. This time it's The Hellenic Professional Society of Illinois that has scheduled its annual cocktail party for

Saturday, January 23rd. Headed by John Christos, one of the finest presidents the HPSI has ever had, the event has been titled, "Frosty Frolic." It will be held in the King Arthur Room of the Sheraton-Chicago Hotel. Hors d'oeuvres will be served and music will be supplied by George and The Aristons.

NAMED......Midwest regional administrator of the Department of Housing and Urban Development is suave George J. Vavoulis, a Minnesota Republican and three-term mayor of St. Paul. The-59- year-old Vavoulis will fill a vacancy created on September 1st when Francis Fisher, an independent Chicago Democrat, moved to Washington to become special assistant to HUD Secretary George W. Romney.

QUOTE OF THE WEEK: "The paradox of age is that it brings wisdom only to those who have retained the capacity to see as a child sees; when the mind's eye hardens along with the arteries, age brings only petulance and prejudice."

"There is one thing infinitely more pathetic than to have lost the woman one is in love with, and that is to have won her and found out how shallow she is."

LAST WEEK....an important event loomed large in the lives of Nicholas, Evangeline and Victor Gouletas. All in their 30's and owners of the Americn Invsco Realty, Inc. (Nick is chairman of the board; Vic is president; and Engie is executive vice-president), they made a mammoth financial investment and it was paying off! Pride in the business acumen of the Gouletas clan, pride in their aggressive spirit, and pride in their perseverance prompted me to write about the purchase of their latest bit of property. No heirs apparent, this trio had no financial wheels spinning for them. They made their own wheels, fashioned them of steel, and they have been spinning them ever since.

Indestructible and super elegant 18-story high rise building is their latest toy. Containing 100 gleaming and opulent modern apartments, The Wellington was purchased at a cost of $4,000,000; $100,000 has already been spent to make the apartments, now selling as condos, more luxurious. Address of this stately and glamorous building, jutting its head out proudly into the skyline, is 360 Wellington in Chicago.

Brain child of Nick, Engie and Victor, 60% of the Wellington condos have already been sold. We point with pride to the Gouletas clan and wish them oversized success.

EVERYONE WHO......knows pretty Debbie Price, daughter of Bill and Holly Price, is raving about this outstanding young miss (a real look alike for Hayley Mills) who was recently selected to "Who's Who Among American High School Students." Rated one of the top two percent in the nation, Debbie is a member of the National Honor Society. Last fall she was selected as an Illinois State Scholar for 1973-74. Debbie plans to attend the University of Wisconsin next fall.

KICKOFF FOR......many elegant social functions held in honor of the Greek Ambassador to Washington, His Excellency John Sorokos, was the perfectly manicured reception given by Consul General and Mrs. Nicholas Macridis at their home on April 7th.

Splashed with international flavor, the mood of the guests was contemporary, and the conversation easy and flowing. While each lady present delivered her own strong message of femininity, Toni Macridis, wife of the Consul General, was sheer sorcery in her black floor length gown mantled in ruffles. Focusing attention on the guest of honor, Consul General Macridis, a vineyard of smiles, charmingly introduced the dignified Ambassador Sorokos, who scored points with his brief and eloquent words. All in all, a glorious evening.

THE BENEVOLENT.......lasses of the GWUC certainly have a calendar painted heavily with special social activities: On April 21st, volunteers delivered Easter packages to Greek Orthodox patients at the Oak Forest Hospital donated courtesy of the George Costas family of

Carnival Grocery. On May 6th they will present their annual spring cultural event, a piano recital by well-known Nicolas Sothras. On June 9th, the GWUC's will hold their annual spring dance at the Regency Hyatt House.

QUOTE OF THE WEEK: "In this world there are only two tragedies: One is not getting what one wants, and the other is getting it."

"It is the free man who must win freedom for the slave; it is the wise man who must think for the fool; it is the happy who must serve the unhappy."

A WHALE.....of a time has been planned for the members and friends of The Greek Women's University Club and The Hellenic Professional Society of Illinois who plan to attend the jointly sponsored ski weekend of the two groups that promises to rock the uniquely designed Playboy Club in Lake Geneva, on February 26, 27 and 28th. The amply padded weekend package deal would entice even the unenticeable to attend and kick up a storm of excitement at this honey-bunny club fringed by beautiful countryside. Spending a weekend at the Playboy has always meant spinning a web of fun and frivolity, spending a weekend at the Playboy with your friends should unfurl a ball of fire whose blaze will burn just like the Chicago fire.

First, the outrageously inexpensive package deal is only $54.50. This includes deluxe accommodations (double room occupancy), two hot toddies at the Jug of Wine, two continental breakfasts, two ski lift tickets, one free ski lesson and a smashing cocktail party. If skiing is not your bag, don't despair and pass up this bargain. You can use the facilities of the club's indoor-outdoor heated pool, play games people play in the game room, go snowmobiling, or even do a figure eight on ice. If you don't like any of those little goodies, well just sit in the lobby and girl-boy watch or boy-girl watch as the case may be.

Co-chairmen of this weekender, which begins on Friday night, are Maria Pappas, representing the GWUC, and John Prodromos, representing the HPSI.

WHAT A...... show David Frost had recently when he interviewed the colorful and tempestuous diva, Maria Callas. Looking beautiful in color, she appeared to be a great deal younger than her admitted 47 years of age. Candid and a little nervous, she confessed to Frost that she was born a Greek Orthodox, but that she does not go to church often. Her philosophy – "God is always with you – you don't have to go to church." But sometimes she does go and light a candle while asking for God's help. To quote Maria, "Not to have Him give me things because He will give me good, bad, whatever is coming. I only ask the strength to accept what He gives." The 130 pound charmer (from a high of 215) said, "Onassis will always be her best friend." In another interview conducted by *Women's Wear Daily*, she said she likes the midi for it hides her fat legs, and she will never, never, make up with her mother. Said Maria, "She did many, many wrong things to me, and blood is not that strong."

THEME OF.....the annual luncheon fashion show to be given by the Philoptochos Society of Saint John the Baptist Greek Orthodox Church in Des Plaines, will be "Up, Up and Away" of TWA fame. Mrs. James Mokas, chairman, has announced that this little fashion fling will be held at the Arlington Park Towers on February 13th. A spring collection of couturier clothes by Oscar de la Renta, Geoffrey Beene, and Donald Brooks will be unveiled by Saks Fifth Avenue. Mrs. Nicholas Blase, president of the organization, has announced the names of the following committee chairmen: Mrs. Nicholas Collins, theme and decor; Bess Koplos and Mrs. Michael Kotsakis, publicity; Mrs. John Papadenis, program and printing; Mrs. James Kounanis, mailing; and Mrs. Socrates Chakonas, patron.

QUOTE OF THE WEEK: "To thank God that your family was saved from a tornado, while the family across the street was blown to bits, is really to blaspheme against the true God." - Harris

"It is harder to dislike someone you know well than somebody you know even slightly, even a murderer, to those near him, must seem almost as much victim as culprit."

UNRESTRAINED AND......willowy beauties, all post-debs and members of the Junior Debutante Auxiliary of the Saint Helen's Women's Club, will swagger down the ramp in a profusion of chic clothes from fashionable Blums Vogue of Michigan Avenue on Saturday, January 30th, when the auxiliary plays host to a fashion-luncheon show scheduled to take place at the "Athens on Rush." A favored Greek menu will be a vital addition to the delightful event which promises to satisfy even the most impeccably chic woman with its showing of glamorous luxurious fashions. Commentating this event will be a tall-stemmed rose, Terri Colovos, former deb. Following cocktails, lunch will be served. Reservations can be made by contacting the chairman, Terri Colovos (SP 7-0571 or Peggy Mitchell (763-9070). If you have an eye for a pretty face, and a taste for delicious Greek goodies, put this one on your calendar as a "must."

JAUNTY SUPERCOLOSSAL.....setting has been hand-picked by The Greek Women's University Club for its 40th anniversary celebration. The spot – the delightfully nautical Belmont Yacht Club – the date is May 8th. While life begins at "40" for this group on February 21st, the date of natal celebration has been pushed up to May 8th so that the beautifully romantic surroundings of the Yacht Club could be appreciated, and the event could be combined with the organization's annual spring dance. In order to make the celebration a bit special – a buffet supper has been planned by the two able chairwomen, Mrs. (John) Secaras, a past president of the organization, and Eugenia Pilafas, a member who has contributed many services to the GWUC in the past. More coming up on this spring floral bouquet real soon.

A LITTLE……spade work on a recent advertisement for Manos' Discoteque managed to unearth some fascinating information – just in case you should be planning a trip to the Orient in the very near future. Located in crowded Tokyo, Japan, is a swinging pub called Manos' Discoteque. Consisting of two floors, it is operated by the three Koutsoulis brothers, formerly of Somersworth, New Hampshire. The first floor is devoted to a cocktail lounge with no cover charge; the second floor is given over to dancing to a foreign band. If you should take a trip to Tokyo and feel a wee bit forlorn, go to Manos' Discoteque and have the Koutsoulis clan show you what action is – Japanese style.

SON OF….the late Demetrios Michalaros and Helen Michalaros, hostess of the Greek Athenian Sunday radio program, was recently caught in the tender trap. Groom to be, Anthony, recently succumbed to the charms of Charlene Brown. The wedding has been set for May.

ONE LONG……legged bird this columnist forgot to report on was the one that delivered a daughter to Ernie and Jeanette Nassos of Glenview. Jeanette, vice-president of The Greek Women's University Club, recently gave birth to a daughter, Laura Marie. The Nassos' also have two sons.

QUOTE OF THE WEEK: "Braving obstacles and hardships is nobler than retreat to tranquility. The butterfly that hovers around the lamp until it dies is more admirable than the mole that lives in the dark tunnel."

"Courage is rightly esteemed the first of human qualities because it is the quality which guarantees all others."

HAVING A…..press pass is the greatest thing that can happen to a girl. It's a magical pass key that can get its bearer into almost anything and almost out of anything. One of the nicest things that it recently did for me was to get me into the Drake Hotel press conference conducted by the unique and unassuming Katherine Hepburn. Meeting this irrepressible blithe spirit is an experience I will never forget.

As I sat on a divan huddled in a frozen heap (she had flung her windows open to the top) I watched the delightful Miss Hepburn in action. A moving lounge lizard, she flung her arms and legs about with abandon while chatting incessantly in a valiant attempt to answer the ridiculous questions being hurled at her by all the nosies in the room who wanted to leave her not one iota of privacy. Completely disarming in approach, she put on the most charming performance for members of the press endearing her to many of us with her refreshing candor. Her opinions were well molded and they were all expressed quite candidly.

Certainly not vying for a position on the best dressed list, she wore a less than ordinary pant outfit topped with a conglomerate headpiece consisting of a cap and tightly knotted scarves firmly entrenched around her slender neck. But what she wore didn't really matter – for she is that kind of person. Clothes to Miss Hepburn are just a necessary accessory that accompanies this carefree and nonchalant individual who magnetizes you the moment she enters a room. For example – her opinion on clothes – short skirts are quite indecent; long hair is a bore. End of subject.

The three-time Oscar winner had such an unrestrained approach to the questions tossed at her that I found myself really not listening at all to her aimless chatter but just watching the fascinating electricity which spurted from her eyes. I have a feeling that this is one woman who could be at home equally well in a twenty-room mansion or a one-room attic apartment. Master of herself, she has come to grips with life and has emerged a winner tossing aside all superficialities, pretenses, and phoniness. This is really one hell of a woman.

WITHOUT A.....ripple in the tide, the following parishioners were elected, and in some cases re-elected, to serve as officers of the parish council of Sts. Peter and Paul. Executive committee members include; Dean G. Phelus, president; Dr. John P. Fotopoulos, vice-president; Evan Ypsilantis, secretary; Peter S. Panos, assistant treasurer. Other executive members are James Corolis and Chris Pappageorge, both past presidents.

LAST CALL……for sculptures, artists, painters, etc. to display their wares is being made by the St. Demetrios Cultural League, sponsors of the Sixth Annual Art Show scheduled to take place on Sunday, March 14th at the Cultural Center of St. Demetrios Church. All artists over 18 years of age with formal training in the field of arts are welcome to participate. Interested artists may call Mrs. Kakis, chairman, or Mrs. Nicholson, co-chairman.

QUOTE OF THE WEEK: "Perhaps no other factor is more important in understanding a problem than that 'of perspective' – half the time we can't comprehend a situation because we stand too far from it, and the other half because we stand too close to it."

"Quarrelsome marriages are not nearly so likely to explode as politely silent ones. Every marriage chamber should have a framed copy of Nietzsche's observation, 'All unuttered truths become poisonous.'"

LIVELY AND……exuberant Peter Brown of Skokie and Jim Christie (the 1969 Howard Hughes tournament winner) recently participated in the Howard Hughes Golf Tournament held in Las Vegas. Peter's team placed first in the last day of the tournament making both Peter and his Helen jubilant and filled with smiles. The prize? A Panasonic Entertainment Center.

IF YOU….are tuned into the needs of others, you'll make certain that you dig down deep into your pocket when you are approached at the forthcoming 13th Ahepa district conclave with a plea to buy a "Have A Heart" Tag – for what you really will be doing is buying a heart for some little child. Tags will be on sale to all those attending the Ahepa conclave scheduled to take place at the O'Hareport Hotel, February 13-14th. Proceeds emanating from the Ahepa "Have A Heart" tags should net enough money to the Ahepa Heart Fund to bring children from Greece over to the United States for very much needed heart surgery. If you are not planning to attend this event but would still like to contribute to this worthy cause, please send your tag donation to Dena Anastos at 5501 Madison Avenue, Morton Grove.

RECENT REPORT....I read on some of the findings conducted at the annual meeting of the Eastern Psychological Association were quite revealing. For instance, one of the reports gave conclusive evidence that people who don't enjoy eating don't get nearly as much fun out of life as those who do.

In an interesting experiment conducted at Cambridge University in England, scientists demonstrated that introverts can be distinguished instantly from extroverts just by putting four drops of lemon juice on each of their tongues causing an immediate increase in salivary output. The introverts unloosened more saliva than the extroverts.

According to the EPA findings, one way to get a quick line on a person's character and personality is to watch how he eats candy. In a survey directed by a group of industrial psychologists in London, 1,200 people were interviewed about their candy eating habits. They were asked if they were "crunchers," "chewers," or "suckers"? Then they were given personality tests. Those who sucked seemed to be the best adjusted and the most emotionally stable. However, at times they tended to be smug and lacking in initiative. The chewers were cheerful and optimistic, but they tended to lack discipline. They usually started tasks without finishing them. The crunchers were highly excitable and impulsive, but unpredictable in their reactions.

QUOTE OF THE WEEK: "Real evils can be either cured or endured; it is only imaginary evils that make people anxiety-ridden for a lifetime." - Harris

"For every one person ruled by thought, a hundred are ruled by appetite; for every hundred ruled by appetite, a thousand are ruled by custom, fear and inertia."

ON TUESDAY……February, 2nd, the officers of the Greek Archdiocese Welfare Foundation signed an option agreement to purchase The Hollywood House at 5700 North Sheridan Road in Chicago for their retirement project. The agreement was executed at the Chicago Title and Trust Company after 20 months of continuous negotiations. The purchase of Hollywood House will enable the Foundation to provide the services for which it was chartered, namely, the care of the elderly, a foster home placement service, and the conducting of social welfare case work.

"These church related services will alleviate a great need in our community for both the old and the young," stated Alec K. Gianaras, president, in making the announcement of the signing of the option agreement. Speaking for the entire board of directors and women's auxiliary of the foundation, Mr. Gianaras expressed gratitude for the confidence and understanding of the community in the Welfare Foundation and in the determination of the board, auxiliary and volunteer workers to make the project a reality.

"We know our people will assist, contribute and participate in this activity, which will give comfort to those in need," stated Mr. Gianaras in response to questions on how the money will be raised to effectuate the purchase of Hollywood House. Progress reports and further details will be released to all the news media on a regular basis by the Welfare Foundation.

DOUBLE HEADER…..treat is in store for you on Sunday, March 7th when The Greek Women's University Club presents "An Afternoon with Valentino," a lecture discussing movies as an art form together with a film showing the dashing Valentino in action as "The Son of the Sheik." It's not only seeing sexy Valentino in a movie that should be oodles of fun, but the event will be held at Calvin Hall, Mundelein College's new Learning Resource Center. If you recall, quite awhile back, this column featured a story on this new and ultra modern educational structure. Just a chance to go through the building will be a stimulating experience. The $33,500,000 structure features sophisticated audio-visual learning aids, a library with a 250,000-volume capacity, comfort, and a breathtaking panoramic view of Lake Michigan. While the lecture-movie afternoon will be held in the Center's one-tiered Galvin Lecture Hall, I am certain that those attending will be given the opportunity to go through the entire Center. So red circle the date – March 7th at 3:30 pm. You had better come early for the Galvin Hall seats only 350. Chairman of this event is Eugenia "Becky" Sacopoulos of Gary, Indiana.

BOOK BEAT: The author of "Z" Vassilis Vassilikos, is coming out with a new thriller entitled, "The Photographs," translated by Mike Edwards. The new novel is concerned with a young poet and film maker who returns to Necropolis after a three-year absence. It is the city in which "Z" (Gregorious Lambrakis) was assassinated. This is the third Vassilikos book to be translated into English.

QUOTE OF THE WEEK: "One of the main reasons for divorce is the large number of women who marry because their many friends have done so; marriage, to them, has become a status symbol, rather than a vocation." -Harris

"Standing water soon becomes poisonous, and so do standing thoughts which are not fed from fresh sources."

A FRESH……and original program has been planned by members of The Hellenic Professional Society of Illinois to commemorate the 150th anniversary of Greece's Independence. Scheduled to take place at Thorne Hall, Northwestern University's Chicago campus, 750 N. Lake Shore Drive, the spirited event has been set to take place this weekend, Sunday, March 28th.

Deliberately planned to captivate an audience consisting of all age groups, the superb presentation will feature a photographic interpretation of Greece's national anthem by Leon Marinakos, a past president of the HPSI. Other added attractions will include a group of choral renditions by the choir members of the Sts. Peter and Paul Greek Orthodox Church, directed by Mrs. Nicholas Mitchell; and a performance of spirited Greek dances by the Hellenic Folk Dancers from Milwaukee's Annunciation Church, under the direction of Gus Saites.

AND A.......super elegant party was recently hosted by Consul General Nicholas Macridis and his, Toni, in honor of Greek Independence Day. Held at the Illinois Athletic Club, it was delightful for we had the opportunity of chatting with some really special people – always in abundance at any Macridis shindig. This time tall, supple Toni wore a soft black crepe jersey gown, draped here and there, to show off her really slim figure.

PERSONALITIES IN THE NEWS: Lots of hugs and get well wishes to three beautiful people who are ailing: S.J. Gregory of Wilmette, currently recuperating at Pres-St. Luke's; James Poulos, also of Wilmette, in Evanston Hospital; and Peter Farmakis in Wesley Memorial Hospital.

Belated birthday greetings to dashing Costa Govostis, handsome senior citizen widower, who was recently feted by his children and a host of beloved friends on his 89th birthday. Topping this exciting cupcake was a birthday card from President Nixon.

George Kafkis, blond, curly-headed, nine-year old thespian, enrolled in Tom Thumb Players, recently auditioned for a nationwide recording studio. This potential Valentino is the son of Nicholas and Aggie Kafkis.

Exciting travel plans were recently unveiled by Michael Assim who is off to Casablanca for a three-week stint.

Beautiful and most unusual wedding announcement was recently sent out by Mr. and Mrs. George Peter Milonas announcing the marriage of their sister, Electra Maria, to Dr. Louis Demetrios Tarsinos at St. George Eastern Orthodox Church in Spring Valley, Illinois. The Tarsino's are now at home in Princeton, Illinois.

The family of Bessie Geroulis Argiris is wearing its heart at half-mast following her recent death. The sister of Judge James A. Geroulis, she is survived by her husband, Gust; her mother, Anna; two children, Sam Argiris and Anna Karup; one brother, Spiro; and two sisters, Lynne Pullos and Georgia Sarantakis.

Consul General Athanasios Petropoulos was guest of honor at the recent 150th anniversary celebration of Greek Independence, sponsored by the North Shore Service League of the Chicago Maternity Center and held at the Knollwood Club in Lake Forest. The all Greek luncheon (décor, food, costumes, dancers) event was a roaring success. Among those attending were Sam and Dee Tzakis of Lake Forest.

QUOTE OF THE WEEK: "It is impossible to have faith without patience, this is why quick minds generally tend to be skeptical."

"One of our unconscious superstitions is that hard luck is catching – which is why we uneasily avoid those who seem to be losers."

"LET ME......entertain you" has been the theme song of The Greek Women's University Club for nigh on to 40 years – and they have done just that by liberally sprinkling the community with all sorts of social events in the past 39 years. The melody is still sweet and the lyrics still go for the Pearl Mesta's of Chicago's beautiful people have once again spread their veddy social wings. This time they will flutter over miles of beautiful blue lakefront landing squarely on top of the Belmont Yacht Club, home of the city's nautical social swingers. Here, members of the GWUC will officially celebrate their "Life Begins at 40" birthday by hostessing an official candlelight supper and wine bash on Saturday, May 8th. The scenic background, the delicious menu, and the strains of Perry Fotos' music will provide a very special kind of charisma for this very special occasion. Co-chairwomen of this multi-colored rainbow are Mary Secaras and Eugenia Pilafas.

GONE WITH.....the girdle is the very idea that one special pair of Gucci shoes or a single Hermes handbag carries with it guarantees of taste because a few women say so for this is the fashion era in which almost anything goes. Bringing this point across Priscilla Hendricks, merchandising editor of *Harper's Bazaar* in the Midwest area, will be the commentator at the forthcoming luncheon fashion show to be sponsored by the Assumption Women's Club. Titled, "Bouquet of Fashions" the wrapped-up, tuned-in event will feature fashions by Margie of River Forest. For tickets to this little blazer call Mrs. Gus Flessor who is general chairman.

OUR MOST.....sincere get well wishes to Mrs. Ernie (Tasia) Lambesis of Lake Forest, who was stricken while vacationing in Sarasota, Florida. We hope that by the time she returns home, she will be well on the road to recovery.

LARGE DOSES......of hospitality were served by Jim and Percy Betzelos when they entertained a group of friends in their home recently. The re-election of Mayor Richard J. Daley was the reason behind this festive occasion at which Dave Stahl, first deputy assistant to the Mayor, spoke on Mayor Daley's plans for the future. Dr. and Mrs. Robert Vanecko (she is the former Mary Carol Daley) were also stellar attractions at this "mission accomplished" party.

THE CHIC......and creative will draw inspiration when they view the beautiful pieces of art work that will be displayed by the Philoptochos Society of Holy Apostles Greek Orthodox Church on Sunday, May 2nd at the church located in Westchester. This double-header art show will also house a mini boutique shop at which art devotees will be able to purchase hand-made ceramics, decoupages, water color paintings, Colorado rock formations, etc. Special treat will be art displays by the Westchester Art League.

A BEAUTIFUL.....little moppet of a girl, with large, baby blue eyes and a shock of light brown hair, was recently christened, Marianne, by Jim and Adeline Brotsos. This lovely little heartbreaker is the daughter of former Chicagoans, Nick and Stella Contos who now make their home in Greenfield, Wisconsin. Marianne's christening, followed by a dinner held in Milwaukee, was attended by many Chicagoans.

QUOTE OF THE WEEK: "When a parent confesses he or she can't handle a child of 16, it is a safe conclusion that the child was mishandled at the age of six."

"Hitting a child is always a sign of weakness; if an adult can't control a child merely with a look, his own character betrays a lack of authority that should be rectified before the child is blamed."

WHILE THE…word "Churchill" may conjure up images of bravery, V for victory, and the regal and majestic British empire, to many in-town gourmets it means flaming saganaki, chicken baked in lemon juice, olive oil and oregano and crispy barbecued lamb, all taste treats available at the Churchill Restaurant, 535 N. Michigan Avenue. Operated by two brothers of Greek descent, Steve and Mike Balourdos, both staunch admirers of the late British statesman, Winston Churchill, the Balourdos dyad decided to name their place after him when they first opened it. In keeping with the name, they do offer a number of British dishes, however, they have also remained true to their own ethnic heritage by featuring a menu of traditional Greek dishes as well. This one's a British martini with a twist of Greek.

FEET ARE….really big this year as evidenced by the luscious and colorful profusion of sandals on display at shoe salons. These shoes need feet that are in top condition, so if your tootsies need pampering, we suggest you pay a visit to the new and beautiful offices of Dr. Peter J. Chiaculas, podiatrist and foot specialist. A member of the American

College of Foot Surgeons, Peter's new location is in the new Medical Arts Building at 120 S. Kenilworth Avenue in Elmhurst.

GREAT APLOMB.....and Greek cool is still being maintained by buoyant, Jim Betzelos and his delightful wife, Persey, who were recently entertained aboard Aristotle Onassis' yacht the "Christina" anchored in royal Floridian waters. Jim and Persey were afforded all the pomp and circumstance extended to those in the beautiful people set.

THE UNPRECEDENTED....fifth termer, Richard J. Daley, who recently won another four-year term as mayor of Chicago, has been handed his first honor by the Greek American community. Casting aside tradition, the 150th anniversary Greek Independence Celebration Committee will honor the first non-Greek boss, Richard J. Daley as "Mayor of the Century" at the annual Greek Independence Day Banquet to be held on Saturday, May 22nd in the International Ballroom of the Conrad Hilton Hotel. The announcement was made by Pierre DeMets, prominent businessman and philanthropist, who will head the event.

THE STORK.......dropped a bundle of male joy at the home of Dino and Jean Pavlakos whose first little tax exemption will be named, Harold Dino. Lucky Harold was born on Monday, May 17th making him fair of face (Monday's child is fair of face, Tuesday's child is full of grace, Wednesday's child is full of woe, Thursday's child has far to go, Friday's child is loving and giving, Saturday's child has to work for its living, but a child that's born on the Sabbath day, is far and wise and good and gay.)

QUOTE OF THE WEEK: "It is shallow to condemn the younger generation for 'losing their standards' when, in reality, many of them have simply found our standards unacceptable in terms of their self-realization, and are seeking desperately for their own, because they don't like what ours have done to us." - Harris

"Parents are largely incapable of recognizing the absurdity in spending the first two years of a child's life in persuading it to talk, and all the subsequent years in persuading it to keep quiet."

GRIEF HAS.....clutched the hearts of all those who knew the warm-hearted, smiling, happy-go-lucky Angelo S. Betzelos of Glenview, loving husband of Bessie and the father of three daughters. Angelo died in the Illinois Masonic Hospital Center on June 9th after a taxicab smashed into his auto at Halsted and Diversey in Chicago.

Beloved by all those who knew him, the violent and repugnant way in which he met his death should make us more vigilant than ever to the hazards we are faced with daily. Our heart goes out to his lovely wife, Bessie, and to his three daughters; to his parents, Steve and Peggy; to his sister, Mrs. Elaine Palmer; and to his two brothers, A. Steve (Stash) and Jim, who, together with Angelo, were a loving trio. A shining example of true brotherhood and of what a family should be – strong, united, with love, trust and respect for each other – the Betzelos' clan will sorely miss their Angelo. May he rest in peace and may his loved ones be granted consolation.

IMPECCABLE INSIGHT.......was used by the members of The Hellenic Professional Society when they selected Dr. Michael J. Bakalis, Superintendent of Public Instruction, State of Illinois, to be guest speaker at their forty-sixth annual presentation dinner-dance honoring the 1971 university and college graduates of Hellenic descent on Saturday, June 26th. A bright star in the horizon, Dr. Bakalis will undoubtedly attract both the young graduates and their parents, despite the generation gap of clashing life styles, for he is a man who is marvelously compelling – regardless of whether you are sixteen or sixty.

This delightful event has been scheduled to take place at The Guildhall, Ambassador West Hotel. If you would like to blow your mind with tasty glasses of chilling alcoholic nonsense, be sure to be at the Ambassador at 6:30 pm. If you'd rather not imbibe in nonsense of any kind, join the group at 7:30 pm For further information just dial one of these numbers: George D. Karcazes, general chairman (263-

1462); Miss Paulette Condos, graduates co-chairman (869-5219); Dr. Harold Andrews, graduates co-chairman (395-1306).

RADIANT WITH.......happiness is the daughter of Peter and Clara Arvanites of Evanston, lovely, blonde Vicky, who recently announced her engagement to Bill Demas, son of Gust and Angeline Demas, also of Evanston. Well known in Greek Women's University Club circles, pretty Vicky is planning a September Lohengrin.

CRUISING ON...... the shores of Lake Michigan has already become a summer pastime what with so many friends spending their weekends on board their boats: Nicholas Jannes, graphic designer and inventor of the pop-up card, has already begun his nautical jaunts on his "Achilles"; ditto Mike Svouros, on his beautiful cabin cruiser also docked at Diversey; Ion and Ethel Caloger, docked in Monroe Harbor, just purchased a handsome new boat and will spend their weekends riding the crests of Lake Michigan.

AND IT.....was a great ding-a-ling surprise seeing movie actor Pat O'Brien at the Chicago Press Club. The aging, but still handsome actor, seemed very friendly smiling and talking to all.

QUOTE OF THE WEEK: "In life, unlike theater, there are no villains, only heroes who mistake their goals."

"Nobody thinks of himself as ill-bred. If one were to ask the most ill-bred person to describe his manners in a word, he would doubtless reply, 'earthy.'"

SUPERSTARS BUD.....and Georgia Photopulos hosted an open house last week to say both "hi" and "goodbye" to Father Philip Pekras and his wife, Chris (Georgia's sister), who made a brief stop in Chicago on their way to Los Angeles. The event gave the Pekras' an opportunity to visit with their many friends in the area before departing for Los Angeles where they will make their home now that he has been appointed Dean of the Saint Sophia Cathedral – a real floral bouquet for the parishioners of that cathedral. This was a delightfully nostalgic round-up of warm and intimate friends.

THE TENDER TRAP…has trapped non-stop beauty, Terri Colovos, daughter of Steve and Jennie Colovos, and tall, blond and handsome, Peter Mikuzis, who met while in college. The coosome twosome will middle-aisle it on October 30th.

WHILE PUFFING….away on his cigarette with obvious gustatory satisfaction, the freewheeling devil-may-care-rough-and-tough Shishkabob Kid, who made a rare personal appearance at the recent three-day picnic hosted by Sts. Peter and Paul Greek Orthodox Church in Glenview, lassoed me into a corner of the picnic grounds and branded the following red-hot statistics on my forehead before I could escape his iron: The 15,000 people who stampeded the picnic grounds consumed 8,973 shishkabob, 672 pounds of feta cheese, 31,951 black olives, 3,987 plates of loukoumades (multiply this by eight per plate and you get a grand total of 31,896 loukoumades.)

My cosmic picnic egg was cracked further when the Kid filled my ears with tales about how Peter Colis, Peter George, Nick Lianis and the Kid, himself, sent up flares all over the Midwest late Saturday night letting the Beef Sellers of America know that they needed more meat in order to satisfy the voracious appetites that would infiltrate the picnic grounds on Sunday. As slabs of the stuff were delivered and stacked wall to wall in Anton's fruit truck, the ladies (bless them) came through, as they always do, denting their pretty little pinkies early Sunday morning trimming and pampering the beef prior to skewering and preparing it for human consumption.

Peter Childs did a bang-up job as announcer and one parishioner, Bill Kouracos, won the 23" color television set. Bill also ran neck to neck with Dr. John Fotopoulos in the sale of raffle tickets with super salesman, John, a neck ahead.

On Saturday night, Leon and Martha Skan brought distinguished Senator Charles Percy of Illinois and his gracious mother to the picnic grounds giving all those in attendance a chance to hear a few words from the handsome Senator.

THE FAMILY.....of Milton Kuris is wearing its heart at half mast over the death of this beloved gentleman who is survived by his daughter, Angela; his son, Chris (Joanne); and a granddaughter, Layne Jo Kuris.

QUOTE OF THE WEEK: "What the essential difference between the wise man and the ignorant man boils down to is that the wise man will often know without judging; the ignorant man will judge without knowing." - Harris

"The human being is an animal so incapable of standing uncertainty that he drives himself toward a certainty that is far worse than the tension he could not bear."

FASHION ANTIPASTO.....of uninterrupted impeccably designed clothes will be viewed by a bevy of over 500 well-bred fashion-conscious socializers who will grace the portals of the Ambassador West Hotel's Guildhall on Saturday, September 25th. This first, in fall luncheon fashion shows, will be sponsored by the St. Andrew's Women's Club and will have at its helm, pretty French pastry, Mrs. Nicholas (Yvonne) Philippides.

Not the usual comatose fashion show sponsored by so many organizations, this sleek sardine will reek of flawless designs from Bonwit Teller's couture collection guaranteed to make the vital juices of fashion conscious ladies run like spring sap as their eyes feast on a Parisian collection of clothes that are alive and kicking.

According to this year's Paris showings, there is no activity along the hem lines; most skirts are inconspicuously around the knee. Clothes are once again being designed for special occasions and this will be very much in evidence at this showing of designers' clothes.

Reservations to this special occasion, handled on a first come first serve basis, can be made by contacting either of the reservations co-chairwomen: Mrs. Nicholas (Aggie) Kafkis, or Mrs. James (Ann) Poulos.

THE SOCIAL….flag flew overtime recently when Gus and Katie Xeros of Dallas, and their two beautiful offspring, Julie and Peter, came to Chicago to pay a visit to Katie's former hometown. House guests of her brother and sister-in-law, Dr. Harry and Helen Lithas, the Elmhurst couple started the nonstop entertaining with a lavish cocktail party at their home where Katie and Gus were given the opportunity to rub elbows with friends and relatives. From that time on, the "adored by everyone" couple were feted everyday, twice a day, until they left for their Lone Star State.

TRAVEL BUG…..has hit Mrs. James (Lee) Corolis, Dr. Lambros and Euthemia Karkazis, Bill Tsenekos and Fran Mavrogen Zettos, all in Athens – while back home, Jim and Bess Maros of Park Forest and Ted and Ann Zoros of Wilmette, will float down the Colorado River on a raft with other adventuresome types taking the trip offered by Jim Stewart of "Travel to Adventure" fame.

THAT LONG……legged bird recently deposited a bundle of male joy at the home of Peter and Christine Karavites (she's the former Christine Chonis who used to write the GOYA column for this newspaper before her marriage). Weighing in at 7 lbs. 7 oz. little Themis also has a sister named Calliope.

TANTALIZING GOODIES…..were recently served by Mrs. Peter (Mary) Koconis in her Lake Forest home where she entertained many well-known, sweet-smelling ladies at a luncheon given in honor of Mrs. Toula Frengou of Athens, Greece, sister of Mrs. Peter (Ritsa) Angelos. Together with her daughter and son-in-law, Jean and Don Manhard,

Mrs. Angelos and her Peter also entertained for Mrs. Frengou in their Deerfield home.

QUOTE OF THE WEEK: "Increased leisure, without an increased cultivation of the mind and refinement of the senses, is the most dangerous enemy of what we call 'progress' – for boredom, which soon hunts pleasure with a vicious intensity, is the fifth horseman of modern life." - Harris

"Octogenarian John Koupas says that when he began to exchange emotions for symptoms, he knew he had reached middle age."

THE BEAUTIFULLY......shaded black castle imprinted on the deep red invitations mailed out by The Greek Women's University Club was right out of Camelot, the parish in Somersetshire, England, now called Queen's Camel, where King Arthur is said to have held his court. Setting the mood for the group's forthcoming "(K) Night in Camelot Winter Cocktail Dance," the invitation announced that the event will be held in the King Arthur Room of the Sheraton-Chicago Hotel on Saturday, November 29th. Cocktails and hors d'oeuvres will be served and music will be by George and the Aristons. Contributions to the Cancer Society will be made by The Greek Women's University Club from the profits.

CHRISTMAS BAZAAR........with hand crafted items for sale will be sponsored by the Holy Apostles Philoptochos Society, Westchester, on Saturday, November 22nd. Mrs. Betty Booras and Mrs. George Karris, chairmen, have announced that the Christmas boutique will offer items too numerous to mention. For the kiddies, there will be all day cartoon movies, games of all kinds with prizes and a Shriner clown making animal balloons. Other added attractions will include an artist drawing full face caricatures, a silent auction of new items, a resale shop and homemade Greek-American pastries and bread.

PARTY GIVERS......all over the country could take lessons from the members of the St. Andrew's Women's Club who conducted one of the most elegant and elaborate dinner dances of the year. Held at the Gold Coast Room of the Drake Hotel, this scrumptious event was indeed executed with a generous hand – from the hearty prime rib dinner, to the tantalizing rhythms of Perry Fotos and his orchestra. Ladies in brilliantly speckled pants suits, rich brocade cocktail dazzlers, and floor length clingers, spun around the floor merrily with handsome, side-burned gentlemen. It was a super happy event at which smiles were prolific. But the really happy ones – the ones whose faces sparkled like crystal chandleliers – were Mrs. Andrew Tzakis, president; Mrs. Christ Karafotias, chairman; and Mrs. Alec Gianaras, co-chairman, who knew that they had another "hit." With so many behind them, we really wonder what they'll do for an encore.

PERSONALITIES IN THE NEWS: Congratulations to Dino and Helen Koretos on the birth of their second child, first daughter, Dana, born on Armistice Day. Dana has a 2 ½ year old brother, Vance.

Speedy recovery to George Pantelis of Milwaukee, Wisconsin, who was recently stricken with a heart attack. George, far too young for such a mishap, is formerly from Cicero.

QUOTE OF THE WEEK: "Of all the foolish and futile experiments, 'living together' before marriage is the silliest; it is no better an indication of what the marriage will be like than sailing a paper boat in a bathtub is an indication of one's prowess in steering a real sailboat through a storm." - Harris

"Man is the only animal who is frustrated when his desires are not realized, and bored when they are."

EENIE, MEENIE, MINIE, MO.....teenagers won't know where to go – there's so much going on for them during this holiday season. For the pre-Christmas jump set, there is the Red Ribbon dance, sponsored by the Maids of Athens – Antigone Chapter, scheduled to take place on December 21st at the River Forest Golf Club. Chairman Michele Kutrumanes, a freshman at Northern Illinois, DeKalb, invites not only the teenagers, but anyone who has the nerve to bridge the generation gap to attend this frolic.

WHAT'S IN A NAME…..There's a lot in it – or rather, in this case, behind it. "T'was the Night After Christmas" is the apt title branded on this social happening to be sponsored by the Sts. Peter and Paul Junior Goyans on the day after Christmas in the church hall. With the thunderous beat of the Chicago Fire Rock and Roll Band, everyone will do his thing. Swinging Connie and Perry Fotos of Skokie are the generals behind this Peter and Paul platoon.

SPEEDY RECOVERY…..is extended to dear friend Jim Brotsos who was the victim of a brutal beating on the far south side by three thugs who knew no mercy. The still unresolved crime put Jim in the hospital for a short spell. Family and friends are grateful he is mending. Likewise, a speedy recovery to Irene Tzakis' mother who is hospitalized at Passavant.

BLACK TIE……..event on the holiday social calendar is the forthcoming Fourth Annual Debutante Holiday Benefit Ball, "Roses in the Snow," set to take place on December 26th in the Crystal Room of the Sheraton-Blackstone Hotel. Officers of this deb group include: Marion Karras, president; Terri Mikuzis and Peggy Mitchell, vice-presidents; Lynn Karambelas, recording secretary; Cynthia Katsenes, corresponding secretary; and Rosemary Chimpoulis, treasurer.

RECENT VISITOR……..to Chicago was Mary Farmakis of New York City, sister of Peter and Daisy Farmakis. The Farmakis' lavishly entertained their many friends and relatives at a post-Christmas party. Treat of the evening was the viewing of slides taken by the Farmakis' on their recent European jaunt.

ADDITION TO……..the world of little people set is a son, born to Mr. and Mrs. Christ Ellis (Betty Pappas). Congratulations.

QUOTE OF THE WEEK: "All pleasure must be bought at the price of pain. The difference between false and true pleasure is this – for the true, the price is paid before you enjoy it; for the false, after you enjoy it." – John Foster

"It is the dull man who is always sure, and the sure man who is always dull." Mencken

IT WOULD…..be nice to think of this new year as a fresh beginning for everyone-a year in which a sort of moratorium would be called wiping out all of the old year's bad debts and difficulties. It would be nice if this fresh start could begin by putting on a new determination – so to speak. And when the futility of recurring problems and the frustrations of the day loom large, swing back the pendulum of the clock and regain the freshness that the beginning of a new year brings. It would be nice.

A POCKETFUL……..of happiness and mirth spilled out recently at the home of Mary Secaras, president of the GWUC, when the organization's annual holiday party blossomed out in full swing. Pulchritudinous brunette buttercups and tall-stemmed long tressed roses dined in festive hilarity. Kay Karakourtis won the new fashion forecast award for the year as she predicted a new trend in cocktail wear – champagne designs on the bodice of cocktail dresses. Needless to say, the warm atmosphere of the Secaras hospitality made this meeting one of the friendliest gabfests of the season.

PUNCHINELLO'S EAST…..will be the site of the forthcoming cocktail party to be sponsored by the HPSI on January 24th. By this time, maybe the mini-feud which brewed at this nightery because of a two dollar toll slapped on anybody watching Jack Eigen do his thing at Punchinello's Monday night will be over with. Althea Prodromos, who has done a neat job of heading some of the society's blasts, will once again play hostess.

PERSONALITIES IN THE NEWS: Congratulations to Lee Corolis of Skokie for her recent election as president of the North Shore Chapter of the International Society of Professional Teachers, Delta Kappa Gamma. She will be officially installed at ceremonies to be conducted in Springfield.

Speedy recovery to Lou Paulos, DDS of Evanston, who is mending at St. Francis Hospital after breaking his leg in three places while ice skating.

DISENCHANTED WITH…..the troubled American scene, the symbolistic rituals of the teen-age hippies and the yippies, the teen-age blooper with locks and tendrils casually caressing his neck instead of hers; his teen-age playmate who would rather play house than keep house – well hie yourself over to a Junior GOYA meeting at almost any Greek Orthodox parish in the city or suburbs – or for that matter – to a GOYA basketball game, a swimming meet, or even a baseball game – and sit and rap with some of the members of these groups. They're bright, blooming and fun loving – a part of the new breed whose faces shine like new pennies with nary a tarnish on them. They are something to be proud of.

QUOTE OF THE WEEK: "A woman wants to be loved for her inner self, yet she spends 90 percent of her time on her outer self and then wonders why she can't hold a man long after she attracts him."

"Nobody is as dull as a man who reads a lot and remembers all of it."

APPROXIMATELY FOUR…..thousand rock fans jammed the Auditorium Theater recently when Cat Stevens and his whimsical guitar made a personal appearance bombarding the emotional audience with songs from his two very big albums, "Mona Jone Jakon" and "Tea for the Tillerman" while bobbing and weaving around the stage. Even though Stevens (whose name is really Steven Dimitri Georgiou) has just made it big as a pop star, he has been recording his own songs about five years now. His last personal appearance was at the Quiet Knight Pub before reaching personal fame. In his early 20's , Steve was born of Greek parents, and is a black-bearded sort of handsome looking hippy who does his thing in a sweat shirt and bell bottoms.

STIMULATING LETTER……..was recently written by William J. Russis, well-known businessman in the Chicago area. Published in the Letters to the Editor column of the August 10th issue of the *Chicago Sun-Times*, Mr. Russis praises the Greek aid cut and states that we can all be proud of Congress for having shown its independence of the invisible forces responsible for the imposition of the present regime on the Greek people.

ONE OF……the handsomest little boys in the pablum set, tow-headed, long-limbed and fair-skinned, Thomas Constantine, son of Gus and Tula Mazarakis of Skokie, was christened on September 5th at St. Demetrios Greek Orthodox Church by Peter and Helen Childs of Northbrook. Guests numbering well over 100, toasted this little heart-breaker with buckets of champagne and then sat down to a delicious luncheon at Café La Tour, Outer Drive East.

HOW FORTUNATE…..for Chicago fashion devotees that the Assumption Women's Society of Olympia Fields has moved its annual fall luncheon fashion show to the Palmer House in Chicago, instead of holding it at the Olympia Fields Country Club. Scheduled to take place on November 6th fashions will be presented by Joseph's. A Grecian theme will be highlighted and fashions from Greece will be shown. General Chairman is Mrs. Louis Batchos; co-chairman is Mrs. D. Apikos.

ANOTHERANTHONY.....(Zorba) Quinn type restaurant has sprung to life in our town – only this one is just a bit different – because of its locale and its décor. Located in the Gold Coast area of Chicago's near north side, it is quite a handsome spot with its dark wood-grain paneling, its massive red tones, and its framed paintings on the walls. Small candlelights on the tables add a bit of sophisticated glow to the room. Located at 878 N. Wabash Avenue, Homer's boasts of a menu that is authentically Grecian all the way through. Although there is no formal entertainment as such, recorded Greek music plays continuously, and the waiters and busboys put on impromptu demonstrations of circle dances, complete with high kicks and deep knee bends. Homer's is operated by Peter Arvanitis.

THE FAMILY...of Elizabeth Chioles, wife of the late John, is wearing its heart at half-mast since the death of this beloved lady. Mother of Sophia (Nicholas) Demet, Helen (Peter) Childs, and Constantine (Ann) Chiolis, she was also the grandmother of nine.

QUOTE OF THE WEEK: "The only use some women have for their husbands is to flaunt them before unmarried women, as a trophy of no intrinsic value but merely as evidence that they have run the race and won." - Harris

"Instinct is often wiser than reason. The woman who refuses a man and then accepts his proposal because of his persistence usually regrets it; her mind has given assent, but not her spirit."

DIPPING INTO......the same shrimp bowl on the weekend of November 12, 13 and 14th will be the friends and relatives of the parishioners of St. John the Baptist Greek Orthodox Church in Des Plaines, who will participate in a series of events which will mark the celebration of the parish's newly completed neo-Byzantine church edifice. The weekend is so chock full of activity that those participating will require the stamina of a Vic Tanney.

Festivities will begin on Friday evening at Greek Night. George Delis and his orchestra will supply the music and refreshments will include shish-ka-bob with all the trimmings, Greek pastries and other refreshments. His Grace Bishop Timotheos will officiate at vesper services to be held in the new church on Saturday evening.

On Sunday morning, His Grace will officiate at the first Divine Liturgy to be celebrated in the new church, and he will also conduct a special blessing service. On Sunday evening, the culmination of the weekend festivities will begin with the 5:30 pm cocktail hour which will be followed by a New York strip steak dinner prepared and served by one of the Midwest's most famous restaurateurs.

Everyone is welcome to participate in the weekend activities of this parish whose dreams of a church edifice have finally come true after an arduous twelve year financial struggle.

THE OCCASION....was the recent Illinois dinner saluting the President held at the Conrad Hilton Hotel in Chicago on November 9th, and for those of us who were fortunate enough to attend this function, it was a star-studded spectacular. Officially, the salute may have been to President Nixon, but unofficially it was just as much a salute to Vice-President Spiro T. Agnew for during the President's speech, he publicly acknowledged the excellent job that Mr. Agnew had done as Vice-President. The standing ovation Vice-President Agnew received was unbelievable.

One of the most delightful and informal moments during the entire evening took place when Wally Phillips, master of ceremonies until the arrival of Bob Hope, announced that it was Mr. Agnew's birthday. An elaborately decorated birthday cake was brought in for him and the entire audience joined in singing "Happy Birthday." At this largest birthday party on record, Wally Phillips announced that it had taken him all day to learn to pronounce the words, "xronia polla," which he expressed to the Vice-President.

ONE OF……our town's loveliest, Terri Colovos, daughter of Steve and Jennie Colovos, wed handsome Peter A. Mikuzis on October 30th at St. Andrew's Greek Orthodox Church. Terri was a dazzling bride in her James Galanos pale blue wedding gown adorned in pearls and splashes of white lace. The church ceremony was followed by an elaborate wedding reception at the Sheraton-Blackstone Hotel where the beaming couple, their families and friends, had one of the liveliest times on record. The warmth exuded by Terry and Peter and their respective families, permeated the room making this one of the happiest wedding receptions on record.

GATHERING FOR…the in-clan will be held during the Thanksgiving weekend when The Greek Women's University Club will once again throw open its doors to those wishing to attend its winter cocktail pow-wow. The place will be the Venetian Room of the Drake Hotel, and the date has been set for November 27th. One of the first official openers of pre-holiday festivities it will be chaired by Barbara Penn.

QUOTE OF THE WEEK: "If there were no suffering in the world, the arrogance of the human race would become intolerable; even as things stand, the people who haven't suffered much personally tend to be irritatingly smug about their good fortune." – Harris

"A person who is 'hard to know' is generally one who doesn't know himself very well, and seems an enigma to others simply because he has refused to confront his own real nature."

TUNIC WITH…..gold-plated silver disks, a mohair and silk-blend pant outfit, a black jumpsuit topped with a richly embroidered Macedonian peasant vest and a black evening dress chock full of 18-carat-gold embroidery were only a few pieces of the collection of Nikos & Takis shown at a recent fashion show sponsored by the Assumption Women's

Society of Olympia Fields held at the Palmer House. After viewing this fabulous collection of glittering formal wear, it is no wonder that the clientele of Nikos & Takis boasts of such distinguished names as Jacqueline Onassis, Dame Margot Fonteyn and Queen Ann Marie of Greece. Price tags on this incomparable collection of gowns ranged from $200 to $2,500 putting quite a dent in the average family pocketbook.

ONE OF.....the members of the wee little people set was christened recently at Holy Apostles Church in Westchester. Named George, after his paternal grandfather, George Stevens, he is the son of Stanley and Kiki Stevens of Oakbrook. The Stevens' first child, a daughter, was named after her very lovely paternal grandmother, Katherine Stevens

HAPPY BIRTHDAY.......to Scorpios all over the country – but particularly to two – whoops – it has now become three – people who share my particular natal day – November 18th: James Corolis, Daisy Farmakis and Dee Tzakis.

ALL SET......to middle-aisle it is one of the prettiest gems in the GWUC collection, vivacious Maria Pappas, who will wed George Economos sometime in the month of February.

TWO SPIFFY.....parties recently graced this columnist's social calendar. The first was a tremendous cocktail soiree given by Sophia Koretzky in honor of Terri and Peter Mikuzis. The other was a supper bash hosted by Phyllis and Soto Colovos at which this genial couple entertained about 150 people.

WIDE EYED......lovelies, debs of the Junior Auxiliary of Saint Helen's Women's Club, will once again present their charity ball, The event, "Snowflake Promenade" will take place on November 26th at the Drake Oakbrook Hotel. The pretty debs will host the event – each wearing her cotillion gown. The ball will be dedicated to a deserving institution, the name of which will be announced that evening. For further information contact Maria Monzures.

CONDOLENCES ARE…… extended to Charles and Sam Kopley on the recent death of her beloved father,

QUOTE OF THE WEEK: "The pathos in life is not that people have to suffer in order to grow, but that so many persist in suffering without growing."

"It seems short sighted to dislike those persons who marry 'beneath them' for some persons can only feel comfortable in a permanent relationship with someone inferior to themselves; an equal or a superior would be too threatening."

A WONDERFUL…..bit of chilling nonsense will be served at Pentachron 71 – the wine and cheese tasting party to be hosted by the HPSI. This bonanza has been scheduled to take place in the Lyric Room of the Fine Arts Building on Saturday, December 4th. Wine and cheese will be served to the background of the bouncing and rhythmic music of the Athenian Duo. The planning committee behind this splash is comprised of past presidents of the organization: Dr. S.D. Soter, William J. Russis, Themis Tsaoussis, James Brotsos, John Damianos, Aristotle Soter and Leon Marinakos.

ALL THE….nice Greek boy doctors like Dr. Welby, Dr. Zorba, Dr. Kildare, Dr. Casey have promised to attend the forthcoming Third Hellenic Medical Society Annual Scholarship Ball scheduled to take place on January 15th at the Crystal Ballroom of the Sheraton-Blackstone Hotel. According to the stethoscope set, the following will entertain: Denis Dimitreas, singer; Vasilios Gaitanos, pianist; and Thomas Serris from Deni's Den. Dancing will be to the music of another nice Greek boy, Perry Fotos.

ESTABLISHMENT OF……impeccable quality is now located in the sparkling new Time-Life Building, 330 E. Ohio. Christened the Gold

Coast Gift Shop, it's the brain-child of entrepreneur, Dino Tubekis. The new premises are chock full of delightful cards and tasteful gifts that would suit the pocketbook of almost anyone. Besides all that – you also get a chance to chat with perennial favorite, Dino, one of our most charming citizens.

PROOF POSITIVE.....that families can successfully work together in a business arrangement has been proved by the swinging Gouletas family, owners of American Invsco. Operated by two brothers and their sister, this fast-growing firm has made the heads of all realty companies spin in recent months – their sales have been so phenomenal. Officers of this little diamond mine include: Nicholas Gouletas, president, in charge of sales and executive training; Victor Goulet, executive vice-president, legal and finance; and Evangeline Gouletas, vice-president of administration and management. The Gouletas' bear watching for they offer a fresh approach seldom encountered in the wild forest of real estate investments.

ALL THE...beautiful people gathered together at the Deerfield home of Dr. Lambros and Euthemia Karkazis to greet in the new year with glitter and fun. This handsome couple hosted a really supercolossal bash – one which will long be remembered by all those in attendance.

QUOTE OF THE WEEK: "People who are affected are not vain, but suffer from a haunting sense of inferiority; an affectation is a confession that you do not think your natural self is good enough to be displayed in public."

"The past always looks better than it was because the mind has a natural tendency to repress memories of pain and only retain memories of pleasure; this is why humanity keeps repeating the same painful mistakes."

POST HOLIDAY....blues syndromes can easily be dispensed with on the weekend of January 21st – a weekend in which two very special events have been scheduled. On Friday, January 21st, the Sts. Peter and Paul Women's Club is sponsoring a "Hay Feed Hoe-Down" (square dance) that promises to make you spring to life what with fat cat Wally Schultz, the best caller in the Midwest, tipping in all the way from Janesville, Wisconsin, just to show you how to promenade. The event will take place in the church hall and the atmosphere will be informal. Chairing this event are Bess Dedes and Tiana Cocallas.

The scenery changes and the backdrop is the very elegant Sage's East, located in the Lake Shore Drive Hotel, 181 East Lake Shore Drive, Chicago. The date is January 22nd and the event is a cocktail party sponsored by the HPSI. Beautiful extras will include a palmist on the premises who promises to delve into your future.

RAZZLE DAZZLE.....smile of newly christened Harry Pavlakos, son of Dino and Jean Pavlakos, broke up everyone at this wee little tykes recent christening which took place at the Assumption Greek Orthodox Church. Named after Dino's beloved father, Harry was christened by Chris and Pauline Kalogeras. Dinner followed at the Black Steer Restaurant.

DELIGHTFUL GROUP OF........HPSI members gathered together at the home of Peter Chiakulas, HPSI president, and really partied it up. The pre-Christmas event was a perfect blending of old and new members of the HPSI, an organization which has really expanded under the capable leadership of President Peter.

WE POINT....with pride to James Economou and Associates of Chicago, who have started off the new year with a second commission to design a Sheraton Inn in Wisconsin. This commission is for a 128-room motor inn to be built adjacent to the ski slopes of Rib Mountain in Wausau. Since last July, Jim, who heads the firm bearing his name, has been a frequent visitor to Madison, where his other Sheraton Inn project is under construction. Located in the heart of Madison's convention center, when completed in September, this commercial resort hotel will have accommodations for 540 guests in its seven-story twin towers.

THE NAME....of the game is "GLENDI"; the scene is Greek; and the production will feature the pulsating rhythms of Stelios Markogiannakis and company. The date is February 13th and your hosts the Sts. Peter and Paul parishioners. Reservations to this hasapeko can be made by contacting either of the two reservations chairwomen; Mary Koulogeorge or Chris Demetriou.

QUOTE OF THE WEEK: "A truly successful personality knows how to overcome the past, use the present, and prepare for the future. But unless we can first surmount the past, we cannot effectively cope with either the present or the future." - Harris

"Women generally get their deepest conversational enjoyment by talking to one woman at a time, while men much prefer talking with a group of men. This is why grown men rarely have a single best friend as most grown women do."

THE REALLY......"in" people to rub elbows with while in New York City are Jackie, Ariana, or at latest count, Betsy Theodoracopoulos, and your best chance of doing this, unless you happen to have their ding-a-ling number, is to dine in one or another of the Greek supper clubs in Manhattan which most of the jet setters frequent. Aside from reveling in the tasteful joys of smoked octopus and other gustatory pleasures, these clubs really make you feel a part of the New York scene, especially the three I visited.

While in the big apple recently, I was taken to three of what are purported to be the most "elite" of the Greek supper clubs in New York City – Dionysios, Adonis, and the Mykonos. "When I saw the entrance, I knew I was home," is the line the glamorous Melina is rumored to have uttered upon walking through the portals of the Mykonos.

All three clubs make you feel you are in one of the many enchanting open-aired gleaming white stucco tavernas in Greece. They all boast of shiny, imported marble floors – floors which sophisticated East Side New Yorkers can glide on and, in some cases, rock on proclaiming their jet set identity.

In my opinion, Dionysios is the swingiest of them all for the music never seems to stop. There are two bands – one Greek and the other rock. The waiters dance and the warbling of the vocalists gets you right in the mood. Dionysios swings until 4 am; it is located at 304 E. 46th Street, and it thunders with cash customers.

Mykonos, located at 349 W. 46th Street, was the first of its kind to open. It proudly pops its buttons at the thought of the many shipping magnets that call it home, and while the menu may be a trifle expensive, the tab run- up is worth every penny of it. With a traditional blue and white motif, its dining room is one of noisy sophistication, and to be seen there puts you in the beautiful people category.

The last of the top-notch supper clubs I visited was the new Adonis restaurant located at 64th and Second Avenue. Specializing in excellent cuisine, its atmosphere is more typically Greek entrepreneur than swinging jet setter, and its greatest charm lies in the impromptu way Greek business men get up to dance a round or two of syrtaki from time to time, just to let out some steam that may have accumulated in their boiler.

PERSONALITIES IN THE NEWS: Starry-eyed and blissful Mary Manos became the bride of Chris Dangles of LaGrange at the Annunciation Cathedral. Dinner followed at the Hyatt House in Lincolnwood. The Dangles are honeymooning in Hawaii.

One of the members of the pablum set, Daphne, daughter of Gus and Tula Mazarakis, was recently christened at St. Demetrios Church. Godparents of this little heartbreaker are Gus and Joan Pappas. Daphne has a handsome older brother, Tommy.

QUOTE OF THE WEEK: "You can tell more about a person by what he laughs at than by what he cries at: our tears reveal what we would like to be, our laughter reveals what we are."

"Life is the art of riding a horse backwards, without reins, and learning to fall off without being trampled."

DABBED WITH……foreign flavor, but swarming with American tourists was Acapulco, Mexico, recent vacation spot for members of the Chicago Press Club, a group of fun-filled intellectuals who know how to relax when they are not running off to Saigon somewhere to scoop a story for the midnight edition. Rooming with my pretty friend, Elaine Markoutsas, assistant editor of *The Greek Star*, our trip was filled with lots of laughter, lots of camaraderie – much less water and even food – all to avoid getting Mexico's famous "Montezuma's Revenge" – the scourge of all visitors.

The pretty little maids in our home away from home gave us an enchanting introduction to the Spanish disposition – singing as they went about their chores and giggling while I attempted to communicate in stumbling Spanish.

Having been to this enchanting little paradise before, the only comment I would like to make is that it's the same – except a lot dirtier and a lot more polluted. For those of you who may be planning a trip south of the border, I suggest that you seriously look into accommodations at the new and very posh Princess Hotel – a few miles from Acapulco's Airport and next door neighbor to the Pierre Marquis. Owned by an American, the hotel cost $40 million and it took two years to build.

Nestled in acres of green lawn and tropical foliage, its Aztec architecture is startling and unusual. The building is in pyramid style, and its open-air lobby has been designed in courtyard fashion. Rumor hath it that the Princess is booked solid until December 1973.

HAPPY TO......learn that the following fine people were unanimously elected into office for the 1972-73 year of the Hellenic Professional Society of Illinois: Peter Anagnost, president; John Prodromos, vice-president; Georgia Geane, recording secretary; Constance Poulos, corresponding secretary; Althea Prodromos, treasurer; Becky Sacopoulos, historian.

NICE TO.....learn that George Alevizos, who worked with the Commission for the Blind for the Commonwealth of Massachusetts, is assisting the Library of Congress as national coordinator, to establish a language collection of Multilingual Books for the Blind and Physically Handicapped. This bibliographic series lists Greek Language in Braille and can be ordered through the regional library network.

SWEETIE-PIE....Themi Vasils was recently named assistant to the president and assistant secretary-treasurer of the National Confectioners Association. Themi is the first woman to hold these posts in the Chicago-based association's 89 year history.

QUOTE OF THE WEEK: "The greatest gift we can give a child is a sense of delight in being allowed to participate in the wonder of the universe, and a sense of proportion which acknowledges that the universe does not revolve around him. Without these balancing rods, children turn into prosy and petulant adults." Harris

"There is a tremendous difference between a man talking because he has something to say and a man talking because he has to say something."

FROM TIME.......to time I had heard comments on the Greek Welfare Foundation and its newly acquired Hollywood House – some pro, some con. But I personally never felt qualified to give any kind of an opinion on the work of the Foundation, for I knew nothing about it. A few weeks ago, however, when the executive board of the Foundation extended an invitation to members of the press, radio and television to attend a meeting to be held in one of the suites at the Hollywood House, I decided I would jolly well attend to find out what all the folderol was all about.

The first thing that hit me smack in the face upon entering the premises was the atmosphere. It was warm, happy, congenial, and made me feel as if I was in Miami attending an Ahepa convention. Personally, old age has always seemed to me to be a dismal affair – both physically and mentally – for loneliness creeps in and time stands still while waiting for the grim reaper. But time wasn't standing still at the Hollywood House – things were jumping. Way up on the top floor where the sun deck patiently waited for summer to come rolling around, ladies were playing cards while their laundry went through its cycles. Further down the hall, the game room played host to members of both sexes who were fiddling around with their cue sticks on the billiard table.

Downstairs in the lobby, folks were dining in luxurious elegance; others were immersed in books and magazines in the library; still others were sitting in another game room playing cards. A beauty parlor reared its pretty head, as did a drug store, a sauna bath and health club, a therapy room, and a hobby and crafts room. Everybody in the place was participating in some kind of activity and the name of the game was fun and laughter.

For a moment, as I rode up the elevator, I thought of the many seniors I had known who had spent their declining years in abject loneliness and fear: people who had been robbed of their families; people who had nothing or no one to see them through their later years.

At the meeting, we were briefed on the twelve-story structure by the officers of the Foundation. We were told all about the 198 complete units of the building (99 efficiencies and 99 one-bedroom apartments). A report was given on the finances involved in the purchasing of Hollywood House. Briefly, they involve the following: a second payment of $300,000 was placed in escrow at the Chicago Title and Trust last month under the terms of the option agreement for the purchase of Hollywood House. This makes a total of $600,000 now being held in escrow with an amount still due of approximately $700,000. When this payment is made, the Foundation will acquire ownership of Hollywood House subject to the existing favorable FHA long-term low interest rate mortgage balance.

The Foundation's Fund Raising Committee, headed by Peter J. Adinamis, is planning a large scale drive to raise the needed funds – not only to complete the purchase of the building, but also to carry on a welfare program which will include subsidies for those who cannot meet the financial requirements.

Naturally, the Foundation needs money and those who are financially able are invited to share in this philanthropic activity by making a monetary contribution. Officers include: Alec K. Gianaras, president; Chris G. Kalogeras, vice-president; Peter J. Adinamis, vice-president; Peter D. Gianukos, treasurer; Themi Vasils, recording secretary.

As for me, I am completely sold on the whole idea of Hollywood House. The sooner it becomes reality, the better. It will be a way of life which promises to evict the tenants of loneliness and fear and rent only to tenants of love and faith.

QUOTE OF THE WEEK: "The man who marries into a family generally finds that his wife has never married out of it; eventually, he is contending against a clan, and not merely disputing with an individual."

"Real communication between friends consists not in saying a lot, but in being able to leave a lot unsaid, although mutually understood."

ONCE UPON……a time a 17-year-old clear, fresh and unwilting beauty, with feet well planted on the ground, shot at a high target by investing what capital she had into a small piece of real estate property that, like Topsy, "just growed and growed" into a multi-million dollar operation. Since that time she's been holding a royal flush hand.

Sultry Evangeline Gouletas, vice-president of American Invsco, a Chicago based realty firm, eats, breathes, and lives real estate. It's her vitamin pill providing her with wings to fly across the continent drumming up business and hobnobbing with some of the world's most fascinating people.

By no means alone in her successful enterprise, Evangeline is flanked on both sides by two handsome and successful brothers whose ABC business acumen has had other members of the real estate industry raising howls at how American Invsco manages to crackle with such intense flames. Nicholas S. Gouletas, president, is in charge of sales; Victor N., executive vice-president, handles the legal and financial end of the firm; and, of course, Evangeline is vice-president of administration and management.

With her natural feminine charm, Engie, as she is called by her friends, recently held as many as four conferences a day in her recent trip to Greece. One example of what she accomplished involves the obtaining of exclusive rights to purchase or sell a ten-story commercial building located in the heart of Athens.

Another veritable plum that was devoured by Engie while visiting Greece was a deal in which Americn Invsco became the sole realtors of the Grand Chalet Hotel in Kifisia, Greece. A class A hotel, it is surrounded by verandas on the eastern and southern sides and can be utilized for receptions and cocktail parties.

Engie epitomizes the young, aggressive business woman of today. With a background in mathematics, she earned her master's degree at Illinois Teachers College and did post-graduate work at IIT, Johns Hopkins and Loyola. Her greatest toy, however, has always been numbers – and it has proved to be quite lucrative for her.

This human female dynamo would go to any lengths to service a client. Ask a former Chicagoan and owner of a north side six-flat who has moved to Greece – Bill Portoclis by name. Engie recently flew abroad just to deliver a sales contract to him personally.

"I'm up each day at seven o'clock and never in bed before midnight. I have very little social life, but don't mind as I find my work very gratifying."

On American Invsco, Engie says, "We deal mainly with Greeks living in the States who want to buy or sell property anywhere in the world. For those who are living in the United States and would like to sell property owned in Greece, or conversely, for those who own property in the United States which they would like to sell while living in Greece, we'll gladly handle these international transactions with a minimum of trouble."

QUOTE OF THE WEEK: "The reason clever people so often do stupid things is that they are generally so busy talking that they never listen – all they hear is the sound of their own cleverness echoing back at them." - Harris

"It is better to break one's heart than to do nothing with it." M. Kennedy

WARMEST WISHES ……to "lovely-to-look-at-delightful -to-know" goddaughter, Dana Pappas, daughter of Chris and Elayne Pappas of Schaumburg and Panagiotis Nikoloulis, son of Demetrius Nikoloulis of Athens, Greece, who became one on Sunday, January 8th at St. Andrew's Greek Orthodox Church. The reception was held at The Venice – with 200 friends and relatives in attendance. It was a love-in with good food, dancing and merriment.

GOOD FRIEND…..Billy Dare (Sedares) is currently starring at the plush Plantation Club in Mahe, Seychelles. According to Billy, the club lies in a coconut plantation, and is the most beautiful spot in the world. Billy says it is serene, green, lush and surrounded by the lukewarm, crystal clear Indian Ocean. Seychelles lies five degrees below the equator in the Indian Ocean, 2,000 miles off the coast of East Africa. Languages spoken are French Creole and English.

THAT SPARKLE……in the eyes of pretty and vivacious, Melanie Corolis, daughter of Jim and Lee Corolis of Glenview, was put there by Nicholas Chionis, son of Connie and Angelo Chionis of Palos Heights.

Diminutive Melanie, who is a graduate of Southern Illinois-Carbondale, served as president of her sorority, Alpha Gamma Delta, and was chosen homecoming queen at Southern. Nick did his undergraduate work at Loyola U and received his DDS from Northwestern. They will middle-aisle it in September.

THE TENDER.......trap has caught one of my favorite young ladies, pretty Cynthia Tzakis, daughter of Dee and the late Sam Tzakis, and Brent Wrasman. The two met while playing volleyball in Washington, D.C. where they both reside. Mom Dee held a warm and intimate engagement party for them on December 29th at the Michigan Shores Club.

SHOCKED TO.......learn about the sudden death of A. Freddie Kalogerakis, who has been living in Boca Raton, Florida, for quite some time now. Freddie was always a fun-loving, effervescent gal with an infectious laugh, who sang her way through many hearts during the early days of GOYA. We extend our sympathy to her two sisters, Mary Kay Stray of Glenview and Dessa Kallas of New York City.

ORCHIDS TO......Mrs. Christina Peters, whose virtues and selfless dedication to her church were extolled in a recent article in the *Chicago Tribune* written by Sheila Gribben. Mother of Ann Graven, Mrs. Peters first came to Chicago in 1932. Since that time she has baked a couple of dozen loaves of altar bread every week for the parish of Sts. Constantine and Helen.

Every Friday, she gets up at 5am and begins to work on her bread – pouring flour, breaking eggs, etc., and then kneading the dough with loving care. Those of us who have tasted her culinary delights can attest to the fact that she is one superb cook. Ann and John calculate that she has baked as many as 150 loaves of bread during Easter week and, that since 1955, she has baked over 20,000 loaves of bread.

QUOTE OF THE WEEK: "When a statement scandalizes you, when it seems utterly wrongheaded from beginning to end – that is the time to examine it most carefully, for it may contain a truth you have long suppressed, out of fear or embarrassment or rigid self-interest."

"We hope that when the insects take over the world, they will remember with gratitude how we took them along on all our picnics." – Greek Orthodox Church Picnic Committees

ONE OF......our town's brightest and most articulate priests has made many of his parishioners very sad by tendering his resignation as pastor of St. Andrew's Greek Orthodox Church after having served this parish faithfully over many years.

Since the word first leaked out that Father John Hondras would no longer be the parish priest at St. Andrew's, there has been much sadness among those of us who have always felt much affection for this man whose hard drive and determination did much to aid this parish reach the pinnacle of success that it has. Father John's brilliant sermons, the remarkable order that he kept in his church, his delightfully blunt, teasing ways, and, most important of all, his refreshingly honest, "tell it as it is" attitude will be sorely missed in a world grown weary of deceitful hypocrisy.

To Father Hondras, and to his beloved, Lou, she of the twinkling smile and ever kind words: we wish you much good health and happiness in your new parish, and mournfully add that St. Andrew's will never be the same without you.

SUMMER TIME......vibes are generally excellent, especially if the moon is full and you were born under the sign of Scorpio, ascending in Capricorn, descending in Libra, and landing in Cancer. Then you're definitely psychic and can make all sorts of predictions with complete accuracy, just as I did last summer. Only two out of two of my predictions were wrong.

It was Greek picnic time. I predicted that the sale of umbrellas would go up on the north shore on the weekend of July 16-18. This was the weekend that the crew at Sts. Peter and Paul Greek Orthodox Church were holding their picnic carnival, and I was tuned into a weekend weather bummer for them. What happened? The sun was disgracefully bright, and the sale of sunglasses went up at all north shore shopping centers. Vibes also told me I would win the 21-day trip to Greece. Instead I won a Spiro Agnew watch that was recalled because of a faulty mainspring.

This year I refuse to make any predictions. I will just present the facts: the 10th annual Sts. Peter and Paul picnic will be held on July 21-23 on the church grounds. Food will be available. Ten raffle prizes will be offered: a 21-day trip to Europe for two or $3,000 in cash, a 23" color TV console, an upright freezer, his and her's five speed bikes, camera/projector/screen, Polaroid camera model #450, 16" portable black and white TV, boy's Schwinn bike, girl's Schwinn bike.

ONE OF…. my very favorite people, pretty and vivacious Elaine Markoutsas has been ailing at Pres-St.Luke's Hospital. But if good wishes have anything at all to do with getting well, Elaine should be hale and hearty again within a short period of time for she has received hundreds of get-well cards. Fetchingly tied together with colorful satin ribbons, they cover up at least three hospital walls starting what may be a new fad in hospital wall paper for very popular people.

QUOTE OF THE WEEK: "It is useless to advise people not to worry, unless at the same time you can teach them how to think; worrying is often the only activity that saves them from blank despair."

"To be is to do." – Camus
"To do is to be." – Sartre
"Do be do be do." –Sinatra

TALL, BONY.......hollow-cheeked and sophisticated dazzlers will slink down the runway on Saturday, September 30th at the Drake Hotel to give the ladies with fashion know-how a lightening flash into what direction milady's wardrobe will move this fall. The occasion will be the prestigious luncheon-fashion show to be sponsored by the gurus of fashion – the St. Andrew's Women's Club. According to Mrs. Denise Gianukos of Wilmette and Mrs. Pandora Spyrrison of Lincolnwood, co-chairwomen, cocktails will be sipped at the Camelia House at noon and lunch will follow in the Gold Coast Room.

For most fashion-conscious ladies, the St. Andrew's yearly fashion show is a better way of getting high in the sky than smoking pot on a plane – the fashions are that smashing. This year's crop of designer's clothes will be shown courtesy of the chic Kane salon; adorning the clothes will be furs from Alper's.

THICK RED......carpet will be rolled out at the Marriott Hotel on Saturday, October 28th when all the Very Important and Beautiful People, garbed in elegant silks and satins will gather together in splendor to sip and sup at the forthcoming Charity Ball to be sponsored by the Sts. Peter and Paul Women's Club. While Perry Fotos' ten piece band will supply the music for dancing, Mary Ann Blanas, president of the Women's Club, has announced that a special combo has been hired for the evening, which will supply the music for the exciting entertainment which has been planned to round out this glamorous dinner dance. Kept under hush-hush wraps, announcement of the entertainment will be forthcoming shortly.

IF YOU'D......like to "step this way and shuffle right in where worries are lost and smiles begin, as you allemande left and sa shay right with bones so loose and steps so light," make sure you attend the Hellenic Hoedown to be sponsored by the HPSI on October 29th. Featuring Bob Stewart as caller, you'll be able to do your do-si-dos at the Billy Caldwell Hall, 6038 N. Cicero Avenue. In charge of this affair is past president Jim Brotsos, who incidentally is one of the sharpest chess players in these here parts.

FUNDRAISING.....fashion show with pretty bon-bon Georgia Photopulos and her two offspring, Jimmy and Kerry, as models, is being sponsored by the Illinois Division, Inc. of the American Cancer Society on September 26th at Johnnie Wiegelt's Hall, 3900 N. Damen Ave. Handsome Bud Photopulos will be the master of ceremonies.

OLYMPIC AIRWAYS.....was really using the old noodle when it grabbed the very capable John Adinamis and created a position for him. John is now Hellenic Affairs Representative in the Chicago area for Olympic Airways providing those of us in the Midwest with a very adept liaison man – a position which has been sorely needed in this area for a long time. John's office is at 500 North Michigan Ave.

AND WELCOME......to the Chicago Press Club's newest member, Consul General Macridis.

QUOTE OF THE WEEK: "It may be true that 'he travels fastest who travels alone' – but that kind of trip leaves the traveler right back where he started from, for all achievement without love is circular and self-consuming." - Harris

"It's extraordinary how the same people who are so sensitive towards slights from others are so insensitive about the way others react to them; those who most resent being rubbed are usually rubbing others the wrong way."

RECEIVED A.....delightful note from our wonderful Vice-President Spiro T.Agnew in which he expresses his delight in once again being selected as running mate to President Richard Nixon. I'm really hooked on this marvelous man whose utter lack of pretension is one of his greatest assets. Let's hope we continue to get men into political office who are not cringing jello-flabs, but who say what they have to say regardless of the consequences to them personally.

ONE OF.....our town's very special pastors, the Reverend Dennis Latto of Sts. Peter and Paul Greek Orthodox Church recently underwent surgery at Passavant Hospital. While Father Latto is recuperating and getting back his strength, his vast legion of friends and admirers continue to offer up very special prayers for the health of this very special human being who, with his kindness, wisdom and warmth, has done much to make this world of ours a better place to live in.

A MOST.......revered and respected lady, Peggy Betzelos, died on Labor Day. She was the wife of Steve. A. Sr. and the mother of Stash (Irene), Jim (Persey), the late Angelo (Bessie) and Elaine Palmer. Mrs. Betzelos was one of our most gracious senior citizens and she will indeed be missed by all those who knew and loved her.

FOR THE......second consecutive year, a member of the Samuel C. Maragos family recovered the foot-long cross thrown into Lake Michigan behind McCormick Place as part of the exaltation of the Holy Cross ceremonies. This year it was 19-year old Tom; last year it was 17-year old Jim. Both are sons of Cleo and Sam Maragos (he's state representative D-30th) and she is president of the Sts. Helen and Constantine Women's Club. On that day, September 17th, nearly 10,000 members of the Greek Orthodox churches throughout the area attended church services at Arie Crown Theater. Later a delicious filet mignon luncheon was held in the Jane Adams Room at McCormick Place.

NICE TO......learn that Spiro Males will be playing Leporello in the New York City Opera Company's production of "Don Giovannni." Two casts of "Don Giovanni" are being prepared. One cast will do the Mozart opera in Italian, the other in English. Males, who will play Leporello, the Don's male servant, will sing in both the English and Italian versions.

WHAT A....feather in the cap of George Lazarus to have the *Chicago Tribune* buy a whole page in the September 18th issue of the *Wall St. Journal* featuring a one-page ad portrait of him. George, who is now columnist for the *Chicago Tribune*, is referred to as King of the ad-marketing columnists.

QUOTE OF THE WEEK: "Successful marriages are those between two persons who are selfish in the same way for they form a common front against the world. What we think of as a successful marriage is often just an interlocking of similar egos."

"When a young man complains that a young lady has no heart, it is pretty certain that she has his." – George Prentice.

AN IDEA......with lots of heart was the decision of the St. Andrew's Women's Club to honor Lou Hondras at a luncheon held at the Drake Hotel on July 29th, an event which easily attracted over 200 women. Sweet, easy-going Lou, caused many a dowager at the luncheon to lose her cool and swallow hard in order to choke down a tear or two; spirits sagged in a room which was hooked on emotion at the thought that this was really "farewell" and "goodbye" to a very great lady who had put a lot of pazzaz into working for St. Andrew's parish for 20 years. Irene Tzakis, dynamic president of this organization, spoke briefly at the luncheon as did Dena Anastos, chairman, who did a masterful job on décor and menu planning. As a token of their appreciation, the women's club presented Lou with a solid gold watch encrusted with diamonds. A totally affectionate afternoon, its memory shall linger in the hearts of all those in attendance long after the Hondras' have made their home in Florida.

IN EXCESS.....of over 20,000 people gathered together to participate in another Pulitzer Prize-winning chapter of Sts. Peter and Paul's best seller, "The Picnic." This year it was written and produced by Peter Cappas, chairman; Jim Smirles and George Chandiles, co-chairmen; who did a bang-up job. A singular and intriguing feature of this picnic was the fantastic communications system, that had been set up enabling anyone stationed at the communications booth, located up high on a mound on the church grounds, to contact, by phone, the workers in the shishkebob tent, the kitchen, the trailer, etc, not to mention the fact that this system also handled all incoming picnic calls. Set up by James Cardis, it is the only such system I have ever encountered at a local picnic. In charge of the communications booth was Peter Childs, who introduced such notables to the crowd as Leah Poulos, member of the world champion Olympic Northbrook speed skating team; Ann Henning, recipient of the gold and bronze Olympic medals for speed skating; and Jack Brickhouse, WGN-TV channel 9 sports announcer. A delightful event sponsored by a hard-working crew.

DELICIOUS AND……divine dinner party was hosted by John and Ann Graven in their lovely LSD pad honoring Ms. Angela Caruso, recent recipient of one of the board of education's plum positions. A lady with lots of smarts who has worked arduously to achieve her success, Angela was recently made associate superintendent in charge of Area C in the Chicago school system making her responsible for over one-third of the schools in the city. Among the many diversified and interesting guests invited by the Gravens was former three-term Mayor of St. Paul, Minnesota, George Vavoulis and his Beverly. Vavoulis is currently Midwest regional administrator of the Department of Housing and Urban Development.

QUITE A……tea party was recently hosted by charming and serene Dee Tzakis in her Lake Forest home. The tea was given in honor of her very pretty sister, Alexis Lelon of Wellesley, Massachusetts, who had come to Lake Forest for a visit. Alexis, and her husband, Tom, are former Chicagoans who moved to the east coast when he was made assistant dean of faculty at Boston University. An academically brilliant man, last spring Tom was installed as vice-president of Phi Delta Kappa, the world's largest honorary fraternity for educators.

QUOTE OF THE WEEK: "Money and time are the heaviest burdens of life, and the unhappiest of all mortals are those who have more of either than they know how to use." -Harris

"The parent who always prevents a child from acting up in public is more concerned with public opinion than with the needs of the child; and the price for this rigidity in public is the child's private resolution to even matters up when old enough to do so."

PUT A........sparkle in your eye, a bloom to your cheek, and a smashing attire on your beautiful bod and point yourself in the direction of the Marriott Hotel on Saturday, October 28th, where an unbelievable collection of fashionable people will gather together to sip and sup at the Sts. Peter and Paul Charity Ball.

Since the word leaked out that Off the Ground, Inc. will perform at this dinner-dance, telephones have been ringing and reservations have been pouring in – for this group – actually an entertainment product of the North Shore – is one of the most prolifically original musical groups in the country. Featuring entertainment which is similar to an off Broadway type theatrical group, Off the Ground, Inc. was originally organized in 1952 by six couples – all musically oriented. Twenty years later they have not only grown in number, but they have produced 20 smash original musical productions for charity. The board, main core of the organization, does all the writing and producing; cast members are selected by audition. Dee Tzakis will chair this event.

CONDOLENCES ARE.....extended to fellow columnist, Jimmy Mezilson and his family on the death of his younger sister, 39-year old Connie Alevizos of Minneapolis. While the effervescent Connie lived in Minneapolis since her marriage, she was a frequent visitor to the Chicago scene and one of the people I always looked forward to chatting with. Sympathy is extended to her husband, Bill; her son, Timothy;

her daughters, Susan Marie and Mary Jane; her mother, Dorothy two brothers and a sister – all from Chicago.

BEAUTIFUL TEA.....party was hosted by the Ladies Philoptochos Second District Council and the Chapters of Greater Chicago in honor of Toni Macrides, wife of Consul General Nicholas Macrides. Held in the Windsor Room of the Continental Plaza Hotel, the tea party, at which guests were indulged in tasty little tidbits, was an incomparable success, thanks to the organizational ability of Mrs. George Marks, president, and Mrs. Esther Bourbules, chairman. Guests included: Mrs. Aluysio Regis Bittencourt, wife of the Brazilian Ambassador to Austria (she is Mrs. Macrides' mother); Mrs. Macrides' younger sister; and His Grace Bishop Timotheos, whose charm and wit brought peals of laughter from all the ladies present.

WE POINT.....with pride to picture pretty Maria Gleason who was selected to model at society's great gathering, the annual Presbyterian-St. Luke's Fashion Show. I might add, she did a superb job.

QUOTE OF THE WEEK: "A man's intelligence may be measured almost exactly in inverse ratio to the length of time he is capable of holding a grudge."

"There is no delusion more fatal than a man's belief that he can kick and gouge and scheme his way to the top and then afford the luxury of being a good person; for no consequence is more certain than that we become what we do."

THE SUN......polished the already bright public image of Leon N.Skan of Wilmette recently when he was named U.S. Productivity Director. President of a Chicago engineering firm, Pollak and Skan, Inc., erudite Leon will direct activities of the National Commission on

Productivity in a six-state region. An electrical engineering graduate of Northwestern University, Leon was one of the organizers and first president of the National Technical Services Association. He is a director of the Admissions Council of the Northwestern University Technological Institute and a member of the Industry Advisory Council of the Engineering College, University of Illinois Circle Campus. The National Commission on Productivity was created by President Nixon to promote greater concern for the importance to U.S. economic strength of continued improvement in productivity. Secretary of Commerce Peter G. Peterson is chairman of the Commission.

ANOTHER BRILLIANT......financial engineer, Minos Zombanakis, recently made headlines in both *Business Week* and *Forbes Magazine.* Zombanakis, a 46-year old native of Greece and a Harvard Business School graduate, has made his reputation by mastering the labyrinth of international finance. He has joined First Boston Corp as senior officer for underwriting and corporate finance in Europe and the Middle East and as a director of the big house.

TRANSPORTED WITH.......joy was pretty Kathy Lappas at the recent bridal luncheon hosted by Florence Dasaky and her mother, Mrs. John Dasaky. The viviacious Kathy will wed Milton Fasseas on December 3rd.

THE INIMITABLE......Nana Mouskouri, who sings as easily as she breathes, will once again entertain her followers at Orchestra Hall on Sunday, March 25th. The talented Nana has built up a tremendous repertoire of fine Greek, French, Spanish and English melodies.

AND LET'S......just use one word to describe the recent Republican tea given in honor of Mrs. Richard Nixon at McCormick Place. DISASTER! Tempers were outraged when the vivacious First Lady finally put in an appearance on stage about 5 pm. Mrs. Hope McCormick, chairman of the event, was lucky she got out of the Arie Crown Theater alive for 6,000 females had repressed their hostilities for about 2 ½ hours. By the time Pat Nixon hit the podium, all the lovely ladies were gnashing their teeth in evangelical fury. The tea was no exercise in compromise for the staunch Republican ladies sitting in the audience, but a strong exercise in self control.

HAPPY TO….learn that a really nice gentleman, Peter N. Mantzoros of Glenview, has been named national director of the Department of Public Relations for the Order of Ahepa. Mr. Mantzoros is editor and publisher of the *Chicago PNYX*.

QUOTE OF THE WEEK: "Events follow feelings more than we realize. To brood excessively about a possible failure is one of the surest ways of making it come true."

"The worst mistakes of judgment are made by people who believe that reason and the passions are opposites; reason does not exist to oppose the passions, but to mediate among them. The man who uses reason to repress his emotions will soon be as mad as the man who permits his emotions to override his reason."

WHEN WE…….received a beautiful party invitation from Bill and Aliki Bryant of McLean, Virginia, inviting us to a black tie dinner at the Drake Hotel on Thanksgiving weekend, we pondered a great deal over the capitalized words included in the invitation: "A VERY SPECIAL EVENING." Apparently, we were not the only skeptics who mulled over these four little words. As close friends and relatives of the Bryant's began gathering into the Walton Room of the Drake Hotel on Friday, November 24th – and the zero hour approached – speculation was at its highest. The answer came following dinner when our host, handsome and amiable Bill Bryant, son-in-law of S.J. and Rita Gregory of Wilmette, announced the engagement of his sister-in-law, Dina Gregory Papas to Nicholas Bacaintan, formerly of Cleveland,

Ohio, and now of Washington, D.C. Nicholas, a close friend of Bill's, was best man at Bill and Aliki's wedding thirteen years ago. On hand to receive the best wishes of those attending the dinner party were the bride's parents, S.J. and Rita Gregory, and her children, Maria and John Gleason, and Gregory Papas. This will be the bride's second marriage and the groom's first. Dina is the widow of the late and beloved Spiro J. Papas. The wedding will take place on December 29th.

ONE OF.....Sts. Peter and Paul's greatest talents in the field of graphic arts and photography is George Maniates of Glenview, whose originality has now been put to the test at one of our town's smoothest ad agencies, J. Walter Thompson. Getting George as a creative art director was one of the smartest moves J. Walter Thompson ever made.

GRIEF HAS.....clutched the hearts of all of us who knew and adored young, handsome and fun-loving, Constantine (Dean) Lamperis who recently met his death in the tragic and senseless Illinois Central train wreck. He was the only son of Helen and the late Nicholas Lamperis.

I will always remember Deanie as a youngster, his laughing eyes filled with mischief, playing all kinds of pranks on his two cousins, Helen and Alice Anthony, while spending summers with them at the Anthony's Grand Beach, Michigan summer home. Then time marched on and Deanie grew up. He attended and graduated from Northwestern Military Academy. A pre-dental student, 18-year old Deanie was on his way to the University of Illinois Circle Campus when he met his death violently and without warning, making us all realize how quickly and unexpectedly even the candles of the very young can be snuffed out.

We extend our sympathy to his bereaved mother, Helen, and to all the other members of his family who simply adored him: his beloved aunt and uncle, Maria and George Manus; another uncle, Peter Ganas; and all of his first cousins, Helen and Alice Anthony, Irene Manus, Irene and Terry Ganas.

QUOTE OF THE WEEK: "Nothing makes one feel so ashamed of his own good fortune as walking through an office building late at night and observing old women on their hands and knees scrubbing floors. Granted, somebody has to do it, but in a sane society it would be the young just starting out, and not the old, who have earned a little dignity."

"What many persons want is not to be happy, but to be envied – and they will endure the most private misery as long as they feel that they are publicly enviable."

PEOPLE ARE....talking about the St. Nicholas Theater Guild's forthcoming presentation of Woody Allen's "Don't Drink the Water," produced by special arrangement with Samuel French, Inc. and sponsored by the St. Nicholas Ladies Auxiliary. This hilarious two-act comedy, which was originally produced by David Merrick, will be given at the St. Nicholas Education Center, 10301 S. Kolmar, Oak Lawn. Performances will be on November 24-26. Ticket information may be obtained by calling Tina Savas. Constantine Lampros of Oak Lawn is directing the performance. The cast includes: Martha Anderson, Gus Anton, Jim Ganas, Helen Gardeakos, Connie Lampros, Dena McDowell, Andrew Nickas, Philip Noplos, Jim Patras, Marianne Powers, Pat Savas, Chris Sarlas, Jim Sinandinos and Ida Trakades.

Stella Lampos, chairman, has announced that all proceeds of the event will be donated to the St. Nicholas Building Fund. It is highly commendable that this organization has raised over $85,000 for this building fund in the past 20 years.

IT WAS.....great fun attending a surprise 50th birthday party for Peter Koconis of Lake Forest given for him by his vivacious wife, Mary. Pike, a fellow Gargle (hail, hail Spiro Agnew), and a family friend for many years, is one of the most capable architects in our community. A bit battered by the surprise, helpings of friendly hugs provided the emotional glue that put surprised Pike together.

VOCIFEROUS CHORUS......of approval has been voiced by the biggies at St. Andrew's Greek Orthodox Church over the reactivation of the Jr. GOYA group of that parish which had become defunct over a long stretch of years. With the kids clamoring for more group activities, the wheels began to churn and Jr. GOYA has now become reactivated with a new athletic director, Christ Kalamatis at the helm. Newly elected officers include: Nick Anastos, president; Vicki Leventis, vice-president; Kathy Varney, recording secretary; Arlene Siavelis, corresponding secretary, and Renee Vaselopoulos, treasurer.

AND DON'T......forget to attend the magnificent annual holiday cocktail party and dance being planned for you by The Greek Women's University Club on December 9th. Entitled, "Mistletoe Magic," this spiffy splash will be held in the Governor's Suite of the Continental Hotel. Barbara Penn is chairing the event.

FOR THOSE......of you who might be planning a holiday trip to the Big Apple, my eastern spies tell me that there is a new zingy chanteuse who is making it big in Manhattan. The lady in question is Joanna Makris who does her thing at the Trio Romantico at the 17th Street Hideaway. Joanna, a spectacular international warbler, can sing in eleven languages, and word has it that she is super in all of them.

QUOTE OF THE WEEK: "The most dangerous thing about a beautiful woman is that it takes a long time for a man to discover she may have no sense of humor – which is the only characteristic that redeems beauty from dullness." - Harris

"Superiority of the body – as with athletes – makes us respectful; but superiority of the mind – as with intellectuals – makes us resentful; possibly this is because athletes don't try to tell us what to do, while intellectuals want to make us over."

MEMO FROM.......The Hellenic Professional Society of Illinois informs us that Thalia Cheronis Selz will be the featured speaker at the next Sunday afternoon lecture series sponsored by the HPSI which will take place in the Kingston Room of the Sheraton-Chicago Hotel. Thalia, a member of the society, received a degree from Oberlin College majoring in history; she received her M.A. degree from the University of Chicago with a major in English literature. She is a published author of novellas, short stories and articles in newspapers, magazines and books. Thalia has also been the recipient of an O'Henry Award for a short story and has had numerous residential fellowships in creative writing at artists' colonies in New York, New Hampshire and New Mexico. Her presentation will be entitled, "Lies: The Touchstone of Truth."

CONGRATULATIONS TO...Joanne Vasilomanolakis, a junior at the University of Illinois, Chicago Circle Campus, who recently became the recipient of a $1,000 scholarship from The Greek Women's University Club. Joanne is majoring in chemistry and plans to attend either medical or dental school.

BABY IT.....was cold outside, but inside the Roditys Resturant the temperatures had risen matching the warm spirits of Chris and Gloria Pappageorge of Glenview, host and hostess par excellence, who had spontaneously invited about 50 friends of Lula Latto, widow of the late and beloved, Rev. Dennis G. Latto, to help celebrate her birthday. The name of the game was "surprise party" – and Lula was surprised. Following dinner, she was presented with a magnificent gold pin encrusted with five diamonds – a token of affection from the gang. Some nightcapped it later at Denny's Den.

AND ANOTHER......member of the pablum set was born on February 22nd to George and Roula Karkazis. Their first offspring, he was christened, Demetrius. George is board president of the Hellenic Foundation.

CONGRATULATIONS TO……Sam and Georgia Booras of Lincolnwood who celebrated 25 years of wedded bliss on Sunday, February 16th. They are off to Florida and then on to Jamaica.

A REALLY…….lengthy and dignified spread appeared in the January 26th issue of the Chicago Sun Times Book Week Section on the translations of Theodora and Themi Vasils. The books in question – Nikos Kazantzkis' "Symposium" and "Journeying." The reviews, written by George Anastaplo, were stupendous.

QUOTE OF THE WEEK: "Marriage remains so precarious a relationship because the very qualities that attract us to a person of the opposite sex are not usually the qualities that bind us – and the qualities that bind us are not readily discoverable under the feverish conditions of romance." – Harris

"Perhaps the predominant mark of maturity is the willingness not to accept credit for a good idea that we initiated, even with the acute provocation of seeing someone else take credit for it."

EENIE, MEENIE, MINIE, MO….we just didn't know where to go – there was so much on the agenda on February 16th. But we chose what we know were two of the greatest parties on record. First, we whizzed northwest where Tom and Helen Costopoulos hosted an engagement cocktail party for daughter number one, Jane, who will promise to love, honor and obey Stanton Stitzel sometime in July. Pretty Jane looked smashing in a crimson gown that matched the fire in her eyes – so head over heels is she. Tom and Helen are pop and mom to three of the most warm-hearted girls I have ever met.

From the Costopoulos valentine, we whizzed back east over to the Corner House to wish Nike (widow of Dennis Giannakis) and Frank Phillips a long and happy life together. Partners in business at the Corner House for many years, they were married quietly at St. George

Greek Orthodox Church the day before. There was much merriment, many nippy-tippy cocktails, a delicious buffet dinner and the music of Perry Fotos. Sharing in the glad tidings were daughter, Matia Cocoris and her husband, Bill, who had flown in from Boston for the nuptials. Others who shared in the couple's happiness were Nike's youngest daughter, Sophia Koretzky and her granddaughter, Christa Cocoris, who currently is living in Chicago while attending Loyola University.

A MAN….with a surprising lack of pretension – despite his many accomplishments – is A. Steve Betzelos, supreme secretary of the Order of Ahepa, who will be honored by the Lincolnwood #396 – Shoreline 380, Ahepa Chapter at a testimonial dinner-dance scheduled to take place at the Sheraton O'Hare Hotel on May 18th. Co-chairmen of the event will be Peter Kaludis and Jim Betzelos, Stash's younger brother. Stash, a natural leader, is being honored after 30 years of membership and service to the Order of Ahepa and the Hellenic American community.

THIS WEEK…..we point with pride to pretty and talented Elaine Markoutsas whose celebrity interviews appear weekly in the pages of the *Chicago Tribune*. This talented miss has done a tremendous writing job, especially in her stories on Lucy Arnaz and Bob Newhart.

THE GREAT….gurus of icecreamology have voted Homer's ice cream (1237 Green Bay Road, Wilmette) the richest, creamiest, yummiest, most delicately flavored stuff in Chicago and environs, according to a recent article which appeared in *Chicago Magazine*. Entitled, "The Scoop on Chicago's Ice Cream," the article tells how seven ice cream devotees went through a blind tasting orgy of 28 yummy ice creams to see how they stacked up. On top of the list was Homer's (rated 91.5) which according to the panel "kind of sizzles, exciting, different." Owned and operated by Gus Poulos – one of my father's best friends, I have been eating Homer's ice cream since I was knee high to a grasshopper.

QUOTE OT THE WEEK: "The most utterly lost of all days is that in which you have not once laughed." –Chamfort

"People with affectations are not vain, but suffer from a haunting sense of inferiority; an affectation is a confession that you do not consider your natural self to be good enough to be displayed in public."

PLANTING ANOTHER……rosebud in their garden of successes is the north shore parish of Sts. Peter and Paul, Glenview. This rosebud will come to full bloom on June 24th at a summer spectacular scheduled to take place at the Chateau Ritz in Niles. On tap will be cocktails, dinner, dancing and treasured raffle prizes. But first – a bit about the fantastic musical attraction.

It won't be the music played at Manhattan's hot rock clubs – the Peppermint Lounge or the Ritz – that's strictly for the punks with high voltage energy. It will be the sophisticated music of the big bands – the bands of the '50's – the magical sounds of Tommy Dorsey, the dancing rhythms of Jimmy Dorsey, the trumpet blares of the inimitable Harry James; the sweet, romantic, hold-me-close tunes written just for you and your squeeze. It's the jitterbug, the cha-cha, the mambo. It's the Perry Fotos Big Band, flying in from Naples, Florida, just for this spectacular. In the past, we've loved his music; we've danced to his music, we've listened to his music. Only this time we'll be dancing to the "Best Big Band in Southwest Florida" – a coveted title recently received by the Perry Fotos Big Band.

How would you like to indulge your taste for outrageous luxury traveling in the grand style of Edward and Mrs. Simpson – or for that matter – Mata Hari? This opulent manner of travel will be aboard the most magnificent hotel on wheels – the Orient Express. As you board this legend and take your seat aboard luxurious surroundings, you will sip a chilled glass of champagne while dining on an elegant continental breakfast. Later – you will transfer to Hollingbourne Station where you will take a short coach ride to England's beautiful Leeds Castle. When you do rejoin the Orient Express, you will once again be served a three-course lunch while sipping on champagne. If this kind of travel interests you, be sure to buy raffle tickets being offered by the raffle committee. Who knows? You may be the lucky winner. So bring your wallet with you and join Georgia Photopoulos and Elaine Tarant, co-chairladies, at this spectacular.

WE EXTEND…..a warm welcome to pretty Danielle Eleni, daughter of George and Denise Karp of Palatine, who made her debut into the world of wee little people on April 18th. Popping their buttons with pride are Michael and Callie Panagiotou, grandparents.

AND A……lovely cocktail bash was recently hosted by Consul General John Zeppos and his charming wife in his LSD pad in honor of internationally famous, Mikis Theodorakis. With wall-to-wall people in attendance, it was a most delightful event. Best known for his film scores for "Zorba the Greek" and "Serpico," Theodorakis has been all over the political map.

RESTAURANTEUR ALEX,……Dana and Jim Kaulentis recently organized an annual golf outing at Olympia Fields Country Club to benefit the John J. Kaulentis Memorial Scholarship Fund. The fund is named after Jim Kaulentis' 19-year-old son who was killed in a Lake Michigan sailing accident last summer. It will provide scholarships for graduating seniors at Deerfield High School and Loyola Academy. A tuition grant also will go to a deserving student at Holy Cross Grammar School in Deerfield. The younger Kaulentis attended all three schools.

QUOTE OF THE WEEK: "I'll think it over and let you know," means "Please wait until I find a mutually acceptable way of refusing."

"Experience can be the worst teacher as well as the best; all that experience teaches a delinquent is to grow rich and successful enough to be able to afford a top lawyer."

ONE OF.......the nicest reasons for writing a column is that it gives me the opportunity to express my feelings about some of the really great "super" people we have in our community. One of these really super guys is a family friend of many years standing; a man who, in my opinion, has done a great deal in his lifetime, to make the world a better place to live in. A noble man, who has aided and abetted humanity collectively, as well as individually with his many financial contributions. I have never known him to turn down anyone who needed any kind of help. He can most accurately be described as a philanthropist with a loving human heart, an outstretched helping hand, and the gentleness, kindness and courtesy found in one who is a true humanitarian. The man I am talking about is James E. Maros of Olympia Fields, who will be singularly honored by the state of Israel on Sunday, May 23rd, in the International Ballroom of the Conrad Hilton Hotel. At this dinner tribute, he will be named "Man of the Year" by the state of Israel and will be presented with the coveted Israel Silver Medal for his tremendous response to the needs of ethnic groups throughout the world. The announcement of this much deserved honor was made at a kick-off luncheon at the Hilton on April 17th. Honorary chairman of the dinner is Marshall Korshak; general chairman is John Daros.

Just to give you an idea of the host of tributes coming Jim's way, let me name a few of the individuals and banks that purchased Israel bonds in Jim Maros' name during the kick-off luncheon: Bank of Greece, $250,000; Gus Zappas, $100,000; First National Bank of Oak Lawn, $100,000; Louis Kuchuris, $10,000; John Daros, $10,000; Jim Munger, $5,000.

TIE A........red ribbon around your finger to remind you to attend the forthcoming four-day Second Archdiocesan District Clergy-Laity and Philoptochos Conference scheduled to take place on May 12-15 at the North Shore Hilton Hotel in Skokie. General chairman of the event is James Betzelos. The four-day meeting is being hosted by the parish of Sts. Peter and Paul Greek Orthodox Church, Glenview. His Eminence Archbishop Iakovos will be in attendance as will His Grace Bishop Timotheos. Under their spiritual guidance, a program of challenging topics has been formulated in order to create healthy discussions and planning concerning individual parish and diocesan needs.

IMPECCABLE FOOD....served in a blissfully relaxing atmosphere is the menu offered by one of the really "in" spots on the southwest side of our town. Only a few months old, Nikos is owned by Nick Skountzos and his partner, Nick Verveniotis. The New Orleans style dining spot is tastefully constructed of stone, stucco and brick and a real feather in the architectural hat of Ted Theodore. Its dining room features an easy-on-the-eyes Spanish décor and melodious-on-the-ears mariachis whose lilting love songs linger in your memory long after you've gone. It is open seven days a week for lunch, dinner and late snacks.

WE POINT.....with pride to one of our most gracious philanthropists, William S. Deree, Chicago, and Scottsdale, Arizona bank-financier. Mr. Deree, chairman of the Development Program Committee of Pierce College, Athens, recently made a statement of intent to the school's board of trustees. To honor this statement, the college voted a name change in its institution. The college level school will hereafter be known as Deree College, and its corporate name as Deree-Pierce Colleges.

QUOTE OF THE WEEK: "To know which illusions must be dispelled, and which are not worth puncturing, is the first and almost the whole art of being a good friend."

"Most second marriages are either duplicates of the first, or else complete opposites; in both cases, the person has committed a second error – either that of repetition, or of assuming that the contrary of something bad is necessarily something good." – Harris

WE POINT.....with pride to Spiro T. Agnew, former vice-president of the United States, for conducting himself so beautifully on the recent

Irv Kupcinet show. Kup did everything in his power to destroy Agnew's dignity, but Spiro kept his cool and answered all the questions thrown at him with the wisdom of a Solomon. I, for one, lost all respect for Kup for his lack of good manners and good taste. He had apparently invited the ex-veep on his show to discuss Mr. Agnew's book, "The Canfield Affair," but no one would have known it. Agnew was met with a barrage of questions concerning his stance on Israel which would have made even the most stalwart of men falter. I have been informed that many upset and disgruntled onlookers have written to the station stating their opinions on Kup's abusive behavior. Good for these people.

Kup's conduct was very distasteful.

CONGRATULATIONS TO......one of the top educators in our fair city, John Graven, principal of Taft High School, who recently became the recipient of a doctorate in education. So beloved at Taft is John that the staff and students recently honored him with a gigantic birthday celebration.

HAPPY TO......learn that Thomas V. Askounis, son of Bessie and the late George Askounis, has been appointed special assistant attorney general of the state of Illinois. The appointment was made by Attorney General William J.Scott.

IT WAS.....a very special evening on Saturday, June 19th, for on that day two very special people, William and Martha Russis, celebrated 50 years of marital bliss – indeed an occasion in this day and age. On that particular day their two children, Katherine Heard and James Russis, and their respective mates, Chuck and Connie, gave a surprise party in their honor at the Seven Eagles Restaurant in Des Plaines. Many beloved friends and relatives attended this festive dinner party – some of whom had flown in from afar especially for the occasion. On hand from out-of-town were: Tony Matsoukas (Mrs. Russis' brother) and his wife, Mary, from Los Angeles; Mrs. Mary Poulos (Mrs. Russis' step-sister), her daughter, Georgia Anasis, and her granddaughter, also from Los Angeles; Ms. Euthemia Matsoukas of New York City (niece of Mrs.

Russis and daughter of Nick J. Matsoukas, fellow *Greek Press* columnist from the *Streets of Athens* who is Mrs. Russis' younger brother); Phoebe and Doug Campbell of Oklahoma (niece and nephew of Mr. Russis) and Steve Poulos of Louisiana (nephew of Mrs. Russis).

Many old-time friends, the majority of whom are stalwart members of the Hellenic Professional Society, along with Mr. Russis, spoke eloquently on the virtues of both Bill and Martha. Among them were their koumbaro John Prassas, D.S.D. Soter, Spiro Apostle, Dimitri Perry, James Nichols, Dion Cheronis and Victor Yacktman. Toastmaster for the evening was James Russis.

The couple has five grandchildren: Diana, Carla and Chuckie Heard, and Martha and Vasili Russis.

QUOTE OF THE WEEK: "When people are made to feel secure, important and appreciated, it will no longer be necessary for them to whittle down others in order to seem bigger by comparison." - Arcastle

"In times of misfortune, we are prone to reflect that we do not deserve such unhappiness, but in times of felicity, it rarely occurs to us that we are equally undeserving of such happiness."

SPARKLING COLLECTION.....of deliciously feminine gowns were modeled at the fashion show luncheon sponsored by The Women's Board of the Combined Cardiac Research Fund on August 20th in the Gold Coast Room of the Drake Hotel. The 100 pieces of totally today apparel, all bearing the distinguished mark of international designer George Stavropoulos, were not only glamorous, but gowns that looked as if they wouldn't go all to pieces if you kept them out late. Stavropoulos' collection reeked of elegance, and his opulent creations came in super rich chocolate shades, classic navy, fashionable black, shades of flanelesque gray and hues of burgundy wine. The master craftsman showed wide flowing sleeves, full graceful skirts, blanketing giant shawls, and whirligig capes cut so that the most gentle of breezes would provoke them into movement.

I was fortunate enough to meet George Stavropoulos at a cocktail reception held at the Riviera 400 Club, Outer Drive East Condominiums, and hosted by Evangeline Gouletas, executive vice-president of American Invsco and chairman of the fashion show luncheon. He was equally as charming and as interesting as the fashions he displayed. Along with Mr. Stavropoulos, I had the distinct pleasure of meeting our new and distinguished Consul General of Greece, Spyridon Dokianos and his pretty wife.

WE WISH....Steve Colovos, Peter Mikuzis and Bill Pappas a great deal of success in their latest acquisition, the House of Windsor located at 6565 North Mannhim Road, Rosemont. The restaurant opened in August, and we were fortunate enough to have Terry Mikuzis guide us through the premises. An immense establishment, the House of Windsor has banquet facilities that will accommodate anywhere from 15 to 850 guests.

AND ONE.....of our town's coolest couples – Stuart and Eva Polydoris of Lake Forest – attended the veddy, veddy social Bicentennial Costume Ball given by none other than Bonnie Swearingen. According to Eva, it was the most beautiful party they have ever attended.

SEX SYMBOL....Telly Savalas did his thing in Newton, Massachusetts on Sunday, October 3rd at the Marriot Hotel when the Greek-American community in Boston honored Senator Edward M. Kennedy at an appreciation dinner. From what I heard – Telly stole the show with his charm and aplomb.

FIVE BRIGHT......attractive and articulate members of the Greek Parliament were recently feted by Consul General and Mrs. Spyridon Dokianos at the Illinois Athletic Club. With patience and stamina in their hip pockets, Demetrios Papaspyrou, Nicholas Anagnostopoulos, Nicholas Papaioannou, Michael Gelenianos, and Constantine Giatrakos stood in line with the Consul General and his wife and Vice-Consul

John Cambolis, to greet the hundreds of Greek-American leaders who had been invited to attend the posh cocktail party honoring the five distinguished international figures.

QUOTE OF THE WEEK: "It is weak men, not strong men, who are cruel – for cruelty is almost always an admission of failure of character in the past, and a desperate effort to rectify by pain what should have been prevented by firmness."-Harris

"The fundamental problem in life – as in business, in art, in politics, and in most human activities- is how to be stable without becoming stagnant."

FOUR HUNDRED…..beautifully dressed people, with turned on smiles shining brightly like the crystal-clear chandeliers under which they stood, waited patiently in line at the Ambassador West Hotel on Saturday, January 20th, to wish fragile, beautiful and radiant, Irene Manus, and her handsome, dark-eyed bridegroom, Jack Singh, a lifetime of happiness together. The couple had just arrived at the Ambassador after being married at Sts. Helen and Constantine Greek Orthodox Church. His Eminence Archbishop Ezekiel of Australia, the Reverend Basil S. Gregory of New York, the Reverend Byron Papanikolaou, and the Reverend Alexander Karloutsos officiated at the ceremony.

Standing alongside the happy couple in the receiving line were the bride's parents, the groom's brother, and a bevy of wide-eyed, shiny-tressed young beauties, dressed in ice blue satin floor length gowns, petal smooth in femininity. A two-hour champagne reception, at which Perry Fotos and his orchestra supplied the music, was followed by dinner in the Guildhall.

Host and hostess for the evening were the bride's parents, George and Maria Manus –George resplendent in his tails – and Maria in her luxurious gown of muted pastel shades and white mink.

From the pale blue satin envelopes, indicating each guest's table seat, to the pale blue satin match boxes and napkin holders which adorned each table, guests were indulged in beauty, good taste, and originality, all equally apparent in the table centerpieces – the most unusual I have ever seen. Four tiered, the base consisted of a rounded bouquet of pink hued and white blossoms.

Three more bouquets, replicas of the balloon like base, jutted up and out from the blue satin center branch of the centerpiece, each one higher than the other. Brainchild of the bride's mother, Maria, a floral wizard in her own right, they were a genuine work of art, flawless in perfection.

George Legaros of Minneapolis, godfather of the bride, was the best man. His wife, the former Connie Nikopoulos of Chicago, accompanied him – and charmingly so, I might add, for the pink satin sling in which her maimed arm rested, matched her gown to perfection.

RADIANT WITH......happiness is Eugenia S. Georgoules, who announced her engagement to Herman Joseph Seifer at a recent party hosted by her brother and sister-in-law, Thomas and Vicki Georgoules at the Pump Room of the Ambassador East Hotel.

EIGHT DESERVING......students will share in scholarships worth \$4,300 at the forthcoming Annual 13th District Ahepa Scholarship Ball scheduled to take place on February 10th at the luxurious O'Hare Inn. Most of the monies derived from this social event will go toward the Peter D. Gianukos Ahepa Scholarship Fund in which eight students will share that evening. Also sharing in the evening's scholarship program will be the American Farm School in Thessaloniki, Greece, in the amount of \$1,100.

QUOTE OF THE WEEK: "For every one person who is bored with his surroundings, there are a thousand who are bored with themselves, because they have not planted enough foliage in the landscape of their personalities."

"The divorce rate will not diminish until many more persons contemplating marriage stop concentrating on whether the other is the 'right person' and start reflecting on whether they are the right person." –Harris

SCHOLARS ON....Greek Americana will present papers on, "The Greek Experience in America," on October 29-31, at the University of Chicago's Center for Continuing Education. Sponsored by the Modern Greek Studies Association, in cooperation with the University of Chicago, the major academic and cultural event is being funded in part by the American Revolution Bicentennial Administration in Washington, D.C. and the Illinois Bicentennial Commission. It is endorsed and recognized as a national bicentennial event and has received attention on the floor of the U.S.Senate and in the public mass media. Leading scholars and civic individuals will be in attendance. Co-chaired by Alexander Karanikas, PhD, and Andrew T. Kopan, Ph D., the event promises to explore the Greek reality in America from the perspective of varied disciplines.

ONE OF.....the handsomest little boys in the pablum set, tow-headed, long limbed, and fair-skinned Steven Peter, son of Peter and Terry Mikuzis, and grandson of Steve and Jennie Colovos, was christened on October 2nd at St. Andrew's Greek Orthodox Church by Milton and Kathy Fasseas. Guests numbering well over 200 toasted this little heart-breaker during the cocktail reception which was followed by a delicious dinner and an evening of dancing at the House of Windsor in Rosemont.

A BIGGIE......you can look forward to attending is the 45th anniversary celebration of The Greek Women's University Club, which will be celebrated on December 5th at a dinner-dance scheduled to take place at the Lake Shore Club. This gala event deserves the support of all members of the GWUC, as well as its friends, for the organization will award two $1,000 scholarships to two university or college students of Greek descent.

LATEST DUO……to be caught in the tender trap is lovely, Maria Papas, daughter of Mrs. Nicolas Bacaintan and the late Spiro J. Papas, and oh so charming, George Cantonis, son of Ann and Michael Cantonis. Since their engagement became official, Maria and George have been wined and dined around the clock. One of the most delightful dinner parties given in their honor was hosted by Maria's grandmother, Mrs. S.J. Gregory, one of our town's most gracious and elegant ladies. The cocktail-dinner bash was held in the Camelia House of the Drake Hotel, and it was indeed one of the most enjoyable evenings I have ever spent. The coosome twosome will tie the knot on January 22nd.

CONDOLENCES ARE…..extended to a very dear friend of many years standing, Leon Marinakos, on the death of his beloved father, Constantine. I had the pleasure of meeting the soft-spoken Mr. Marinakos many years ago and he was, indeed, a most charming man. He is survived by his wife, Mary; a daughter, Yiota (Rev. Dr. Theodore) Thalassinos, and two grandsons.

QUOTE OF THE WEEK: "Success is not a ladder, as the popular metaphor has it, but a labyrinth – not a climb upward, rung by rung, but a maze filled with false turnings and dead ends; failure does not consist in falling from the ladder, but in becoming so involved with the labyrinth that one no longer desires to reemerge into the sun light."

"Love in France is a comedy; in England, a tragedy; in Italy, an operatic aria; and in Greece, a melodrama." – Pinkington

ONE OF…..our town's greatest benefactors, S.J. Gregory (Sklavounis) of Wilmette died on August 31st at Grant Hospital in Chicago. While he had been physically ill over a lengthy span of time, the 83-year-old S.J. had been mentally active, conducting his business empire, up until the time of his death. A captain of industry who could lock heads with the most sagacious business tycoons in the country, he was a pioneer in the motion picture arena. Founder and president of the well-known Alliance Amusement Company, his business operations also included McDonald's restaurants and cable TV systems.

One of the greatest philanthropists of our era, S.J. never turned down any requests for funds from any charitable group. He served as chairman of the Building Fund Committee at St. Andrew's Greek Orthodox Church. His financial bequests were numerous amassing monies for the church he loved so well. In deep appreciation, the St. Andrew's Community Center was named after him. He is survived by his widow, Rita, and three daughters: Dina Bacaintan of Wilmette, Eugenia Stassinopoulos of Athens, Greece, and Aliki Bryant of McLean, Virginia.

AND A......surprise birthday party was recently given by Sam and Dee Tzakis of Lake Forest for their koumbara Jean Collias. The Tzakis' treated a group of friends to a concert presented by the Lake Forest Symphony Orchestra at Barat College (Victor Aitay conducting). The concert was sponsored by the Community Music Association (Dee is president of the womens' committee). Later guests adjourned to the Tzakis home where they sipped and supped in honor of Jean.

THE FAMILY....of Aristides Athens is wearing its heart at half-mast since this senior citizen's death in Trenton, Michigan, a few weeks ago. The affable Mr. Athens is survived by his widow; his sons, Thomas and Andrew Athens, two of the most respected names in our community; another son, Dr. William Athens, and two daughters, Tula Georgeson and Mary Diveris.

SYMPATHY IS .....also extended to the family of John G. Skontos who succumbed recently. He is survived by his wife, Mary; his son, George; and a daughter, Constance Marinakis. His death was really a shocker for it followed right on the heels of the very lovely party sponsored by George and his, Kathy, honoring Ted Anastos.

QUOTE OF THE WEEK: "The man who is proud of knowing his own mind often doesn't know his own heart, and this is why his mind usually betrays him into dangerous absurdities." - Harris

"The moment we can give a reason for loving someone, the love has been diminished and turned into a kind of calculus of emotions; for instance, a baby loved because it is 'cute' faces an awful fate as its cuteness recedes."

THE WORLD…is a lot sadder and poorer since the death of one of our town's most lovable citizens, warm-hearted and affable Peter Gianukos of Evanston, who died suddenly on May 30th. With his lively spirit and his soft grin, he gave as few people do in their lifetime, but the well of Peter Gianukos never ran dry. What he gave he received twice over in the devotion of his endless array of friends scattered all over the country.

The true spirit of Peter Gianukos was caught by *Sun-Times* writer, Michael Miner, who interviewed him a month before his death and whose Topline story appeared in the front page of the Friday, June 7th issue of the *Times*. Reading the dialogue was like having a conversation with Peter for Miner had plainly caught the earthy way Gianukos had of expressing himself. He will be sorely missed by his legion of friends, as well as by his wife, Pota; his son, James (Denise) and two grandchildren.

CONGRATULATIONS TO……Connie Theodore, daughter of Peter and Matina Theodore of Glenview who was recently honored with a Northern Illinois School Press Award.

DITTO TO……Aris Athens, son of Tom and Irene Athens of Wilmette, who received special academic honors at the senior convocation of Lake Forest College.

TO ELEVATE…….your point of view, be sure you read, "The Greek Mystique," written by our very own pretty and talented, Elaine Markoutsas, which will be published in the August 4th issue of the *Chicago Tribune*, Sunday Magazine Section. Writer Elaine has put together an interesting article that promises to be excellent reading for everyone.

LARGE DOSES…..of genuine hospitality, warmth and affection were served to all those attending the recent cocktail party buffet dinner bash given by Andy and Louise Athens in their Hinsdale home. General chairman of the Clergy-Laity Congress, Andy and Louise gave the party in honor of those who worked behind the scenes to make the congress the successful event that it was.

Cocktails and delicate Greek tidbits were served in the patio swimming pool where sturdy trees in the background bowed their heads in reverence to the flock of church hierarchy who were in attendance. The floor show from the Athens North, with Spiro Skouras serving as MC, provided unsurpassed entertainment during cocktails.

A taverna dinner was served on the green where colorful tables and chairs, decked with hurricane lamps and print table cloths, had been set up amid carpets of emerald green lawn that seemed to drift on and on until it met with blankets of blue sky and puffs of white clouds. Hanging proudly overhead, guarding the succulent buffet table, was a large gold tent which covered everything a raindrop could wet. Food was served by girls dressed in colorful Greek costumes.

QUOTE OF THE WEEK: "The only victory over love is flight." - Napoleon

"The seeking after a status symbol is futile and endless-for as soon as enough people have attained it, it is no longer a status symbol; true status is achieved only by those secure enough to live by substance and spirit, not by symbols." – Johnson

NOT EVEN.....the blizzard of '78 could keep the in-crowd from attending a swinging cocktail party sponsored by the Hellenic Professional Society of Illinois. Close to 200 people danced atop the clouds of the John Hancock's 95th to the earthy beat of John Giatris and his Grecian Aires. The exceptional view and delicious hors d'oeuvres set a festive mood that lasted far into the wee hours of the morning. The hostesses of the evening, Antoinette Contos, Lucy Pappas, and Cleo Pappas, wish to thank their record-breaking crowd of guests for braving the still snow-covered streets of Chicago to make this post-holiday revel a smashing success.

MEMO TO........Elaine Markoutsas: I heard raves and raves of praise on your recent feature article that appeared on the front page of the *Chicago Tribune's* "Lifestyle." I thought it was great – and so did everyone I discussed it with. Keep up the super work you are doing.

AND THE....Edith Piaf of Greece (the highest honor I can pay her) Nana Mouskouri, will be back in our town the latter part of the month, where she will croon her tunes in a rare American appearance. The place will be the Opera House; the dates – April 21-23, with one show each evening. The inimitable international stylist and recording star sings in English, Italian, French, German and Greek. Tickets to the concert are available at 29 North Wacker Drive.

CENTRAL DESIGN.....of the new 1978 commemorative postage stamp that will honor Dr. George Papanicolaou is a sketched portrait of the noted cancer research and theme, "Early Detection of Cancer" according to U.S. Postal authorities. The stamp, which will be issued on May 18th at the White House,, with Mrs. Roslynn Carter participating in the ceremony, will honor Dr. Papanicolaou for his development of the "Pap Test" Cancer Detection Procedure.

GATHERING FOR....the in-clan took place recently when Stash and Irene Betzelos held a wing-a-ding-ding in their palatial home. The "everybody in the city of Chicago was there" party, which lasted until the wee hours of the morning, was filled with short people, tall people, blonde people, dark people, fat people, skinny people – people – people – and more people. It was a real love-in for the Betzelos' who are known all over the United States – so active are they both in the Ahepa cause.

CONGRATULATIONS TO……solid citizen, Andrew A. Athens, who has been added to the board of directors of Talman Federal Savings and Loan Association. Jet-propelled Andy fills a vacancy created by a recent board decision to expand its membership from eight to nine directors.

ONE OF……our town's top educators, Dr. Andrew T. Kopan, addressed the recent Hellenic Symposium which took place at Cyrus Durgin Performing Arts Center, South Campus of the University of Lowell, Lowell, Massachusetts. An associate professor of education and director of the Division of Educational Foundation, School of Education, DePaul University, Andrew took the big bird to Lowell to address the group on "Greek Language and Education."

QUOTE OF THE WEEK: "No one grows old by living – only by losing interest in living." – Marie Ray

"Love is a gift that one person makes to another. It is a gift of the heart, and the heart signs no documents." – E.M. Forst

IT'S THAT……time of year again. That time of year that is known as "primary time," when we should all go to the polls, declare our party affiliation, then vote for those we consider qualified enough to run in the big race. No apathy – no saying, "I should have, but I didn't" because this is what puts the wrong people into office.

An exceptionally qualified candidate will be running in the primaries this March. His name is familiar to all of us – Associate Circuit Judge Peter Bakakos of Wilmette. He is the Republican candidate for Judge of the Circuit Court of Cook County in the suburbs, and his name will appear on the Republican Suburban Cook County ballot in the March 31st primary election.

Those of us who are privileged to know Peter, know that there is no better man suited for the position of the Judge of the Circuit Court. A distinguished man of sound moral character, his judgment, integrity, and lengthy experience qualify him to serve the people of the state of Illinois as Judge of the Circuit Court. With Peter Bakakos on the bench, the flames of justice will certainly burn brightly in our state.

Currently, Peter is an Associate Circuit Judge, bringing a long and impressive career to his present candidacy. He is Supervising Judge of the Circuit Court Surety Section and Chairman of a Study Committee on Bail Procedures of the Illinois Judicial Conference (the latter is a federally funded project recommended by the Illinois Supreme Court Committee on Criminal Justice Programs to review and recommend improvement of the state's bail laws).

Prior to his present assignment, Peter presided for ten years in the north and northwest suburbs, including courts in Evanston, Arlington Heights, Skokie, Winnetka, Glenview, Northfield and Lincolnwood. Since space precludes my listing all of Peter's professional accomplishments, let me sum up by saying that he has been rated qualified by the Chicago Bar Association and the Northwest Suburban Bar Association. He was endorsed by all major newspapers in the primary and two out of three in the general election candidacy for Appellate Court Judge.

THE FAMILY.....of James Nichols is wearing its heart at half-mast since the death of this beloved senior citizen. A founder and a former president of St. Andrew's Greek Orthodox Church, the affable Mr. Nichols was very well known in the Chicago community for, indeed, he was one of our town's most beloved gentlemen. He is survived by his wife, Constance; his three daughters and sons-in-law: Caleroi (Peter) Boukidis of Los Angeles; Elaine (Peter) Kokoris; Dorothy (John)

Kavooras of Birmingham, Michigan; nine grandchildren; a sister, Marion Anagnos; a sister-in-law, Ida Chamales, and a brother-in-law, Christ Chamales of Florida.

BULGING AT.....the seams with beautiful people was the recent cocktail reception hosted by our very warm and congenial Consul General Spyridon Dokianos and his lovely wife, Maria, who entertained over 200 people in honor of the Ambassador of Greece, His Excellency Menelaos Alexandrakis, and his charming wife. It was a party filled with the crème de la crème of Chicago and high chic glamour fever was the temperature of the evening. Color it a "Who's Who" gallery of Greek personnages in our town.

QUOTE OF THE WEEK: "To love is to admire with the heart; to admire is to love with the mind." –Theophile Gautier

"There is nothing wrong with education that a good haircut wouldn't cure." Anonymous

FELLOW COLUMNIST......Jimmy Mezilson and his sister, Fay Machinis, are wearing their hearts at haf-mast since the death of their beloved brother, Christ. Married and the father of three children, Christ was a former board member of the Chicago Hearing Society. His death was sudden – making a total of three deaths for the Mezilson clan in a comparatively short period of time. Helen Pappas of Salt Lake City was the first to go; she was followed by another sister, Connie Alevizos of Minneapolis.

A ONCE.......in a lifetime event that will be much more than the usual fond remembrances and rewarding accomplishments of a very special human being, has been scheduled to take place on June 9th in the Grand Ballroom of the Palmer House. At this time the United Hellenic

American Congress will honor our beloved Archbishop Iakovos, the spiritual leader of the Greek Orthodox faithful in the United States. The National Banquet will commemorate the 20th anniversary of the enthronement of a spiritual leader who has provided and who continues to provide strength and direction to all of his faithful. A man who ignores the obstacles at his feet and always keeps his eyes on the goal above, His Eminence has uplifted our minds with his words of hope, love, and charity, and his good works bear powerful testimony to the church's growth.

I doubt that any man in our community has done as much as Andrew A. Athens, national chairman of UHAC, to aid the Greek cause. Andy gives of himself as freely as the water flowing from an endless fountain of generosity. A man with an elevated point of view, he is as warm and friendly as the boy next door; as clear and bright as the most flawless diamond; and a man who wears his spirituality as comfortably as a pair of old slippers. With such a man in the driver's seat, the banquet is bound to be a solid gold Cadillac.

Honored guests at this event will include such national luminaries as: Walter Mondale, Vice-President of the United States; Congressman John Brademas, Senator Paul Sarbanes, Congressman Edward Derwinski, and Congressman Martin Russo. Entitled, "A Tribute to Greek Orthodoxy," the banquet promises to provide you with a delightfully social evening, a spiritually rewarding evening, delicious food, and a chance to see anybody who is anybody in our town.

FUNERAL SERVICES…..for Pierre A. DeMets, retired restauranteur and prominent figure in our town, were held on August 13 at his beloved Saints Constantine and Helen Greek Orthodox Church for which he had diligently worked during his lifetime. A deeply respected man in the community, Pierre DeMets gave unselfishly to his church, his community and to his legion of friends heading many mammoth projects and devoting himself totally to philanthropic and church work.

In the late 1950's, the late Mayor Daley appointed him chairman of the Pan American Olympic Games. He arranged with the government of Greece to have the Olympic Torch flown to the United States and brought to Chicago and to Soldiers Field lit all the way from Athens. In 1958, he was honored by Archbishop Michael with the medal of St. Paul. But his greatest ecclesiastical honor came from his All Holiness Athenagoras, who conferred him with the exalter title of Megas Archon Skevophylax (protector of the Patriarchal art and relics). He is survived by his wife, Thula.

QUOTE OF THE WEEK: "Many a deep secret that cannot be pried out by curiosity can be drawn out by indifference."

"One of the most ominous signs of disturbance in modern American society is that wives, by and large, are more mature and less content than their husbands; and a social order can flourish only when the men are mature and the women are content."

THE FAMILY……of George J. Marks of Lincolnwood is wearing its heart at half-mast since the death of its beloved husband and father, respectively. The benevolent 62-year-old George died on October 22nd following a heart attack at Mount Sinai Hospital. A former board chairman of St. Andrew's Greek Orthodox Church, he held the title of Mega Archon Fronimon bestowed on laymen for service in the church and he was named, "Man of the Year" of the Federation of American Hellenic Societies. My condolences to his widow, Beatrice; his two sons, John and Christopher; and his brothers, Andrew, Nicholas and Dean.

TO COMMEMORATE….its 50th anniversary, the Hellenic Professional Society of Illinois, will sponsor a Golden Anniversary Celebration on Sunday, October 26th, in the Grand Ballroom of the Conrad Hilton Hotel. Aspects of the celebration have been in the planning stages since the beginning of the year, according to Leon Marinakos, former president of the society, and general chairman of the dinner-dance.

HEARTS AND.....flowers to Mrs. George (Christine) Annes of Wilmette, who took the time and trouble to write me a beautiful birthday ode. Her kind and gentle words will serve as an inspiration to the future writings of this column.

A Birthday Ode to Stacy

It's easy to go out and buy
A big birthday card from a guy,
But to truly send your best wish
To a warm and lovely miss
A person should sit down and write
What is really in one's heart.
She greets you with warmth and love
With smiles, wishes and hugs
At all the big social rugs,
So to this sweet little Greek bug
I send my heartful tug
Happy birthday, my sweet dove
May God keep you with love.

As always, Christine Annes

"It may be true that 'only the brave deserve the fair,' but that's because only the brave can live with the fair; it takes a man who is quietly confident of his powers to handle a beautiful woman."

APPLAUSE, APPLAUSE.......to Tom Kapsalis, Commissioner of City Planning in our town, who was recently appointed to yet another top spot – this time by Mayor Jane Byrne – in the Aviation Department. Tommy will take over operations at O'Hare International Airport, which will give Aviation Commissioner Pat Dunne an assist.

Tom is a very special friend. Back in the late 1950's, Tommy, my late and beloved cousin, Euthemia Russis, George Conomikes, who originally hailed from New Rochelle, New York, and who currently makes his home in California, and I met for lunch faithfully, every Wednesday at Mayor's Row. It was fun time in all of our lives. Then, in 1962, Euthemia lost her bout with cancer. We were all shattered by her death, but our friendship provided us with the emotional glue that slowly helped us get it all together again. Today we remain stalwart friends.

WITH A……sparkle in her eye and a bloom in her pretty cheek, Vicki Leventis, daughter of Dino and Maria Leventis of Lincolnwood, became one with Russel Dulany on June 23rd at St. Andrew's Greek Orthodox Church. A dinner reception followed at the beautiful Highland Park Country Club.

WEARING THEIR……..hearts at half-mast is the family of Gus E. Poulos, founder and owner of Homer's Ice Cream Company in Wilmette, who succumbed recently. When I was growing up, he and my late and beloved father were very close friends (which means we polished off an awful lot of ice cream, courtesy of Gus). My sister, Irene, had the honor of baptizing second son, Jon. Gus was a marvelous human being with a great sense of humor. He is survived by his wife, Angelyn; his three sons, who operated the business with him – Stevie (Priscilla), Jon and Dean – a brother, two sisters, and two grandsons.

AND YET……another well known gentleman, Nicholas G. Kanellos, a most faithful devotee at St. Andrew's Greek Orthodox Church, died recently making everyone in the parish a little bit sadder. He had served the parish for 30 years and could be seen every Sunday, come rain or shine, at the pangari. An officer and member of the parish council, Mr. Kanellos was presented with an award for his service during the 50 year celebration of that parish. A grocery executive, he was co-founder and charter member of the Grocerland Cooperative, and he owned and operated the Shop and Save Food Mart, the Gain More Food Mart, and the Land-O-Foods Store on North Sheridan Road. He is survived by his wife, Mary.

LOVE NOTES.......are sweet and they crooned the sweetest tune at the recent marriage of Maria Kountouris, daughter of Mrs. Emanuel Kountouris of Toledo, Ohio, and the late Emanuel Kountouris, to Gregory Michael Brown, son of Peter and Helen Brown of Northbrook. The handsome couple took their vows on September 1ST at Toledo, Ohio's Holy Trinity Greek Orthodox Church. A reception followed in the Crystal Room of the Commodore Perry Hotel. Maria and Greg met seven years ago during the Ahepa's educational journey to Greece – and it has been hearts and flowers ever since.

QUOTE OF THE WEEK: "A person who insists that he listens 'to both sides of the question' fails to add that he listens to each side in quite a different manner; with his ears critically cocked to the side he tends against, and with his ears flopping pleasurably to the side he tends to favor."

"The greatest mistake you can make in life is to assume that you can see others more clearly than they can see you." – Harris

ONE OF......our town's brightest female educators, Anastasia Graven (Mrs. John), principal of Boone and Decatur Elementary Schools in Chicago's north side, was recently interviewed by Casey Banas, education editor of the *Chicago Tribune*. An edited transcript of the interview appeared on the front page of the *Chicago Tribune* (September 3rd).

A continuing concern is how parents can work closer with educators to help improve school for their youngsters. In her interview, Ann answered a series of questions offering a principal's perspective on cooperation between parent and teacher.

CONGRATULATIONS TO…….Realtor Tony Antoniou who is taking over the Regency Orleans Building on East Superior. He will convert it into a small hotel to be known as the Abbey-Regency. Tony's other acquisitions include the Abbey and Interlaken resort hotels in Lake Geneva.

ANOTHER HONOR…was perched on the shoulders of Engie Gouletas and her brother, Nicholas, real estate tycoon, who is chairman of the board at American Invsco, when they were invited to attend a reception at the White House on Thursday afternoon, January 3rd. Nick and Engie accepted the invitation extended by First Lady Rosalyn Carter and took the big bird to Washington, D.C. to attend a salute to Poetry and American Poets reception.

OUR TOWN…….is a lot sadder since the death of beloved Helen Lamperis on Christmas Day – ironically enough – on her birthday. Helen, a lady of great courage with a delightful sense of humor, succumbed to a heart attack. She had lost her handsome, 18-year-old son, Constantine (Dean) Lamperis in the biggie – the Illinois Central train crash about 7 years ago. But courageous Helen continued to walk the path of life gallantly – despite her great loss. She is survived by her sister and brother-in-law, Maria and George Manus; four nieces – Helen and Alice Anthony, Irene Manus Singh, Irene Ganas; and a nephew – Terry Ganas.

GATHERING OF…….friends and relatives of the late and beloved, Nick John Matsoukas, who succumbed in Athens, Greece, on December 19th, gathered together at a memorial service held in his honor on Sunday, January 13th, at the Radisson Chicago Hotel. It was given by the family of William and Martha Matsoukas Russis, brother-in-law and sister of Nick John, respectively.

It was not a melancholy gathering – but rather – a Nick Matsoukas kind of gathering – one which had color, humor, intelligence and the best of friends and acquaintances paying him tribute and revealing humorous anecdotes about charismatic Nick. Had he been tuned in he would have been both pleased and amused – such was the nature of the man.

James Russis, nephew of the deceased, coordinated the entire program, which featured such well-known speakers as Harry Mark Petrakis, Nicholas J. Melas, Mrs. Dimitri Perry, Julius Echeles, attorney, and Harry Barnard, renowned biographer.

One of the nicest features about the memorial was the fact that all of Nick's children had flown in from New York City to attend: Euthemia, Avra, Niki, David and Peter John.

QUOTE OF THE WEEK: "Experience can be the worst teacher as well as the best; all that experience teaches a delinquent is to grow rich and successful enough to be able to afford a top lawyer."

"Some persons seem to do good publicly so that they can build up a supply of 'reputation credit' in order to do evil privately." -Harris

THE WORLD......is a great deal sadder since the death of lovely 44-year-old Connie (Mrs. George) Legeros of Edina, Minnesota. A former Chicagoan, Connie Legeros was the oldest daughter of one of our town's most socially prominent families, the George Nikopoulos family. A Northwestern University graduate, and a member of St. Andrew's Greek Orthodox Church in her formative years and up until her marriage, Connie was active socially and had a legion of friends and admirers for, indeed, she was the epitome of gracious charm. Her desire to make this world a better place to live in spurred her on to involvement in many charitable organizations where she gave of herself in abundance. She is survived by her husband, George; her sons, Christopher and Nicholas; two sisters Doria Karampelas of St. Petersburg, Florida, and Delphi Harrington of New York City; and a brother, Paul Nikopoulos of St. Louis, Missouri.

CHUCKLE OF....the month came from Northbrook's Tom Mantice who took a nasty spill outside of Ted Smith's "Town and Country" only to notify Ted that his famed eatery will soon be known as "Tom and Ted's."

A DELIGHTFUL…..afternoon will be spent by all those kiddie lovers who plan to attend "Bunny Hop Fashions," sponsored by the PTA of St. Andrew's Greek Orthodox Church on Sunday, April 4th at the S.J. Gregory Auditorium. Here you will be able to feast your eyes on numerous pretty saucy-eyed moppets and little boy pranksters who will model a collection of kiddie fashions designed especially for the world of wee little people. A sunny afternoon for the kiddies as well as the adults.

DON'T FORGET….to take the tour offered by The Greek Women's University Club – a guided architectural tour of Frank Lloyd Wright houses in Oak Park to be conducted on April 13th .

CONGRATULATIONS TO….Ann Graven (Mrs. John) who was recently appointed principal of Boone Elementary School by the Board of Education. Hubby John is principal of Taft High School.

SPECIAL CONGRATULATIONS…also go to Alec K. Gianaras, well-known businessman, philanthropist, and a long-time champion in the field of mental retardation, who was recently honored at a testimonial dinner given by Little City for retarded children. It was held in the Guildhall of the Ambassador West. President and chairman of the Board of Transformer Manufacturers, Inc., Alec is currently serving his second term as president of the Little City Foundation. A loyal and dedicated member of the board, he has served with distinction as a dinner chairman of the Little City Testimonial given in honor of His Grace Bishop Timotheos.

QUOTE OF THE WEEK: "He who loves you will make you weep, but he who hates you may make you laugh." – Spanish proverb

The achievers I have selected for this book wear many faces—educators, doctors, business people, attorneys, etc. I don't know how you feel about those I have chosen, or if you even know them. But to me, they have reigned supreme in my Greek-American world. I know there are many others who wear the same badge, but space has precluded me from including them. Think about whom you consider to be an achiever, and perhaps, in subsequent writings, we can accord them the honor they deserve.

James V. Apostol, M.D. (right) was an assistant professor of surgery at Northwestern University when he retired from the active practice of surgery after having served as an exemplary surgeon since 1965. He is currently retired and living in Tucson, Arizona. George Andrews (left) worked at Hughes Aircraft as chief scientist for over 25 years designing communication satellites and surveillance (spy) satellites. He was awarded four patents for significant inventions in his field. Pictured in the center with her husband and brother, is Cleo Apostol Andrews, educator, who co-authored a workbook on English grammar.

Andrew A. Athens has received numerous awards and honors, each recognizing his outstanding services to his faith, his Hellenic heritage, public affairs and philanthropy. He founded the United Hellenic American Congress, after the invasion of Cypress, to advocate for human rights and religious freedom for all Hellenes living in Diaspora. Under his leadership, diplomatic relations between Greece, Cypress and the United States have been strengthened. Pictured above with UHAC Chairman Athens are His Grace Bishop Iakovos, His Excellency Nicholas Martis, Senator Paul Sarbanes and Dr. John Brademas.

Becky Bisoulis, internationally famous dress designer specializing in combining fabrics and textures in unusual ways, is pictured above at the Field Museum with (from left to right): first cousins Gloria Besbekis, Georgia Kotsiopoulos and Dennis Marlas. Among the many honors bestowed upon her are "Woman of the Year" by the City of Hope, "Designer of the Year" by the Apparel Industry Board and New York's Prix de Cachet Award.

Dr. Angeline P. Caruso received her Bachelor's Degree from Chicago Teacher's College, her Master's from Northwestern University and her Doctorate from Harvard on a Fellowship. Having spent almost 40 years serving children in the Chicago Public Schools, Dr. Caruso was appointed Interim School Superintendent for the Chicago Public Schools.

Well-known as the former owner of Century Broadcasting Company is George Collias. Next to him are: Dee Tzakis, Stacy Diacou, and Persey and James Betzelos.

Peter Fotos started his band in Chicago in 1950. Many years after, he moved to Naples, Florida. Much too young to retire, he started another band in Naples and was soon recognized as a great guru of big bands in southwestern Florida. *Gulf Coast* Magazine voted Perry Fotos' Big Band the "Best Big Band in Southwest Florida."

Alec K. Gianaras, industrialist, civic leader, and philanthropist, was president of Transformer Manufacturing Inc., a most prosperous electronics firm. A key supporter of Little City and City of Hope, and his beloved parish, St. Andrew's Greek Orthodox Church, he has been recognized nationally and internationally for his service to Greek-American causes. He is pictured above with his son, Alex, when Alex was a teenager. Color him ambassador of human relations.

The Gouletas triumvirate, Nicholas, Evangeline and Victor, set off a condominium blaze that still crackles with the flames of success. American Invsco converted posh high-rise buildings into condos giving everyone an opportunity to own prime property. Parents of the triumvirate are Steve and Maria Gouletas.

Dr. Michael C. Govostis began his medical career as a general surgeon at Wesley Memorial Hospital and later went on to become a professor of surgery at Northwestern University Medical School. Such an outstanding surgeon was he that his reputation, particularly among the Greeks, was flawless. Every family that had need of a surgeon utilized his surgical skills at one time or another. He was not only known for his surgical skills but also for his diagnostic skills. His favorite pastime was fishing. Dr. Mike's brother, James Govostis, DDS, was one of the first Greek dentists. Jim practiced for 62 years.

John P. Graven served as assistant superintendent of Chicago Public Schools following a tenure as principal of Taft High School. Anastasia P. Graven was principal of Daniel Boone School and Decatur Classical School concurrently. Together they received the Tree of Wisdom Award for outstanding service rendered to children and youth.

Successful entrepreneur, Nicholas Kafkis, is pictured above with his wife, Aggie. Nicholas is founder and CEO of Kafko, a highly recognized chemical specialty manufacturing company.

Tom Kapsalis, Chicago's Commissioner of Aviation, is shown above with Helmut Jahn, architect (arm outstretched) with aviation staff and consultants during O'Hare's $2 billion development program in 1981 (in today's dollar it would be about $20 billion.)

Shown during a reception are Commissioner Tom Kapsalis, Senator Carol Moseley Braun, Mayor Harold Washington, Attorney General Neil Hartigan and Senator Ted Kennedy.

Andrew T. Kopan, Ph.D., professor of education at DePaul University, is shown addressing a crowd at the university. A brilliant researcher, he has done a definitive history of Greeks in Chicago and has published numerous books in the field of education and ethnicity. Andrew has long been a part of the Greek legacy and throughout his lifetime he has embraced it proudly and shared it with all of us. Color him a distinguished and much published historian.

Nicholas J. Manos, one of the most outstanding bankruptcy attorneys in the country, served as reorganization counsel for the Rock Island Railroad. He is pictured above at a dinner held by the Gargalianon Society honoring Vice-President Spiro Agnew at which he served as toastmaster. Others shown above are Governor and Mrs. Edgar Whitcomb of Indiana and chairman of the event, Stacy Diacou.

Leon Marinakos, engineer par excellence, has been part and parcel of the United Hellenic American Congress since its inception. With this extraordinary talent for putting together highly original color illustrated lecture presentations, his work was so recognized by the Greek government that he was appointed honorary cultural attaché to the counsel general of Greece.

Nicholas J. Melas has had a long and distinguished career in public service. Among his most significant accomplishments being elected a commissioner of the Metropolitan Water Reclamation District for 30 years, the last 18 of which he served as president of the Board of Commissioners. Among his great accomplishments is the construction of the Tunnel and reservoir plan, a massive 3.5 million engineering project that protects the region's drinking water.

Charles C. Moskos was a sociologist of the United States military and a professor at Northwestern University. Described as the nation's "most influential military sociologist" by the *Wall Street Journal*, Charlie was often a source for reporters from the *New York Times*, *Washington Post*, *Los Angeles Times*, the *Chicago Tribune* and other periodicals. He was the author of the "don't ask, don't tell" policy which prohibited homosexual service members from acknowledging their sexual orientation. Shown above at a lecture at Northwestern University is Charlie with his son, Andrew.

Harry Mark Petrakis is the author of 24 books. He has twice been nominated for the National Book Award in Fiction. His work has been adapted for film and television and is also translated in numerous countries around the world. He has lectured extensively and holds honorary degrees from a number of universities including the American College of Greece in Athens.

Profiles in courage is the best way to describe Georgia and Bud Photopulos—she for being a 43-year cancer survivor, and he for always being there for Georgia despite a distinguished career as a correspondent and producer for ABC that kept him hopping. Promising to help others if she survived her cancer diagnosis, Georgia founded the Cancer Call-Pac (People Against Cancer); she was a consultant to the National Cancer Institute and helped establish their nationwide info line 1-800-4-cancer. Color them very courageous.

The Honorable John J. Stamos, a brilliant and distinguished barrister, has served as assistant corporation counsel, City of Chicago; he has been appointed states attorney of Cook County, elected to the Appellate Court of Illinois; appointed to the Illinois Supreme Court. The currently retired Justice Stamos is pictured above with his wife, Daisy.

John H. Secaras, the U.S. Labor Department's top attorney in the Chicago region, has received the Presidential Rank Award of Meritorious Executive in recognition of his sustained exceptional efforts and contributions to the development of all laws enforced by the Labor Department. He was twice honored with the distinguished career service award—an award rarely given twice in an individual career.

The research specialties of George Thodos, Ph.D., professor of Northwestern University, included heat and mass transfer, thermodynamic and transport properties and solar energy. Dr. Thodos conducted research for Phillips Petroleum Company and Pure Oil Company where he developed processes for the purification of petroleum. This work resulted in the awarding of seven patents. He was also awarded the prestigious Walter P. Murphy Distinguished Professorship.

Irene Tzakis, the only woman in the history of the St. Andrew's Greek Orthodox Church to be elected into the high office of president for three consecutive terms and the most successful fundraiser, is shown with Archbishop Kokkinakis and her husband, Andrew, president and founder of White Stokes Company.

Paul G. Vallas was the first CEO of the Chicago Public Schools from 1995 to 2001. He had previously directed the budget arm of the Illinois State Legislature and served as budget director for Mayor Richard M. Daley. He resigned the office of CPS CEO and unsuccessfully ran for Governor of Illinois. Following the election, Vallas was appointed CEO of the School District of Philadelphia. He became the nation's most sought after superintendent by bringing order and energy to Chicago's moribund school system.

Theodora Vasils has translated six published works on Nikos Kazantzakis. She has also recently published, "Hold Fast the Mountain Pass," an historical novel based on the life and the world of Kazantzakis. A brilliant writer, she received an Honorary Doctor of Letters degree from Dominican University in recognition of her growing international reputation, particularly for her response to the challenges posed by Kazantzakis, the most renowned writer in Greece of our time.

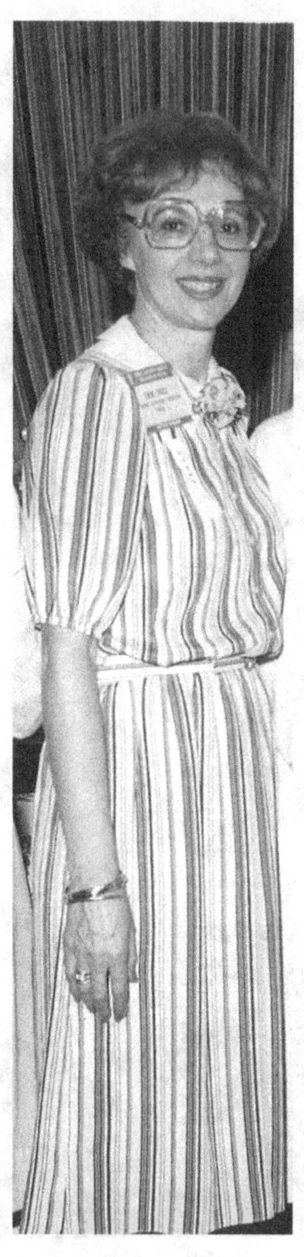

Themi Vasils was formerly managing director of the National Confectioners Association and was honored by the National Candy Wholesalers Association. Directory and volunteer worker for the National Hellenic Museum since 1991, she has served as its president. The Orthodox Clergy Association of Greater Chicago honored her "for outstanding contributions to all the Orthodox Churches in the Orthodox jurisdictions of metropolitan Chicago through the press and other media."

Harriet Geannopoulos was executive director at Star Employment Service from 1954-63. In 1968 she co-founded Thirty-Three Personnel Center dedicated to the placement of college women; in 1970, with the changing of the laws, the agency placed both men and women. Harriet received the Lincoln Award, a state wide award given by the Illinois Employment Association for integrity. She is pictured above with her husband, Nicholas, a successful business man in insurance and real estate.

"A woman would be more charming if a man could fall into her arms without falling into her hands." – Bierce

RESERVATIONS HAVE…..been closed by the Sts. Peter and Paul Women's Club to "A Night at the Plaka" scheduled to take place this Sunday, February 18th at 1401 Wagner Road, Glenview. Since space is limited, the committee has announced that tickets cannot be purchased at the door. The Glenview fire ordinance forbids the further sale of tickets because the maximum quota for the capacity of the hall has been sold.

STILL GASPING…..is pretty Debbie Gallios, daughter of Pete and Sue Gallios, over her meeting with handsome, raven-tressed Olympic champ, Mark Spitz, at the Gallios brothers really "in" Miller's Pub. Debbie was hosting at Miller's one day when in walked the fabulous Spitz – in town for the Houseware Show. Debbie, who hasn't been the same since, attends DePauw University in Greencastle, Indiana.

Another frequent nightly visitor at Miller's is long time favorite, Virginia Mayo, star of the musical, "No, No, Nanette," currently playing at the Shubert Theater, according to Jim Gallios. Jim is the Gallios who is always where the action is for he often hosts at both Miller's and the beautiful and newly renovated Vannie's, named after Van Gallios, brother number four.

WELL KNOWN……pediatrician, James Nicklas, M.D., eloquently allayed the fears of parents who often feel guilty when their child suffers a "crib death" at a recent interview on Channel 2 TV Sunday 6 o'clock news. Long-time family friend Jim did us all proud with his intelligent and easy-to-understand explanation of "crib-death."

SPECIAL RADIANCE……..exudes from Myrsini Terzis since her engagement to George Karkazis, M.D., radiologist at Chicago's Billings Memorial Hospital. A very active member of The Greek Women's

University Club, the effervescent Myrsini recently received her master's degree in guidance and counseling. Round-up time will be in May.

SPELLBINDING MUSICAL.....artist, Nana Mouskouri, the singer with a surprising lack of pretension, will appear in concert with the Athenians at Orchestra Hall on March 25th at 3 pm. Prime seats for this concert have been reserved by the 13th District Lodge of the Daughters of Penelope. A ticket purchased for the Mouskouri concert will help support the Daughters of Penelope twin projects which are the Daughters of Penelope Scholarship Fund and the Greek Welfare Foundation Fund.

GOOD TO......see both George Valos and Dino Tubekis walking around again, both hale and hearty following surgery.

QUOTE OF THE WEEK: "Like the measles, love is most dangerous when it comes late in life." - Huxley

"Love is a form of intelligence, its highest form, and the evidence is that stupid love usually crushes or deforms whatever it embraces, like an unintelligent parent who cripples a child with a burden of misdirected love."

THOSE ON.......the Greek Independence Day Parade Committee are saying such terribly nice things about Tom Costopoulos, chairman of the committee, whose intelligent appraisal of all the mini and maxi details of this peripatetic event promise to make it one of the best parades on record. This annual parade has been very ably handled by past chairmen (like my good friend, Nicholas Manos, who did such a super job last year). Just as old wine improves with age – so has the parade, lessening the growing pains it first endured.

According to Chairman Costopoulos, this year there will not be the usual competitive queen contest. Instead, each community shall select a very fresh, very with-it young pretty, between the ages of 17 and 20, who will represent her church group in the parade. In total, there should be approximately 15 young beauties, with freshly washed and ironed hair, in white or blue gowns, lighting up State Street with their brilliance. A hush-hush committee is also currently meeting to select this year's "Man of the Year" – a difficult and burdensome task for there are so many outstanding achievers in our community. Much ado about something.

ACCORDING TO……the very musical Mrs. Nicholas (Georgia) Mitchell, president of the Second Archdiocesan Choir Federation and choir director at Sts. Peter and Paul Greek Orthodox Church in Glenview, a Church Musician's Workshop will be held this weekend at St. Benedict's Center in Madison, Wisconsin. The first half of the weekend session will be dedicated to the presentation of new music; the second half to a workshop on the common problems and solutions of our choirs.

During the weekend, the executive board of the Federation will also meet. Georgia welcomes choir directors, organists, choir members, and all interested parties to attend. While it may seem too late to attend this workshop, we are certain that those who do decide to make a last minute trek to Madison will be most welcome.

WONDERFUL EASTER……weekend was spent by Chris and Elayne Pappas of Elgin, and their two offspring, Gary and Dana, for they drove to Drake University to spend Easter with son number one, John, a freshman at Drake. Handsome John will be one of the escorts at the forthcoming Debutante Cotillion to be sponsored by the Saint Helen Women's Club.

LATEST NEWS…..from The Greek Women's University Club is that these damsels sponsored a special lenten meeting at St. George Greek Orthodox Church. An informal coffee hour followed the services. Later, Ioannis Terzis, Byzantine artist and iconographer, who has done most of the church artwork, pointed out the symbolism in the Byzantine art and icons. Mr. Terzis is the father of GWUC member, Myrsini Terzis.

QUOTE OF THE WEEK: "Those obsessed with health are not healthy; the first requisite of good health is a certain calculated carelessness about oneself."

"A woman nags her husband not because she wants to dominate him, but because he has been unsuccessful in dominating her. Nagging is almost always an expression of a woman's unsatisfied need to be dependent."

TAWNY SKIN.......summer-streaked hair, and a look as earthy and delicious as a great big luscious Mediterranean peach can all be yours way before summer if you decide to get away from the Midwestern slush and visit the sun-drenched, blue-skied, clear-watered resort islands off the coast of Florida. A preview of the kind of fresh, sparkling wardrobe you will take with you will be shown by models (slim enough to go skinny-dipping off a boat in the Bahamas) at the forthcoming "Getaway" luncheon-fashion show to be sponsored by the Women's Club of Sts. Peter and Paul this weekend. The cruise fashion event has been set to take place at the spanking new North Shore Hilton in Skokie. According to Mrs. George (Eileen) Maniates, chairwoman, international fashion designer, Noriko, will be on hand, and if you're hooked on Calypso music, you'll get more than your fill at this event for a calypso band is being flown in from Trinidad for the occasion.

A WHALE.....of a time has been planned for members and friends of the stethoscope set who plan to attend the Fifth Annual Scholarship Ball sponsored by the Hellenic Medical Society. President E. Stephen Kurtides, M.D., has announced that this year's smashing wingding will take place on February 9th in the Guildhall of the Ambassador West Hotel. Chairing the event are Mr. and Mrs. Nicholas Dunkas. More on this sugar-coated pill later.

AND A….very warm and cordial welcome is extended to our newly appointed Proistamenos at Sts. Peter and Paul in Glenview, the Rev. George J. Scoulas; his wife, Mary; and their two daughters, Alexandra and Catherine. Father Scoulas officially took over as pastor of the parish on Sunday, February 10th. In his first sermon to his new flock, Father Scoulas, wearing his spiritual strength and intellectual fortitude like a second skin, focused on the times with a very fresh, very with-it attitude. Following the Divine Liturgy, 400 parishioners, with shining smiles and filled with eager anticipation, welcomed the Scoulas family at an informal family-type luncheon held in the church hall.

It was a mutual love affair, for as the luncheon progressed, you could sense that the charisma of the Scoulas family had permeated into the hearts of all those present. Chairman Bill Liaros, assistant vice-president of the parish, cohesively tied the luncheon together. Rev. Scoulas has been given the task of "carrying the torch" lit by the late and unforgettable Dennis Latto. We welcome Father Scoulas to our town and wish him many years of prolific service in his newly acquired parish.

GOOD FRIEND…..Ann Smenos has a special radiance and allure since the faculty and students at Morton Junior High School named her the "Sweetheart of Morton High" on Valentine's Day. Along with the name came the party game at which Ann was wined, dined, kissed and hugged by the entire faculty and student body.

QUOTE OF THE WEEK: "We can justify anything by turning it in a different light: after all, the sadist can point out that he is really being kind to the masochist by providing what he wants and needs." – Harris

"The best argument against promiscuity is not a moral one, but a psychological one. As Rosenstock-Huessy tersely put it 'Sexuality throws

no light upon love, but only through love can we learn to understand sexuality.'"

COLOR THEM.......super great – those kids who are members of the GOYA at Sts. Peter and Paul Greek Orthodox Church in Glenview – for working overtime to raise money to buy a "Consecration Key." (Sts. Peter and Paul will be consecrated on November 18-19 and all those contributing a minimum of $1,000 will receive this key.) The funds collected will be used exclusively for the purpose of retiring the existing mortgage of the church. This time the group will present, "A Family Glendi" on Saturday, September 23rd at 7:30 pm. The event, which will be held at the church, will feature the Aristons.

Chairing this Glendi are Peter Betzelos and Tom Kanelos. According to my young friend, Peter, GOYA is working overtime to try to raise $1,000 so that the organization can turn this sum of money over to the church and receive a symbolic key that will open the door to the baptized church. Tickets to this event can be purchased by calling the church. So do what you can to help these marvelous kids. Their motives are pure and beautiful.

TWO WEEKS......ago our town suffered a devastating blow with the passing of a most beloved and respected citizen, Sam N. Tzakis of Lake Forest, who fought the good fight with all of his might. The candle of Sam's life was snuffed out on Friday, October 21st, at the Wesley Pavillion of Northwestern Memorial Hospital, leaving his family and friends a lot sadder, a lot lonelier, but a lot prouder for having known this very valiant human being. A man with beautiful enduring qualities, Sam was a very devoted Christian who served his church in many capacities in his lifetime – particularly as a long-time active member of the parish council of Sts. Peter and Paul.

Personally, I will always cherish the memories of our Scorpio parties, the lovely holiday concerts at Barat College, the trips to Whitewater, Wisconsin, to visit Peter and Mary Koconis, and, oh, so many other precious times remembered by all of us who knew and loved Sammy. We extend our sympathy to his wife, Dee; his three children, Nick,

Marcia and Cynthia; his brother, Andrew Tzakis; his sister, Tessie Andreakis; his brother-in-law, George Michaels; and his sister-in-law, Alexis Lelon.

THE TENDER.......trap has caught pretty Eugenia Rexinis, daughter of Rev. and Theano Rexinis who has pledged her troth to Nicholas George, son of Harry and Mary George of Seattle, Washington. Wedding bells will ring in the spring of 1979.

PARTY GIVERS.......all over the nation could take lessons from Persey Betzelos who invited over 100 people to a birthday bash for hubby, Jim. Gourmet cook that she is – Persey cooked and baked everything herself – but everything – for this delightful party. All those present went home a lot fatter – but a lot happier for generous Persey had really indulged her guests. It was a real blast!

QUOTE OF THEWEEK: “The most constant and prevalent of all human traits is that of overestimating something we want and do not have, and then underestimating it after we have obtained possession; the laws of emotional perspective are the opposite of physical perspective – things distant seem large, and things near by seem small.”

“We think that our opinion of someone depends on what we see in him; it does not. In most cases, it depends on what he makes us see in ourselves.”

THE PARISHIONERS.....of Holy Apostles Greek Orthodox Church in Westchester are excited and elated with the progress being made by the committee in charge of the Consecration of Holy Apostles Greek Orthodox Church scheduled to take place on the weekend of May 31-June 1. Consecration of this prize-winning edifice will begin at 7 pm on Saturday, May 31st at vesper services and will culminate on Sunday evening with the Consecration Banquet and Ball which will be held at the beautiful Sheraton-Oakbrook Hotel. Sincere and tireless efforts are being expended by General Co-chairmen Arthur J. Andrews of Elmhurst and Sam G .Gordon of LaGrange, together with the spiritual leader of the parish, the Reverend William S. Chiganos, who is serving as honorary chairman, to make this the most outstanding event in the history of the parish, and from the energy being expended, it most certainly will be.

His Eminence Archbishop Iakovos and honored clergy will lead the vesper procession the evening before the day fixed for the Consecration – in this case, May 31st. Immediately following vespers, a reception will be hosted by the youth of the parish in the Fellowship Hall.

On Sunday, June 1st at 8:30 am, the clergy will again assemble in the new church and the service of Orthros (Matins and Lauds) will begin. Following the Divine Liturgy a reception will take place in the Fellowship Hall that will be hosted by the Philoptochos Society.

Social festivities will be in full swing that evening at the Consecration Banquet and Ball. Honored guest will be His Eminence Archbishop Iakovos. Starting at 6 pm, a 45-minute reception will be held. Dinner will begin at 7 pm. Following a brief program, there will be dancing to the music of Perry Fotos and his orchestra.

I would certainly be remiss in the writing of this column if I did not name the distinguished committee members who have worked and are continuing to work day and night to make this weekend a succss: Dr. John Gallios, James Youlios, Phyllis Gordon, Ann Smenos, Ulysses Backas, Dr. and Mrs. Andrew Tomaras, Steven Pappas, John Gramas, Elias Kusulas, George Mannos, Nathan Principato, James Psyhogios, Michael Cotsilis, Demetra Chiganos, and Steve Vanides.

To commemorate this event, the parish of Holy Apostles is publishing a Consecration Album. Designed by Steve Vanides, the album will be devoted to the activities of the parish – past, present and future; another section will be commemorative in nature – honoring departed loved ones; biblical passages and symbols of our faith; and still another section will include messages and greetings from contributors.

QUOTE OF THE WEEK: "The things we say bear little resemblance to what is on our minds; for instance, the important questions we ask usually conceal some other question we are too ashamed (or too unaware) to formulate in words; and this is why the answers we get rarely satisfy us – because they do not answer the hidden question, only the verbal one."

"People should hang out their minds for an airing every so often, if they want their opinions to smell as fresh and sweet as their linen; the sour odor of stale convictions clings to most of us like a mist."

THIS WEEK……..I point with considerable pride to the Gouletas triumvirate – Nick, Engie and Vic – the real estate giants of the Midwest, the land barons who buy and sell, the high-rise face lifters who have transformed Plain Jane buildings into buildings of statuesque beauty and who now reign majestically over Condominium Land. These three wizards of buying and selling have mixed massive doses of know-how, enthusiasm, and self-confidence and injected them into the veins of their sales staff – all of whom have become prolific as hares in the selling of condominiums all over the country – making the Gouletas story the success story of the year.

At a recent Amer-Invsco Awards Banquet, held in the Grand Ballroom of the Palmer House, guests numbering 1,200 were in attendance. The majority were employees and their spouses from Chicago and its suburbs; Houston, Texas; Milwaukee, Wisconsin; and Atlanta, Georgia, and many other cities throughout the United States, employees who had taken the big bird in to share in the excitement of annual awards given to those who had climbed the mountain of successful selling and were now perched precariously on its tip. Some fell – not quite ready to attain the heights; others touched the sky; by next year – many will zoom like spacecrafts into the magic land of success. However, one thing appeared certain that evening, the Gouletas triumvirate was a threesome honored, respected and loved by their employees.

So – as a friend, as an admirer, as a columnist – I point to them with a great deal of ethnic pride: First – as individuals – each with a particular brand of knowledge to impart to the team; second, as compassionate employers – creating opportunities for their people; third, as dreamers – with enough reality to look into the big picture – the long haul; fourth, as generous contributors to charities – especially to their church; and most of all – as a family – whose love and respect for each other has been the cohesive force in helping them to reap their harvest of plenty.

NOTE FROM.......Louis G. Malevitis, general chairman of the 25th anniversary celebration of the Plato Elementry School, announces that the Parochial School of the Assumption Greek Orthodox Church needs donors to financially assist and help reduce the yearly school deficit of the Plato Elementary School. (Last year's deficit was $79,815.) Whatever gift you care to give will be included in the "Friends of Plato School Donor Book."

CONGRATULATIONS TO......one of our town's greatest guys, Andrew A. Athens, national chairman of the United Hellenic American Congress, who was chosen to serve on the Advisory Board of Senator Charles Percy of Illinois, in creation of the private non-profit, "Alliance To Save Energy" which was announced recently by the White House.

AND SOME ....of our nice Greek boys have done it again – made the Social Register of Washington, D.C. – that is. The names of the gentlemen who bear the distinction of being in the Green Book include: Senator Paul Sarbanes, Congressmen John Brademas, Gus Yatron, Paul Bafalis, Paul Tsongas, John Nassikas, Dr. Achilles Sakellarides, John Constandy, Mike Manatos and John Naktos.

QUOTE OF THE WEEK: "One of the chief ingredients of maturity is the calm recognition that the best one can get out of life is a draw." -Harris

"No woman is responsible for her face, but every woman is for her expression; and, especially after thirty, a woman's attractiveness is only one-fourth face, one-fourth artifice, but fully one-half expression; if the latter is greedy, or mean, or sullen, or discontented, the other half goes for nothing."

ST. ANDREW'S.......Greek Orthodox Church has been making history for years– and last Saturday night, December 11th was no exception. The event was the 50th anniversary dinner- dance of the parish, held in the elegant ballroom of the Ritz-Carlton Hotel. Here, under dazzling crystal-clear chandeliers, 550 guests sipped cocktails and exchanged some meaningful and some not so meaningful dialogue. Gentlemen, resplendent in black tie, were in abundance, escorting beautiful women in gowns of quiet richness, dazzling colors, floaty fabrics, ravishingly romantic, and seductively alluring creations. It was a resplendent evening that memories are made of, and the priceless ingredient of class was in the air. It was an evening of nostalgia – and of recollections – and one guest – a very special cousin – Eugenia Stassinopoulos, sister of the chairman, Dina Bacaintan, had flown in from Athens for the occasion.

Twenty-two men served as parish council presidents in the 50-year history of the church. They were: Paul Demos, E.M. Chirigos, John Papas, James Nichols, William Cotseones, C.G. Kakarakis, George Arvites, Andrew Margarites, George Phillips, George Nikopoulos, Thomas K. Valos, C.N. Johnson, Constantine J. Papas, Nicholas Prassas, Peter Gianukos, George J. Marks, Alec K. Gianaras, S.J. Gregory, Michael Cantonis, George J. Annes, Christ N. Karafotias, Theodore J. Theodore. Of these, only eight are living.

All past presidents were honored that evening – for it was a special evening dedicated to them. Each was presented with a beautifully inscribed gold medallion. The living, of course, accepted their own plaques; the remainder were presented posthumously to the widows of the past presidents or to close members of their families. A special gold medallion was presented to Mrs. Basil Stevens, widow of the single greatest benefactor in the 50-year history of St. Andrew's Greek

Orthodox Church, Dr. Basil Stevens. Gus Assimos and Nicholas Kanellos were the recipients of silver medallions for their dedicated service to the parish.

Your columnist, who wrote and edited St. Andrew's 50th Anniversary Album, was presented with a lovely plaque with a silver medallion on it. Nick Andoniades, art director of the album, was presented with a similar plaque. Third recipient was George Maniates who did special layouts and designs on this album.

Speaker of the evening was His Eminence Archbishop Kokkinakis of Great Britain, who had flown in from London, to participate in the evening's festivities. His Eminence had served as parish priest back in 1940 prior to his elevation to bishop and then, subsequently, to archbishop. Another honored guest was the Rev. John Hondras who had served as parish priest for 20 years. He and his, Lou, had taken the big bird in from Jacksonville, Florida, for the occasion.

Accolades to Dina Bacaintan, chairman, and her daughter, Maria Papas, co-chairman of the dinner-dance; Irene Tzakis and Christ Karafotias, co-chairmen of the entire 50th Anniversary year; and to Ted Theodore, president of the parish, who worked tirelessly to make this event the smashing success that it was. An orchid to my sister, Irene, reservations chairman, who worked arduously to process the hundreds of reservations that poured in for this auspicious occasion.

THE STORK......dropped a bundle of male joy at the home of Peter and Terry Mikuzis whose second little tax exemption will be named Constantine Peter. Born on January 15th, he weighed in at 7 lbs. 6 ozs.

QUOTE OF THE WEEK: "It is always well to remember that success is a ladder not an escalator." – Warren Hull

"The basic contradiction in the human animal was summed up long ago by Seneca, when he observed: 'We are always complaining that

our days are few, and then acting as though there would be no end to them.'" - Harris

THIS WEEK…..we point with pride to one of our town's most gracious and most involved citizens, beloved Andrew A. Athens, president, Metron Steel Corporation. Andy, always a spokesman on national and international situations, has not only been asked to serve on the Advisory Board of the private non-profit, Alliance to Save Energy but he recently became the recipient of an award by the Resource Ellis Island Committee. Sensitive to the problems facing all of us today, Andy was asked to serve on the Advisory Board of the Alliance by its chairman, Senator Charles Percy, bringing to the organization the perspective of industry. In addition to Andy, the board is comprised of 53 distinguished individuals from such areas as commerce, industry, government, labor and the academic world.

Andy received the coveted Ellis Island Award at the first Ellis Island Award ceremony held on Ellis Island on April 30th. The ceremony was simple, but symbolic, and focused on the ethnic strengths of our country.

"LULLABY AND…..Goodnight" could have been the song sung at the recent christening of Peter Rummel Trilikis, son of Mr. and Mrs. George P. Trilikis, so quickly and quietly did this little cherub fall asleep following his recent christening by godparents, Mr. and Mrs. Nicholas Chaimes of Peoria at Sts. Constantine and Helen Greek Orthodox Church. The reception was held at Niko's Restaurant. This little latest addition to the pablum set, who is the grandson of Bill and Zoe Rummel, was named after his paternal and maternal grandfathers, Peter Trilikis and William Rummel.

MEANINGFUL GESTURE…….of love was recently made by Michael Hatsos well-known and beloved Chicago personality who gave a donation of $1,000 to The Greek Womens University Club in memory of his wife. The donation was presented as the "Anna M. Hatsos Scholarship."

WE WISH.....long-time family friend, Gus Pappas of Lincolnwood a quick and complete recovery. Gus recently underwent surgery at the Northwestern Pavillion under the magic hand of Dr. Mike Govostis. He has recently received a phenomenal amount of cards from his legion of friends.

TANTALIZING GOODIES.....certainly were in abundance at the recent cocktail reception sponsored by the Greek National Tourist Organization to celebrate the official opening of its new Chicago office located on the sixth floor, 158 North Michigan Avenue. The invitation was extended by the very gracious Dimitri N. Vlachos, midwest director.

QUOTE OF THE WEEK: "No man knows himself until he has come face-to-face with calamity. It is only in crisis that we learn our true identity. Many a man has gone through life thinking he was strong when he was only safe."

"Those who make a habit of flattery lack the capacity to love; flattery is always a sign of emotional impotence, seeking to achieve the effect in words it cannot attain in deed."

THE BRIDAL.....spotlight has been shining brightly for the past couple of months on one of our town's prettiest, Pamela Koconis of Lake Forest, who recently wed Dean Boosalis of Denver, Colorado. Following the ceremony at Sts. Peter and Paul, 200 beautifully dressed people, with turned on smiles shining brightly like crystal chandeliers, waited patiently in line at the Michigan Shores Country Club on Saturday, May 31st, to wish beautiful and radiant Pam, and her attractive dark-eyed bridegroom a lifetime of happiness together. Clustered around them were handsome ushers and fresh wide-eyed, shiny tressed young bridesmaids adorned in skinny-strapped, off-white sheer gowns splashed with pastel colored flowers. Waist-length capes and wide-brimmed picture hats – petal smooth in femininity – completed their outfits. Dinner followed the long champagne reception.

Host and hostess for the evening were the bride's parents – Peter and Mary Koconis. Pike was resplendent in his rich brown dinner jacket, and Mary looked like a long breezy summer evening in her flowing blue, pink and white chiffon print. Equally handsome in their finery were the groom's parents, John and Kay Boosalis of Lincoln, Nebraska. The handsome couple honeymooned in San Francisco.

"WHAT WILL....you do with your tax rebate?" asked pretty Elaine Markoutsas, one of the *Chicago Tribune's* most prolific writers, when she called me one sunny afternoon. "What will I do with it?" I retorted, tongue-in-cheek. "Well, if the rebate is a dollar, I'll buy some bubble gum, and if it's $100, I'll convert it into 100 one dollar bills, wallpaper my closet, and maybe save for a rainy day." Well, foxy Elaine typed out my thoughts, as well as the thoughts of such biggies as Floyd Kalber, news anchorman, Channel 5; Irving Seaman, Jr., president of the National Boulevard Bank of Chicago; insurance mogul W. Clement Stone; Bonnie Swearingen, wife of Standard Oil tycoon and many others. We were all quoted in her article, "The Taxing Problem of Spending That Extra Rebate Money" which appeared in the May 22nd issue of the *Trib*. It's really super having a celebrity friend!

A REAL......tragedy was the death of handsome and delightful, Alex Tubekis, a 30- year-old family friend who died on July 30th. The victim of a hit-and-run accident, he was killed exactly one block away from his home in Medina. Alex is survived by his wife, Phyllis; two children; his mother, Rita; and a sister and brother-in-law, Candy and George Lelos.

THAT TENDER.....trap has caught Cari Tsaoussis, daughter of Themis and Frances Tsaoussis, and Peter Pappas, son of Gus and Joan Pappas, who recently announced their engagement. Both good-looking, educated and really with it people, they plan to wed sometime next year.

RECENT PARTY......hosted by Nick and Aggie Kafkis gave everyone an opportunity to meet their cousins and houseguests, Bobby and Mary Vovos of Athens, Greece. It was indeed a fun evening which brought together good friends and relatives of the Kafkis family. Bobby and Mary and their two children, Anda and Aris, have been staying with Nick and Aggie for the past month.

QUOTE OF THE WEEK: "With some exceptions, it is generally true that beautiful women have no sense of humor – possibly because they fear that laugh lines will mar their pulchritude." -Harris.

MERRY CHRISTMAS AND A HAPPY NEW YEAR TO ALL

For this year's Christmas column, I thought it might be fun to ask some of the outstanding personalities in our community plus some friends to send their answers to the question: "If you could be granted one Christmas wish, what would it be?"

Samuel C. Maragos (D) state representative, 30th district: "To be able to legislate health, happiness and no taxes for the people of the state of Illinois."

Georgia (Mrs. Bud) Photopulos: "When faced with a life-threatening illness – living becomes your first priority, and you become aware of how precious life really is. I am especially blessed with a dedicated, compassionate husband – wonderful children – close family and dear friends. My Christmas wish??? With the grace of God – to live a full, productive life."

Dana Pappas of Elgin (my pretty 10-year old goddaughter): "If I was given one Christmas wish, I would want a puppy. A puppy that is soft, cuddly, cute and playful – a playmate of my very own."

Mayor Nicholas Blasé of Niles: "Peace for everyone – more love between people. Daughters that will listen and obey. Two good boys for husbands on my daughters' 18th birthdays."

Leon Marinakos: "Christmas is Christ or should be. And Christ as the revealed affirmation of expectations. My wish then would be that each of us comes to know this truth and make it our own experience."

Brian Smenos of Berwyn: "I'd like a date with the beautiful chick who writes this column."

S.D.Apostol: "To be able to walk the streets of our city of Chicago at two o'clock in the morning, as I did in the streets of Athens in the summer of 1967, without the fear of being mugged, robbed or killed."

Joy Childs of Northbrook: "I wish that for a moment, on this special day called Christmas, the world would stop and all the happiness, peace and joy of this day be spread around the world thoroughly like the crème filling in an Oreo cookie."

Peter Brown of Skokie: "My one Christmas wish would be good health and happiness for my family and all my friends. Without these two – you have nothing in life."

James Chrones: "My fondest wish for Christmas would be that every human being looked at every other human being as a living, breathing fellow human – to be judged alone on his own merit and not as a Greek Orthodox, as a black, as a Jew, as a millionaire, and so forth."

Nick Kafkis, the bard of Rogers Park: "Diamonds and pearls and kegs of gold; travels, adventure and deeds so bold. Then the fantasy ends and fades away, and my wish for all is good health and joy on this Christmas day."

"The only way to attain one's ideals is to abandon one's illusions; but this is impossible unless we learn to separate the two."

TOTALLY AFFECTIONATE.....group of people, still filled with pazzaz and that fiery O.Y. spirit, gathered together at the recent Orthodox Youth Reunion (St. George Church Hall) to throw some more coal in the furnace to keep their enthusiasm, love of life, and love of the organization that brought them together some 20 to 25 years ago, warm and intact. After much back-slapping, hugging and kissing, the 300 former stalwart members sat down to a delicious beef dinner which was served by volunteers from the St. George GOYA. On hand to demonstrate the talent that rocked former O.Y. shows were Danny Poulos and Jimmy Pappas who put on an impromptu comedy act polishing their show biz image which, in my opinion, has kept its luster throughout the years. Helen Maharis followed the comedy act with a vocal solo.

Seated at one of the front tables were four of the following founding daddys of the O.Y. who addressed the group humorously and nostalgically: Peter J. Adinamis, Chris G. Kalogeras, John Graven (who gave credit to the women who have served the O.Y. – God love him) and Andrew Kopan. Their puns and acknowledgments were caviar to all those present.

Orchids to the committee which did a magnificent job of putting this wing-ding together: Nick Lianos, chairman of the reunion and president of St. George, and his Peggy; Sophie Kopan, Christ and Athy Lamnatos, Steve and Mary Sfondilias and Helen Troy.

AND WE'RE......certainly very proud of Gus Assimos who recently received a medal from St. Andrew's Greek Orthodox Church commemorating 35 years of faithful service at that church, most of which were spent as a member of the parish council. The Assimos clan, one of the nicest families in our town, is comprised of Gus' charming wife, Angeline, and his three children: Mary (Peter) Koconis of Lake Forest, Mattina Malas of Chicago, and George (Helen) of Wilmette.

HIGH TARGET…..has been hit by Anthony Michalaros, son of Mrs. Ellie Michalaros of Greek radio fame. An interior designer, Anthony has been commissioned to design a one million dollar villa in Palm Beach, Florida. He recently returned from Europe where he searched throughout Venice, Florence and Milan to find the necessary equipment for his project. Anthony, whose office, Interior Graphics, is located at 313 West Hubbard in Chicago, just finished a job in Sun Valley, Idaho.

AND WE….all owe a great big "thanks" to many of the prominent business executives in our community who so generously treated the 26 handsome and virile-looking evzones and the Greek Independence Day Committee to delicious dinners during the five day stay of the evzones. Unfortunately, I was only able to attend one of these dinners (the magnificent one hosted by Toni Antoniou at his Holiday Inn in Hillside). A salute to Toni, the hosts of the Diplomat Restaurant, the Ambrosia, and to Diana's Opa for their generosity. Another salute to Jim Maros of McDonald fame, who offered to charter a bus which would take the evzones on an extended tour throughout our city and then wind the whole bit up by treating them to McDonald's famous burgers.

QUOTE OF THE WEEK: "If children grew up according to early indications, we should have nothing but geniuses." – Von Goethe

"Women make better mothers than wives – which is a fortunate thing, because for every one man who is looking for a wife, ten are looking for a mother."

WELL THE…..Koconis family is back in the news again. On Saturday, August 16th, we attended the grand opening of a dazzling new McDonald's in Whitewater, Wisconsin. Newly acquired toy of Peter and Mary Koconis of Lake Forest, this McDonald's is vibrant with color

– both inside and out, large in size and booming with activity. There, to the beat of marching bands, sunny skies and the love and good wishes of hundreds of good friends – the official red ribbon of this latest in the link of McDonald chains was cut and the official ceremonies begun. At noon all the well-wishers who had driven to Whitewater for the occasion were wined and dined at the Duck Inn – owned and operated by Tony and George Gargalis.

Following lunch, a caravan of cars swung over to Richland Center, to spend the weekend at George Collias' farm – nestled in the rambling and picturesque green hills of Wisconsin. Pretty Gene Collias had extended a weekend invitation to Richland Center to attend a birthday celebration for her brother, George, who, incidentally, was a super special host. The fun began when the great guru of farmland tucked us all into a large open wagon, attached to a tractor, furnished us with bales of hay to sit on, and gave us a guided tour through acres and acres of beautiful countryside. But the hostest with the mostest, Gene Collias, together with her sister, Danae Collias Kornaros, worked their buns off cooking and preparing a buffet dinner for about 60 people. Later, with delicious abandonment, we polished off four home-made birthday cakes topped off with fresh, creamy gobs of ice cream.

A BEAUTIFUL……collection of over 200 people, all bedecked and bejeweled in their finery, attended the recent regal dinner party hosted by Andrew and Irene Tzakis of Lincolnwood. Held at the Ambassador West on September 7th, it opened the fall social season with a bang. The dinner party marked the occasion of the Tzakis' 25th wedding anniversary. But this was a well-guarded secret until the dinner hour when Nicholas Tzakis, oldest of the three Tzakis offspring, proposed a toast to his parents.

During a most delightfully long cocktail reception – guests mingled together as they drank and munched on delicious hors d'oeuvres. Dinner was served in the Guildhall and from the deep red tablecloths to the burgundy floral bouquets adorning each table, it was obvious that guests were being indulged in beauty, good taste, and luxury. Hostess Irene was resplendent as ever in an exquisite white Norman Norell gown, while Andrew looked super elegant in his quietly rich, chocolate brown dinner jacket.

Following a delicious dinner, guests danced to the music of Perry Fotos and his orchestra.

QUOTE OF THE WEEK: "The fundamental and unresolvable contradiction in the male nature is that no father of forty wants his daughter to do what he wanted other men's daughters to do when he was twenty."

This week I dedicate this column to a first in the annals of the Greek Orthodox Churches in Chicago and outlying suburbs – a parish library – the brain child of the Reverend William Chiganos, parish priest, Holy Apostles Greek Orthodox Church, Westchester, Illinois.

ONCE UPON A TIME…..the seed of an idea flickered across the mind of a young, idealistic, and dedicated young priest. The seed was nourished until it ripened: it will bear fruit on Sunday, November 16th, when the parish library of the Holy Apostles Church will open its doors at official dedication services.

This new learning resource center, the first of its kind in a Greek Orthodox Church community, will provide its parishioners with materials for spiritual and emotional growth, leadership, adult religious education programs, pupil exploration, and family-church-interrelationships.

Functioning as an integral part of the program of the church, the library will provide a healthy menu of good books, pamphlets, and non-book materials selected to whet the spiritual appetite of Sunday school teachers, pupils and members of the church.

For children – toddlers to teenagers – there will be Bible stories appropriate to their particular age level, stories of the life of Jesus, prayers and graces, stories to enrich day-to-day Christian living, fiction stories of Biblical times, and books about children both here and abroad.

For teenagers, the library will supply books which will further the concept of God and Christ, stories on the Bible, books inquiring into the Christian faith and other religious, devotional books, materials on dating, marriage, school life, inspiring biographies, books about the church and religious heritage and books on ancient and modern Greek history. For adults, the parish library will house books on the relationship of God to man, biblical translations, the life and teachings of Jesus, enrichment of prayer life, family living and other religious topics.

Members of Holy Apostles Greek Orthodox Church are especially proud of one of its flock, Mrs. Robert Smenos of Berwyn, IIllinois, whose dedication to this parish library has been phenomenal. Mrs. Smenos has been a single, driving force behind the actual working formation of the parish library. Without her knowledge, drive, dedication and organizational acumen, the library would not be in existence today. Holding a degree in library science from Rosary College, Mrs. Smenos has many years of library experience behind her, and it is this knowledge that has made her a positive and active force in the actual setting up of the parish library which now houses 600 books.

Other highly instrumental parishioners who participated in the formation of this project are the members of the parish guild, affectionately known as the parish "angels," a group that generously donated both time and dollars to this worthy project. Headed by Mrs. Chris Kirkeles, president, they have made this resource center a project to be proud of. Others who have given generously of themselves to help organize this "first" parish library include: Mrs. Peter Goetz, Mrs. Paul Lolakes, Mrs. George Chipain, Mrs. Steven Pappas and Miss Becky Chiganos.

"How many travelers would bother to take trips if they were bound to a vow of silence about the venture upon their return." – Harris

THE PARISHIONERS……of Sts. Peter and Paul Greek Orthodox Church in Glenview are excited and elated with the progress being made by the committee in charge of the Consecration of their parish which is scheduled to take place on the weekend of November 18-19.Consecration ceremonies will begin at approximately 7:30 pm on Saturday, November 18th at vesper services and will culminate on Sunday evening November 19th with the consecration banquet and ball which will be held at Marriott's Lincolnshire Resort.

Tireless efforts are being expended by all members of the parish, led by Nick Dennis, president of the parish council and general chairman of the consecration, and the Reverend George J. Scoulas, spiritual leader of the parish, to make this a most outstanding event. Reservations chairmen are George and Maita Houpis.

I would certainly be remiss in the writing of this column if I did not name the distinguished committee members who continue to work day and night to make this two-day event a big success. They include: the Rev.George and Mary Scoulas, Nick and Mary Dennis, James and Lee Corolis, George and Maita Houpis, Constance Dumas, Dee Tzakis, Jim Betzelos, Constantine Kangles, Lou Sigalos, Mary Anton, Euthemia Karkazis. All in all, the weekend of November 18th promises to fulfill the expectations of all of us.

AND IT…..was a beautiful Sunday at the parish of Sts. Peter and Paul on October 15th for it brought back memories of a beautiful human being, Sam N.Tzakis. On this Sunday the Sam Tzakis family held a one year memorial service for their husband and father, respectively, at which the Sam N. Tzakis path was unveiled. Built to facilitate people in wheelchairs or others unable to climb stairs, it was constructed to assist those who had difficulty in going up stairs thus depriving themelves of attending church services. This is what happened to Sam in the last few months of his life. And so – his dream of having such a path constructed was fulfilled by his widow, Dee, and their three children - Nick, Marcia and Cynthia.

WEARING THEIR…..hearts at half-mast are members of the George J. Annes family of Wilmette. The 75-year old Mr. Annes succumbed on

June 9th leaving vast voids in the hearts of those who knew and loved this beneficent gentleman. Famed for his Johnny's Steak House and Broker's Inn, Mr. Annes was the owner of a chain of seven restaurants, the first of which was founded 55 years ago. At the time of his death, Mr. Annes was board president of St. Andrew's Greek Orthodox Church. He is survived by his wife, Christine; a son and daughter-in-law, John and Virginia; a daughter and son-in-law, Rhea and Louis Bournakis; and five grandchildren.

CONGRATULATIONS TO.........Maria Kotsinis and Sophia Giannakopoulos, who chaired the fundraiser on behalf of Kosta Zografopoulos. Held in the S.J. Gregory Auditorium of St. Andrew's Greek Orthodox Church, it was a real winner. As we all know the handsome 33-year-old Kosta met with a tragic accident a few months ago. This remarkable young man has fought the good fight with all of his might. But while his darkest hours are slowly fading from the horizon and he can see a light at the end of the tunnel – Kosta still must face the gremlins of pain, readjustment and horrendous hospital costs that show no mercy. The benefit served as the major contributor to the fund that will benefit Kosta's medical needs.

QUOTE OF THE WEEK: "An old man complaining that 'things aren't the way they used to be' rarely includes himself in that appraisal."

"The paradox of age is that it brings wisdom only to those who have retained the capacity to see as a child sees; when the mind's eye hardens along with the arteries, age brings only petulance and prejudice."

OFFICIAL DEDICATION......of The Reverend Dennis G. Latto Memorial Center took place on October 6th, at elaborate ceremonies conducted in the newly constructed center, located on the grounds of Sts. Peter and Paul Greek Orthodox Church in Glenview.

From the opening ceremonies to the last opa dance in the courtyard of the magnificent new structure, the event was a smash for a cloak of love encompassed the entire crowd. And though the weather was bleak and cloudy, the sun shone brightly in the happy faces of all the parishioners for a solid foundation of love, faith, and sacrifice, once a gleam in the eyes of the Reverend Dennis G. Latto, had at last become a reality.

Ribbon cutting ceremonies began at 4:30 pm when Mrs. Dennis (Lula) Latto, widow of the late Reverend Latto, former pastor of the church for whom the center was named, snipped the yellow ribbon adorning the door of the new edifice. She was followed into the building by immediate members of the Latto family, some of whom had flown in from the south to pay tribute to their late and beloved, Danny; His Grace Bishop Timotheos, who was followed by members of the clergy and guests.

Bishop Timotheos officiated at the agiasmo and the melodious choir, conducted by Mrs. Nicholas (Georgia) Mitchell, participated in the service. Visibly moved by the occasion, Lula Latto then stepped forward and graciously presented the parish with a magnificent painting of her beloved late husband. Then the Reverend Peter Georgakakis of Hammond, former schoolmate and dedicated friend, spoke briefly about Father Latto and the singular honor which had been bestowed upon him by the parish of Sts. Peter and Paul.

Bill P. Liaros, chairman of the entire event and assistant vice-president of the parish council, was indeed a most charming master of ceremonies handling the entire program with ease and aplomb. After acknowledging past presidents of both the parish council and the woman's club, he thanked some of the "unsung heroes" of the parish who had assisted him in his capacity as chairman. He then introduced the speakers of the evening.

George Cotsirilos, made an acknowledgement on behalf of the Latto family.

Congratulations are extended to Chairman Bill Liaros for a job well done, and to his Dolores, who handled reservations for this very memorable occasion. May the Reverend George Scoulas continue to carry the torch put down by Father Latto so that its flame shines brightly throughout the hallowed halls of The Rev. Dennis G. Latto Memorial Center.

ONE OF.....our town's prettiest teenagers, Tina Mantice, daughter of Tom and Helen Mantice of Glenview, was picked among a bevy of beautiful high school juniors to reign as one of the attendants in the queen's court at Glenbrook North High School.

QUOTE OF THE WEEK: "Ask yourself whether you are happy, and you cease to be." – John Stuart Mill

"Most criticism is a form of egotism. The more different kinds of people a man does not like, the more right we have to suspect that he wholly approves only of those who are precisely like him. But the neurotic inconsistency in such a critical person is that, if we probe deeply enough, it will be found that he doesn't like himself very much at bottom." – Harris

TWO LUMINARIES.......in the field of education, Dr. John Graven, and his beloved wife, Ann, celebrated 25 years of togetherness, at a beautiful bash thrown by George and Marina Alexander of Winnetka, friends of long standing. The event, attended by approximately 125 people, was held at the 95th in the John Hancock Building. A couple irresistibly hooked on education, John is principal of Taft High School, and Ann is principal of Daniel Boone Elementary School.

On hand to share in the evening's merriment were relatives, friends, and star-studded educators like handsome and personable, Dr. Joseph P. Hannon, Superintendent of Schools in Chicago; Dr. Angeline Caruso of the Chicago Board of Education; Dr. Nicholas Mannos, principal of Niles West High School – to name a few. Speaking rare and nostalgic stuff was another long-time friend of the Gravens – Harry Mark Petrakis – who has remained miraculously unscarred despite his literary fame.

Tom Manos, godson of John and Ann, was spokesman for all of their godchildren in attendance (too numerous to mention) and bouquets were thrown at Ann's mother, Mrs. Peters, who beamed with pride at both of her children. The Gravens: A shining light in today's darkened caverns of marriage.

GREECE WILL......never be the same since two devil-may-care teenagers, George Kafkis of Skokie and Nicholas Brown of Northbrook, paid a visit to that country for three weeks. The handsome teenagers have a lot of interesting stories to pass along to their friends. George and Nicky traveled with the Ahepa group and had man-about-town, Nick Anastos, also of Skokie, as head honcho of their group.

NOTE FROM......Presbytera Rexinis announces the availability of three $1,000 scholarships, via The Greek Women's University Club route. In order to be eligible for one of these educational gravy trains you must have a grade point average of 3.5, based on a 5 point scale; must be either a sophomore, junior or senior, as of September 1977; must be attending a metropolitan Chicago area college or university; and must be a U.S. citizen of Greek descent.

In the past three years, The Greek Women's University Club has presented scholarships to five young ladies. This year the club has received a donation of $1,000 from Michael N. Hatsos to be presented as the "Anna M. Hatsos Scholarship," in memory of his beloved wife. For an application, or for further information, write or call Eugenia G. Pilafas, 4733 N. Rockwell Street, Chicago 60625 or call 334-6199.

THE RICHES....that accompany a good traditional marriage, blessed with the priceless ingredient of love, are riches that can never be surpassed – as evidenced by the long-standing marriage of two of our town's most respected citizens – Spiro and Mary Apostol – who celebrated their 50th wedding anniversary on September 18th at the elite Saddle and Cycle Club. The dinner party honoring the Apostols were given by their two children – Dr. James Apostol of Chicago and Mrs. George (Cleo) Andrews of Los Angeles and their respective spouses.

QUOTE OF THE WEEK: "Women seem to talk more than men, not so much because their total verbiage is greater, but because psychologically most women cannot tolerate a lull in the conversation, and will rush in to fill the void, no matter how irrelevant or needless their comment."

"There's something topsy-turvy in a society like ours, where people introduce us to others by our first names – because they haven't known us long enough to recall our last names."

SNOBS, BLUENOSES......chauvinists, liberationists, glamorous ladies, mustached gentlemen, conformists of various hues, old people, young kids, and just plain ordinary folks, all colorfully and elegantly dressed, attended the recent and unforgettable Annual Celestial Soiree and Debutante Cotillion sponsored by The Saint Helen's Women's Club, auxiliary of the Sts. Constantine and Helen Church, which took place serenely amid outdoor torrential storms on June 16th in the Grand Ballroom of the Conrad Hilton Hotel.

Here, twelve well-bred radiant beauties, with long shiny locks tenderly caressing their shoulders, dressed in neo-classic white gowns which fell gracefully from the waist and gently skimmed the floor, were escorted by their bursting-with-pride fathers, donned in white tie and tails. The setting was movie-like romantic extravaganza, and the evening a super splashdown directed by one very pretty lady, Mrs. George (Kathy) Skontos and her two co-chairwomen, Mrs. Gus L. Malleris and Mrs. Stephen Manta.

The escorts of this year's deb crop numbered 24 – each one more interesting than the other – and a joy to see – for they looked super clean, super intelligent, super fun to be with, and super handsome. Actually, they reflected the really new today trend that bright and knowledgeable kids are following - their very own individualized life style – thereby coming up on top of the heap.

Guests of Nick and Kay Manos of Riverside, who had their own lovely,

Stathia, bowing in this year's group, we enjoyed the intermingling with friends, the winning of the beautiful floral centerpiece, the presentation, the atmosphere of the Cotillion, and the whole idea behind it.

DID YOU.....know that a Hellenic Couples Invitational Tennis Tournament was recently held in Chicago? Charles and Sam Kopley won first place trophy. Other winners included: second place, Dino and Maria Leventis of Lincolnwood; third place, Tom and Helen Mantice of Northbrook; fourth place, Nicholas and Aggie Kafkis. Plans are currently being formulated to expand and hold tennis tournaments for singles, also.

MEMBERS OF........the Gus Harris family have had many occasions for celebration these past few months. In July, Gus and his wife, Eugenia, celebrated 50 years of marital bliss. Their daughter, Kay, and her husband, Constantine Duros of Arlington Heights, invited 65 of their close friends and relatives to a dinner party held at Lancer's Restaurant in Schaumburg to celebrate the occasion.

On September 3rd, their grandson, John Duros of Evanston, son of Connie and Kay, married Peggy Kmieciak of Wilmette. On September 18th, Connie and Kay celebrated their 30th wedding anniversary.

QUOTE OF THE WEEK: "Apart from all other considerations, the deep psychological reason that we need someone to love us is that we can freely confess our faults and our defects only to someone who acknowledges our lovability."

"The only way a man can get a woman to tell him a secret is to pretend no interest in it; this so infuriates her congenital sense of curiosity that she is forced to assail him with the secret." – Harris

OUR TOWN.......is a great deal sadder since the death of our beloved Bishop Timotheos who had really endeared himself to so many with his sparkling personality, his fine leadership, his wisdom, and his spirited inspiration. The energetic bishop's messages were always clear – that life is not an everlasting picnic, but on the contrary, a matter of struggle, a mixture of triumph and failure, joy and sorrow – but his sermons were never somber – for he had the ability to sprinkle them with gayety and wit – making him so easy to listen to. At the end he traveled a difficult road, but we are certain that his tremendous faith eased the pain of suffering that was a part of his illness. May he rest in peace.

A RECENT....smash hit evening was sponsored by the parish of Sts. Peter and Paul - the first in a series of scheduled fund-raisers for the Rev. Dennis G. Latto Memorial Center. An antipasto of well-bred, well-coiffed and well-groomed people walked through the portals of Second City to gather together and sip cocktails – a prelude to the gourmet dinner which followed at That Steak Joynt and for the specially seasoned rave review, Et Tu Kohoutek, held back at Second City. Not the usual comatose, still-watered fundraiser, this one was bathed in oceans of enthusiasm and refreshing diversity.

It was a solid gold Cadillac from the start, for one of our town's most brilliant attorneys, George Cotsirilos, was in the driver's seat. While he proposed, executed and chaired the entire event, tis rumored that pretty Terry Cotsirilos' nimble fingers did the walking.

On behalf of Sts. Peter and Paul, special thanks are extended to affable Bernard Sahlins, producer-director of Second City. A childhood friend of George Cotsirilos, this event certainly would not have been possible without him.

General chairmen of the Rev. Dennis G. Latto Memorial Center Building Fund Campaign are Andrew A. Athens and Thomas A. Athens. Chris G.Pappageorge is serving as campaign director.

LAUGHTER IN.....the aisles that will be heard for miles and miles will be the reaction to the forthcoming new production to emanate from St. John the Baptist Church in Des Plaines, Illinois, if past performances are any indication. This northwest suburban parish has, from time to time, come up with some hilarious productions all in the Greek language and, as we understand it, the forthcoming one will be the best yet to come. The production is called, "Grecian Holiday '78" and it will consist of two all Greek language plays. The Greek laugh-in will be "Stravoxilo," and the musical will be, "A Night in Athens." Opening night will be February 25th at 7:30 p.m.

SOCIAL DOYENS…….crowded about in the apartment of Sophia Koretzky recently to wish affable Nicholas Kafkis many happy returns of the day. The surprise event was kept hush-hush – and though everyone thought Nick suspected something – he seemed wide-eyed and dazed – and really touched that cousin Sophia had given such a lovely party in his honor. Hostess, Sophia, who always entertains lavishly, had brought together different cliques of Nick's friends – all who knew and enjoyed each other's company. Phyllis Colovos had made a scrumptious Leaning Tower of Pisa cake which easily handled the entire crowd. Nick's wife, Aggie, was so relieved when the surprise was finally over – for it took quite a bit of doing to hide the party facts from suspicious Nick. All in all it was a gathering of handsome, spirited well-wishers.

QUOTE OF THE WEEK: "We forget kindnesses far more easily than we forget injuries; for we unconsciously regard a kindness as something that is our due, while we regard an injury as utterly undeserved, even when it is not."

"One of the wittiest rebukes to egotism must be credited to the anonymous appraiser who remarked about a vain contemporary, 'I'd like to buy him at my price, and sell him at his.'" – Harris

SOME OF…..the most capable people in our town are working long and hard hours to complete plans for the 22nd Biennial Clergy-Laity Congress of the Greek Orthodox Church of the Americas, scheduled to take place from June 29-July 6, at the Conrad Hilton Hotel. With capable Andrew

Athens of Hinsdale at the helm as congress chairman, the event promises to be one of coordinated clergy-laity effort at which administrative, educational, financial, philanthropic, interchurch and social and moral issues and problems will be solved. A few program highlights follow: June 29th, the feast day of Sts. Peter and Paul will be celebrated at Sts. Peter and Paul in Glenview with His Grace Bishop Paul from Mexico officiating. On Sunday June 30th, St. Nicholas Church will be consecrated in Oak Lawn with His Eminence Archbishop Iakovos officiating.

The Greek Orthodox Ladies Philoptochos Society, the philanthropic and charitable arm of the church, will hold its conference simultaneously. General chairwoman, Bea Marks of Lincolnwood, has announced that this is the first National Philoptochos Conference to be held in Chicago since 1933.

DIPPING INTO.....the same fruit bowl were approximately 150 women who attended the recent luncheon given by the St. Andrew's Women's Club in honor of its past president, Mrs. Andrew (Irene) Tzakis who created a legend by serving a successful and unprecedented six year term. Teary-eyed and touched at the tribute paid to her, fireball Irene spoke eloquently thanking everyone present for helping to make her term of office the extraordinary one that it was. The St. Andrew's Women's Club presented Irene with tokens of their appreciation thus ending the term of office of a lady whose extraordinary drive for perfection did much to make the past six years of the club one of the most profitable periods in its history.

BULGING AT....the seams with people was Harmswood Stables in Morton Grove, where Bud and Georgia Photopulos recently entertained 500 people on Memorial Day weekend. "The Photopulos 500" was easily the raciest event of the weekend what with such well-known celebrities as Channel 7's John Drury (easily the handsomest man present) and Joel Daley (replete in cowboy hat and boots) in attendance.

YOUNG LADY....loaded with intellectual ability and with a surprisingly lack of pretension despite this ability is Kathy Porikos, daughter of Mrs. Georgia Porikos and the late and well-known Chicago attorney, George Porikos. Kathy, who graduated Phi Beta Kappa from Carleton College, recently received her PhD. in clinical psychology from Columbia University.

QUOTE OF THE WEEK: "When a deep injury is done to us, we never recover until we forgive." - Paton

"If you are calm and collected when everyone else is losing his head, maybe you just don't understand the situation."

ONE OF......our town's most illustrious citizens, Nicholas J. Melas, president of the Metropolitan Sanitary District of Greater Chicago, was recently honored by the Anti-Defamation League of B'nai B'rith for distinguished public service at a dinner held in the Grand Ballroom of the Pick Americana Hotel. Guest speaker was United States Senator Paul S. Sarbanes.

The Distinguished Public Service Award is presented to persons who have outstanding records of community service. Nick's contributions as a public servant span many decades. His efforts to improve our city, making it a better place to live, have earned this honor for him.

Nick Melas is an achiever. He has served as project director at the Industrial Relations Center of the University of Chicago. In his capacity as director, he was responsible for organizing and directing management development programs for executives of major corporations. Later he became administrative assistant to Joseph Lohman, then sheriff of Cook County. In 1961 Richard J. Daley appointed him City Sealer of Chicago. In 1962 Nick was elected commissioner of the Metropolitan Sanitary District of Greater Chicago. He is now serving his fourth term. Simultaneously, in 1975, Nick was elected president of the MSD Board of Commissioners, a position he holds today.

AND HANDSOME.......Christopher Brown, son of Peter and Helen Brown of Northbrook, participated in the recent Olympics held in Colorado Springs, Colorado. The 15-year old Chris, a weight lifter, was the only student in the north suburban area to qualify for the Olympics in the freshman and sophomore category. Athletes from all over the country were chosen to participate in the sports event which was sponsored by the U.S. Olympic Committee. Naturally, Peter and Helen popped their buttons. They are oh so proud of their Christopher.

FOR THE......fifth consecutive year Peacock Ice Cream Company in Evanston entered its ice cream in the Illinois State Fair Dairy Foods Competition and walked away with Blue Ribbons. The Illinois State Fair Judges for Dairy Products award a Blue Ribbon for first place, and rate ice cream on the point basis for flavor, body and texture, melt-down, color and package. Peacock's, owned by George and Kathryn Bugelas of Evanston, again received the highest point score of any of the other premium ice cream brands submitted this year for evaluation. All judging and grading is done on a Blind Identity Basis.

AND IT'S.....always great fun being invited to the home of Don and Demi Dadas in Lake Forest., This time it was a piano concert and the artist, David Burk, was given the opportunity of playing his entire repertoire before Don's guests two days prior to presenting his piano recital to the public.

QUOTE OF THE WEEK: "You don't really know yourself unless you are capable of changing those aspects you know about and don't like; self-knowledge as an intellectual exercise can go for a lifetime, like a chimpanzee, scratching the same place, but never getting rid of the flea."-Harris

"The most obnoxious affectation is the affectation of blunt candor when it is only malice masquerading as honesty."

MEMBERS OF......the James Poulos family of Wilmette are wearing their hearts at half-mast since his recent death at Evanston Hospital. Jim was well known on the North Shore for his affable manner while playing host at his Sweet Shoppe in Winnetka. His close friendship with my father goes back many years in which we, too, got the opportunity to get to know the real man – the warm and sensitive human being that Jim was. A member of the St. Andrew's parish council, he contributed a great deal to this parish in his lifetime, both financially and otherwise. As a matter of fact, when the new St. Andrew edifice was completed, back in 1957, and cornerstone services were held, members of the community began bidding for the honor of being the first to put the key in the new church door. The honor went to Jim, the highest bidder, at $5,000. He is survived by his wife, Anne; four children – Steven, Niki, Connie and Nancy; and many brothers and sisters. One of his brothers, Gus Poulos, is owner and operator of Homer's in Wilmette.

MEANWHILE BACK........home our house guests, cousins John and Irene Merakou took the big bird and flew back home to Athens after a 45 day trip to the states where John underwent extensive heart surgery for the second time in four years at St. Luke's Hospital in Houston, Texas. While receiving tender, loving recuperating care at the Diacou Clinic in Chicago, John told us about the personalized daily efforts, time and energy extended by the ladies of the philoptochos in Houston to all hospitalized patients of Greek extraction. These unselfish self-appointed Florence Nightingales make their daily vigils to both St. Luke's and Methodist Hospitals daily assisting patients in every way they can – particularly those with language barriers. Their chatty feeling of intimacy is a real healing balm to those afflicted with both surgical and nostalgic wounds.

CHEAPER BY THE DOZEN.......About 12 gals from The Greek Women's University Club have volunteered to demonstrate Greek ethnic dances at the Greek Independence Day celebration to be sponsored by the Hellenic Professional Society of Illinois. The ladies are also spinning their cultural cocoon preparing for the modern classical piano concert to be presented by Nicholas Sothras on May 6th in the Fine Arts Building.

BRILLIANT AUTHOR……Harry Mark Petrakis is at it again – probably with another best seller. His newest book, "In the Land of Morning," due to hit the bookstores next month, is a story of a Chicago Vietnam veteran who returns to his old neighborhood (on Halsted Street) to find his family full of hate and vengeance. Another study on the violence we do to each other.

QUOTE OF THE WEEK: "Most couples who elope do so not for romantic reasons but because they are afraid that if they wait much longer they might return to their senses."

"The kind of joke a person cannot take about himself is a surer index of his character than the kind of joke he relishes about others; what he does not find 'funny' about himself is always the weakest part of his nature."

ON TUESDAY…….evening, October 21st, in the Grand Ballroom of the Conrad Hilton Hotel, the United Hellenic American Congress will honor one of our town's most beloved benefactors, Andrew A. Athens, president of Metron Steel Corporation. This first national banquet will be a fund-raising event which has as its goal the sale of a minimum of 1,000 tickets.

A deeply respected man in the community, Andrew Athens has been the catalyst in the formation of the UHAC in Illinois, and his untiring effort for the creation of the National UHAC were recognized in his selection as the first national chairman of the organization. But

Andrew Athens needs no introduction in Chicago, in the United States, and, for that matter, on foreign soil for he has produced mammoth worldwide projects. A man with psychological depth and understanding of his fellow man, he has always organized around a single charitable force, and with imagination and power has built an empire of good works. In his lifetime, Andy has headed innumerable organizations and has responded to his fellow man with rapport, pathos and an unselfish singleness of purpose – the accomplishment of the goal at hand. It is, therefore, appropriate that the first fund-raising effort of the United Hellenic American Congress should honor this man who has given of himself consistently in order to further the goals of humanity.

Following the cocktail hour and dinner, one of the most poignant films I have ever seen will be shown. A tear jerker, it is called "A Boy Named Panayiotis," and it has been made and will be distributed through the efforts of Reverend Spencer Kezios and Reverend Evagoras Constantinidis. Once you see this film, you will realize that the $50 donation UHAC is asking for is a small pittance to pay to aid the children of Cyprus.

Dinner chairmen are Nicholas Gouletas, Frank Kamberos and Frank Kuchuris.

THE THREE…..owners of American Invsco – real estate tycoons Nicholas, Evangeline and Victor Gouletas – recently hosted a biggie at which they honored members of the consular corps in Chicago It was an extravaganza – what with the continental type buffet, the unending bottles of champagne, and the enchanting music of Franz Benteler and his Royal Strings straight from the Consort Room of the Continental Plaza Hotel. All three mingled with the uninterrupted stream of fascinating people who never seemed to stop coming through the door. The evening was four star.

WE WELCOME…..Rev. Peter Karloutsos, second priest at St. Andrew's Greek Orthodox Church, to our town. Rev. John Kutulas, senior priest at this parish, has announced that Father Peter was ordained deacon by His Eminence Archbishop Iakovos on September 4th. He assumed duties on October 1st and will be ordained a priest at St. Andrew's by His Grace Bishop Timotheos on Sunday, October 19th.

Father Karloutsos is the son of the Very Rev. Michael Karloutsos, pastor of St. John's Greek Orthodox Church in Cedar Rapids, Iowa, and the brother of the Rev. Alex Karloutsos, formerly of Sts. Constantine and Helen Greek Orthodox Church in Chicago.

QUOTE OF THE WEEK: "Whenever I meet a man who seems guarded, I feel that his spirit is not at one with itself; for the guarded attitude does not so much imply suspicion toward others but lack of confidence in one's own strength."

"The surest way to remain uneducated is to fear exposing your ignorance; false pride is the greatest enemy of knowledge."

WITH A.....sparkle in her big, brown Mediterranean eyes, a blush in her cheeks, and a sensational fresh young smile, Stathia Manos was married to eligible bachelor attorney, Thomas Askounis, on Saturday, September 17th at 5:30 pm at the Assumption Greek Orthodox Church. While the sun had teased and taunted all day threatening to disappear in its entirety, from the moment the bride entered the church, it shone in a special radiance.

Daughter of Nicholas and Kay Manos of Riverside, Stathia was by far one of the loveliest young brides this town has ever seen. Breathtaking in her mother's ivory satin wedding gown, which set off the tiniest of waists, the heavy satin gown slid down onto the hips landing in gracious folds on the floor. The long train followed – gently spilling out on the white runner.

Following the ceremony, guests stood in the receiving line in the French Room of the Drake Hotel to wish the newlyweds a lifetime of happiness together. Standing alongside Stathia and Tom were the bride's beaming parents, Kay and Nick; the groom's mother, Bessie Askounis of Oakbrook; the best man, Dean Govostis; and a bevy of wide-eyed, shiny-tressed young beauties, dressed in peach color floor-length gowns, petal smooth in femininity and accompanied by their ushers. (One of the most cherubic of these was young George Manos whose smile was meant to melt feminine hearts – both young and old alike.) Guests were then indulged in a lengthy cocktail reception which was followed by a delicious Beef Wellington dinner in the Gold Coast Room.

From the delightfully different super rich luscious chocolate wedding cake, to the vast array of delicately concocted pastries and fresh fruit which adorned the sweets table, the reception overflowed with good food, good wine, and good friends. Later, guests danced to the music of Perry Fotos and his orchestra.

WE PROUDLY.....tip our hat to Elaine E. Caras, daughter of Mr. and Mrs. Louis Caras of Des Plaines, who won the Miss Illinois Teenager Pageant this summer. Judged on scholastic ability, poise, personality, beauty and civic contributions, the 16-year old Elaine came out tops despite stiff competition. A student at Maine West High School, she is on the A honor role.

LIFETIME LOVE.....affair with culture, monthly get-togethers, dances, civic participation activities – these, and many other incomparable social scenes will be offered to the new breed of college graduates of Greek descent who become members of The Greek Women's University Club this fall. Barbara Penn, vice-president and membership chairman of the GWUC, extends a cordial invitation to all Greek women or women of Greek descent who are graduates of accredited colleges or universities to contact her so that an invitation can be sent out to the GWUC's membership tea scheduled to take place on September 29th.

GUESS WHO......the guests of honor will be at the forthcoming 15th Annual Luncheon and Fashion Show sponsored by the Philoptochos Society of Holy Apostles Church. None other than the Chicago Cubs own Milt Pappas and his wife. The date is October 6th; the place is the Grand Ballroom of the Sheraton-Oakbrook Hotel in Oakbrook. The theme is "Woman on the Go and Her Escort."

QUOTE OF THE WEEK: "Men are not worried by things, but by their ideas about things. When we meet with difficulties, become anxious or troubled, let us not blame others, but rather ourselves, that is our ideas about things." Epictetus

"Education consists in supplying the halted mind with a method of work and some examples of success." – Hocking

WHOOPIE, WHOOPIE.......do. What a super weekend is in store for you. That is if you heed my advice:

First, take your connoisseur's eye for fashion and your sinfully rich pocketbook over to the Gold Coast Room of the Drake Hotel this Saturday – at roughly 11:30 am (so that you can imbibe in a freshly chilled cocktail) and partake in a panorama of absolutely smashing clothes – courtesy of the St. Andrew's Women's Club. Here, at this yummy luncheon fashion show, opulent I.Magnin will show you how to laugh at Chicago's winter wind chill factor by simply wrapping yourself in a luxurious floor length mink coat; how to look super seductive in the new black little nothing lingerie dress; how to be deliciously female or whatever else your womanly wiles want you to be. Just call either of the reservations co-chairwomen and pray that you will be able to get a last minute reservation: Aliki Poulakidas (LO 1-6485) or Ann Poulos (AL 1-5272).

AND NICE.......to know that The Parthenon, "home" to Chris and Bill Liakouras, recently won a *Chicago Tribune* Award as one of Chicago's Top Ten Restaurants in our town. I understand that The Parthenon also tied for first place with The Bakery in the October issue of *Chicago Guide*, which carried a rating of Chicago restaurants. Others in the top ten include the Cape Cod Room (Drake Hotel), Berghoff, Blackhawk, Jovan, Biggs, R.J. Grunts, Kon-Tiki Ports and the Magic Pan. The *Chicago Guide* rating is the result of a poll among its readers, not gourmet authorities. Felicitations to the two Greek gourmet brothers whose eatery is always filled with a "standing room" only crowd.

WHILE "DISASTER"........was the name of the game on the second day of the three-day 11th Annual Picnic and Carnival sponsored by Sts. Peter and Paul (due, of course, to the horrendous downpour which fell over our town on September 29) the other two successful days certainly made up for it.

Handsomest 12-year-old on the picnic grounds was Alexander Macridis, son of Consul General Nicholas Macridis, who attended the event with his father. He's a winner – with his twinkling eyes, gracious smile, and charming manners.

"Gone, but not forgotten," was the tender message of love which came through to me as I entered the Narthex of Sts. Peter and Paul to light a candle during the three-day festivities – for on the left wall of the narthex, under an icon of St. Dionysius, patron saint of the late and revered Rev. Dennis Latto, was a gold vase filled with yellow roses. An unforgettable and touching gesture for a man who did so much for this parish.

And a wonderful job of announcing was done by Peter Childs, who sat up in his booth on a church mound making his announcements despite heavy thunderstorms and chilly winds.

QUOTE OF THE WEEK: "It seems short sighted to dislike those persons who marry 'beneath them' for some persons can only feel comfortable in a permanent relationship with someone inferior to themselves; an equal or a superior would be too threatening."

"Pride gets no pleasure out of having something, only out of having more of it than the next man. We say that people are proud of being rich, or clever, or good-looking, but they are not. They are proud of being richer, or cleverer, or better looking than others." – C.S. Lewis

AS COOL……as new sheets on hot dry sunburned skin will be the forthcoming Christmas Bazaar scheduled to take place on Wednesday, December 3rd. Sponsored by the chic ladies in the North Shore parish of Sts. Peter and Paul Greek Orthodox Church in Glenview, the bazaar promises to inject fresh adrenaline into the tired blood existence of the daily afternoon coffee-klutch crowd for it will feature impeccable originality. Fresh, priceless hand-made items, impossible to duplicate at any price in any shop, will be available, as will greenery, beribboned wreath and patchworks, not to mention sought-after home-made candy, pastries and bread. While the rare works of local artists will be displayed at the Art Gallery, look for the prepared tried and true recipes of jellies and preserves, including that special old-fashioned goody "quince."

According to Mrs. Evan (Helen) Papageorge of Lincolnwood, chairman of "Country Christmas Village," a masterful gourmet luncheon will be served in the church's Country Kitchen.

POOPED PARTYGIVERS…..who need to socialize in a quietly luxurious environment would do well to attend the forthcoming fabulous Annual Christmas Ball to be given by the classy ladies of St. Andrew's Greek Orthodox Church. Their buddingly beautiful black tie event will be held in the Guildhall of the Ambassador West Hotel on Sunday, December 7th. Mrs. John (Theo) Bartholomew, chairman, heads the list of regal ladies who are working arduously to make this ball the most elegant in the history of the Women's Club of the parish.

ANOTHER MAGICAL…..annual cocktail party and dance that has been making history for years has been announced by The Greek Women's University Club. It will take place on Saturday, November 29th. "Magical Moments" will be held at Café La Tour, Outer Drive East. Music will be supplied by George and the Aristons.

ONE OF……our town's most eligible bachelors, Nicholas Tzakis, son of Andrew and Irene Tzakis of Lincolnwood, was recently caught in the tender trap by pretty Eugenia Coorlas, daughter of Mr. and Mrs. Stratte Coorlas, also of Lincolnwood. The intimate family and close friends engagement party took place at the Drake Hotel. A July wedding is being planned by the couple.

THE CHICAGO…..*Tribune's* recent supplement, "Chicago '81" recently polished the already bright public image of Tom Kapsalis, who is doing such a special job as commissioner of aviation. Tom has been named as one of the 12 on Chicago's budget team. A super star if ever there was one, he has certainly provided direction to the major rehabilitation and expansion of O'Hare Airport.

WE POINT…..with pride to John Pappas, son of Chris and Elayne of Elgin, who recently made "Who's Who in American Schools and Colleges." John is a junior at Drake.

NEW MEMBER…..of the pablum set is Ioanna, spanking new daughter of George and Kathy Skontos of Glenview.

QUOTE OF THE WEEK: "Ninety percent of what passes for conversation is not communication as much as medication. It is used to make the speaker feel better, either by depreciating others or by inflating himself."

"One of the most effective ways of absorbing knowledge is to remain steadfastly ignorant of things that are not worth knowing; the mind has only so much room and the more bric-a-brac it takes in, the less space remains for the basic furniture of wisdom. This is why persons with a great deal of information so often have a minimum of sense." – Harris

A GREAT…..personality, Alex Gianaras of Bannockburn, has won the coveted presidency of Little City. Prominent businessman, leader in civic and church activities, Al succeeds Chief Criminal Court Judge Joe Power.

ONE OF.....the swankiest events of the year was attended by one of our town's sharpest graphic designers – Dean Nicholas Alexander, son of Nicholas and Menda Alexander, who was invited to the Nathan Cummings' recent champagne cocktail art preview held at the Art Institute. The reception was followed by dinner at the Drake Hotel. Talented Dean, head graphic designer for Planning Design Collaborators of Evanston, handled all the graphic designs for the sales pavilion of Harbor Point at Randolph and Michigan.

AND ALL.....of the sinfully beautiful people had scads of fun at a recent cocktail bash held at the Greek Consulate and hosted by Consul General Nicolas Macridis and his lovely, Toni. Here, in a warm and intimate atmosphere, and in unerring good taste, guests were treated to a diversity of delicate tidbits while sipping a variety of drinks. It was a totally irresistible atmosphere with marvelously quick-witted people.

THE CONTROVERSIAL.......and political figure of Mikis Theodorakis loomed large and powerful on stage at the recent "Theodorakis Conducts Theodorakis" concert which took place at the Arie Crown Theatre at McCormick Place on Friday, October 26th. With arms as powerful as eagle's wings flapping in encompassing gestures, Theodorakis' repertoire, while dramatic, was at times heavy with pathos. In his lighter moments, Theodorakis' arms seemed to grow slimmer as they flew in staccato like movements directing not only his eight piece group of talented musicians, but his very talented singers. With multi-million dollar talent on the stage, it was indeed a shame that the evening had to be marred by a few upstarts seated in the audience who chose to display their politics by foisting an untimely sign in the air with the asinine words, "Remember Greece, Don't Forget Chile." This was followed by the dramatic release of three white pigeons – an unkind gesture at that for the poor pigeons were completely blinded by stage lights. Those who selfishly chose this time to display their political leanings did nothing but take away from the musical splendor of the evening. My special thanks to fellow columnist, Kay Valone, founder and director of Mission Incorporated, whose guest I was that evening.

Proceeds collected by the Benefit Performance Committee, headed by Kay, will go to the very worthwhile worldwide Orthodox Missions for Alaska, Korea and Kenya Missions.

QUOTE OF THE WEEK: "Our opinion of people depends less upon what we see in them than in what they make us see in ourselves." – Sarah Grand

"Husbands want novelty and wives want security; but wives, when they are bored with security, look for novelty; and husbands, when they are bored with novelty, return to security."

GENERAL AMERICAN.........Transportation Corp. recently announced a complex plan for the sale of its LaSalle National Bank to James G. Costakis and Harrison I. Steans, associated in ownership in the Hyde Park Bank & Trust Company, Marina City Bank, the First National Bank of Highland Park, the Bank of Elk Grove in Elk Grove Village, and the Woodfield Bank in Schaumberg. GATX said it agreed to sell about 14% of the bank's stock outstanding to both men – or companies designated by them – for $4 million effective November 30th. GATX also granted the pair options to buy substantially all the rest of the LaSalle Bank shares by January 1, 1977, for about $54 million.

We point with a great deal of pride to Jim and his banking accomplishments and wish him a great deal of success in his financial endeavors. One of our town's most outstanding citizens, he has served on many local and civic committees. The newly named vice-chairman of LaSalle National is a graduate of the University of Chicago. Married to the former Elaine Stevens, daughter of Mr. and Mrs. George Stevens, Jim and his family reside in Lake Forest.

LET'S TALK.....about our very own Elaine Markoutsas. Aaron Gold, the *Chicago Tribune's* Tower Ticker, had this to say about her:"A

PROMISE KEPT": Elaine Markoutsas, writer par excellance, told George Shearing from her wheelchair last spring that she would 'come dancing in' to see him next time he came to the London House. She did just that last Tuesday night when he began another four-week engagement. George greeted her with a standing embrace and said, "I'm so proud of you....you have a will of iron."

On the same day, also in the *Chicago Tribune*, our own Elaine received a byline on a super, terrific story she did on Shearing entitled, "Shearing's back....and so is she." A lot of talent, spunk and drive in our pretty friend, Elaine – and I, for one, am quite proud of her accomplishments. Look for more in a few months.

A ZINGY.......dingy, splish, splashy cocktail reception was recently given by the Big Greek Bird people, Olympic Airways, in the main dining room of the Illinois Athletic Club. The lavish event was a welcoming gesture to Olympic's new Midwest regional manager, Fokas Drakalovich, and an adieu to S.A. Porter, manager-governmental affairs of North America. Everyone who is anyone was there – all clicking glasses filled with the nippy-tippy brew while biting into really scrumptious goodies from an overladen hors d'oeuvres table. H.S. Papadakis is general manager of North America, Olympic Airways, and our town's handsome John Adinamis is Hellenic Affairs representative in the Chicago area.

QUOTE OF THE WEEK: "Isn't it true that all of what we call 'anxiety' consists simply of different forms of fearing one's self?"

"Biographies are inadequate because they show us only one part of the subject; a good biography should show us three things about its subject – the man he was, the man he thought he was, and the man he would like to have been."

WITH AN……innate gift of knowing how to handle things, the Orthodox Youth Alumni Association (1946-1955) had the horrendous task of amassing names and addresses of those who had been active in the organization way back when and then planning a dinner for all of those folks . They did a fantastic job of organization – plus coming way ahead financially. According to Nicholas Lianos, president of the St. George Greek Orthodox Church, a man who loomed large in all of these plans, the committee not only did a great job of bringing together former O.Y. members for an evening of relaxation and enjoyment, but made all of the following donations with money that was left over: $50 donation was turned over to the original churches which comprised the O.Y. during 1948-55 totalling $500; a $50 donation was made to the St. Antonios Chapel of our diocese; and an additional donation of $300 was made to the St. George Greek Orthodox Church for the utilization of its facilities for the evening.

THIS WEEK…..we point with pride to two pretty and hard working ladies for the outstanding work they did on their annual Christmas bazaar: Mrs. Chris (Gloria) Pappageorge of Glenview and Mrs. Andrew (Evelyn) Demetrius of Glenview, co-chairwomen of the Country Christmas Store bazaar sponsored by the Women's Club of Sts. Peter and Paul Greek Orthodox Church. This event was such a smashing success that many of the ladies who came prepared to lunch at the church hall had to be turned away. We tip our hat to both Gloria and Evelyn and to the hard-working crew that assisted them in this – one of the greatest financial successes on record.

WE POINT…..with pride to Nicholas J. Melas, vice-president of the Metropolitan Sanitary District of Greater Chicago, who was recently honored by a committee of Chicago business and labor leaders at a testimonial reception given in recognition of his 11 years of service to the public and his outstanding community participation as a proven elected official. Fireball Nick personally greeted business men, personal friends, and relatives, who all attended the jam-packed reception to extend their good wishes to a man who has contributed a great deal to the local political scene, as well as to the Greek community.

A man with a light bulb brain that never seems to blow out, Nick holds degrees in both chemistry and business administration, and was once named, "Man of the Year" at the University of Chicago. Candidate for re-election to the board of trustees of the Metropolitan Sanitary District of Greater Chicago, Nick has successfully served the district for two terms.

NICE TO......learn that the very capable George Karcazes has been elected president of the Greek Welfare Foundation. A Chicago attorney, George is a graduate of the University of Chicago School of Law. He succeeds Alec K. Gianaras

QUOTE OF THE WEEK: "A friend is a person who knows all about you and still likes you."

"Perfectionists fail to understand that a man's capacities may make us respect him, but it is his foibles that make him lovable; and the person who rigidly represses all his foibles is always puzzled by the world's lack of cordiality."

FEET WELL.....planted on the earth while shooting at high targets is The Greek Women's University Club which recently donated $1,000 to Cooley's Anemia Foundation adding another philanthropic feather to their large brimmed philanthropic hat. The presentation, made by Handa Mallis, treasurer, to Pat Matareese, Chicago area chairman of the foundation, took place at the Rodity's Restaurant and was attended by approximately 35 people. Eugenia Sacopulos, president of the GWUC, gave the greeting and Lee Corolis served as program chairman. Dr. Alan Schwartz, chief hematologist, Children's Memorial Hospital, answered questions on Cooley's Anemia during the question and answer period which followed the presentation.

One good deed deserves another must have been the thought rolling through the mind of Louie Kuchuris of the Mary Ann Baking Company who, dining with his family and friends, happened to be seated near the GWUC group. Following the presentation, Mr. Kuchuris, a philanthropist himself, announced that he had picked up the tab of all those dining in the GWUC group. Orchids to you, Mr. Kuchuris, for your overwhelming generosity.

AND THE.....big bird touched down on American soil bringing us a very pretty cousin from Athens, Greece, Ms Vickie Nicolopoulos. While Vickie hails from Athens, she has been living in Geneva, Switzerland, attending school there and learning languages so that she can fulfill her ambition of becoming a translator. Daughter of Dr. and Mrs. Demetrios Nicolopoulos, Vickie shall be staying with us throughout the Easter holidays. Welcome to our town, Vickie.

CHARMING AND.......utterly feminine Irene Betzelos will be hosted and toasted by the Daughters of Penelope "Danae Chapter" on April 19th at the Golden Flame Restaurant. The dinner-dance event is honoring Irene who served as Past District Governor of the Daughters. Since she is national chairman of the Cooley's Anemia Drive and April has been designated as Cooley's Anemia Month, all net proceeds will be donated to the Cooley's Anemia Fund.

"TWO KNIGHTS".....owned and operated by Chris Pappas of Elgin serves the most delectable veal marseilles dinner. Located at Irving Park, Route 53 in Itasca, Illinois, it was so yummy that I raved about it to all my friends for weeks and weeks. Well, my opinion of that particular dish was confirmed in the April 11th issue of the *Chicago Sun-Times* column, "Let's Eat Out" under the heading "Noble Meals." Not only was my opinion of the veal marseilles dish confirmed, but also my opinion of this really super supper club. So, for those of you who have never had the pleasure of dining at the "Two Knights," I suggest you do so. But be sure to make a reservation - it's that packed nightly.

QUOTE OF THE WEEK: "Every man will fall who, though born a man, proudly presumes to be a superman." – Sophocles

"It is no accident that so many women who think they yearn for a man to dominate them have married men they can twist around their fingers; for the fantasy of being dominated allows them to conceal from themselves their deep fear and resentment of being permanently subjected to such a relationship in real life." – Harris

SUPER BEAUTIFUL……bash was hosted by Evangeline Gouletas of the Gouletas real estate clan (American Invsco) during the holiday season. In a bone, white and mirrored setting, unlike any I have ever seen, in the unique Mies van der Roe building, the backdrop was perfect for the sophisticated crowd that sipped and supped in the Gouletas pad while violins plucked tender and melodious tunes. Engie, always a very charming hostess, paid homage to members of the press and top echelon personnel at American Invsco.

MEMO FROM…..a New Yorker informs me that Aristotle Onassis, the billionaire husband of you know who, is building a 51-story $95 million tower on Fifth Avenue and has launched a costly world-wide campaign to lure big business tenants. The billionaire and his daughter, Christina, recently donned hard hats for an open-air elevator ride to the top of the partly completed Olympic Tower, a pleasure dome that has been compared to the hanging gardens of Babylon. The building consists of 21 floors of offices, topped by 30 floors of condominiums.

REALLY, REALLY……proud of two pretty sisters, Themi and Theodora Vasils who have translated two of Nikos Kazantzakis' books. The reviews of both translations appeared in "Publisher's Weekly." Kazantzakis' lovers all over the land will be interested in purchasing the brilliant translations by these very smart ladies:

"Symposium," T.Y. Crowell. Discovered and first published in Greece in 1971, some 14 years after Kazantzakis' death. It is one of the Greek novelist's youthful works in a faithful translation by the co-translators of "Journeying."

"Journeying: Travels in Italy, Egypt, Sinai, Jerusalem and Cyprus," Little Brown. These early travel pieces by Kazantzakis were commissioned by an Athens newspaper in the twenties. First collected in 1927, a revised edition rewritten by the author appeared posthumously in 1961 as part of his complete works. The journals in this fine new translation are taken from the 1961 edition.

ANYONE CALLING.....out, "Is there a doctor in the house?" while in the Guildhall of the Ambassador West Hotel on February 1st will be deluged with medical specialists of all types for on that date, the Hellenic Medical Society will present its Annual Scholarship Ball.

QUOTE OF THE WEEK: "Love is a romantic island of emotion, surrounded on all sides by expenditures." – Harris

"When will we be grown up enough to abolish the double standard of demanding punishment for those offenders we do not know and imploring understanding of those offenders we do know."

IT IS......also with great sadness that I write about the death of a very valiant lady, Theresa Cotsirilos of Winnetka, who fought the good fight with all of her might for such a long time. Wife of well-known and respected attorney, George J. Cotsirilos, Terry finally succumbed after about a 25-year bout with the cancer. Sister of the late and beloved Reverend Dennis G. Latto, former pastor of Sts. Peter and Paul Greek Orthodox Church in Glenview, she had the same indomitable spirit that he possessed. Terry is survived by her husband; three children, Stephanie, John and George; her mother, Stamo Latto; and a brother and a sister, Nicholas Latto and Urania Alissandrato.

AND WHAT......a kick I got out of seeing my super involved goddaughter, Dana Pappas of Schaumburg, marching in the Orange Bowl Parade in

Miami, Florida on Saturday, December 31st at 7 pm on Channel 5. Dana, who plays both the piccolo and the flute, tap dances, toe dances, etc. marched with the Jas. B. Conant School, Hoffman Estates.

HANDSOME ADDITION......to the mush and pablum set is George Singh, a 6 lb. 7 oz. bundle of joy, born to Irene and Jack Singh on April 29th at Northwestern Memorial Pavillion. Grandparents George and Maria Manus are beaming with happiness at their first grandchild.

TAKING ANOTHER.....step into the future is legal-beagle George Skontos of Glenview, who recently received an appointment to serve on the newly formed Cook County Republican Platform Committee. No one is more deserving than the very qualified George who is slowly coming up as a top banana on the Illinois Republican scene.

BUDDINGLY BEAUTIFUL....tribute was recently made to State Representative Samuel C.Maragos when he was selected as an outstanding alumnus of The John Marshall Law School Alumni Association. Sam was presented with one of the Distinguished Alumnus Awards at the school's 75th anniversary dinner held on May 4th at McCormick Place. Sam is chairman of the Illinois Commission on Atomic Energy, Minority Spokesman of the House Judiciary Committee, and a highly respected, active and involved member of the Revenue Committee.

QUOTE OF THE WEEK: "Half the trouble in the world is caused by people who are trying to run away from reality. The other half is caused by people who are trying to force their version of reality on the rest of us."

"It is surely one of nature's mischievous ironies that the qualities that attract us to a person are often the most superficial ones – thus, the reasons couples stay married has little to do with the reasons they got married."

AN ARCHITECTURAL…masterpiece of flawless design, a showplace of exquisite taste, and a home reflecting the warmth and beauty of two very special people, Jim and Bess Maros, is the "castle" we had the pleasure of viewing at a sneak preview champagne cocktail bash given by the Maros' on Saturday, April 27th in Olympia Fields. We were not quite prepared for the estate setting – but there it was – a magnificent sight. Walking on a red carpeted plank to the front door, we were greeted by Bess and Jim and then treated to a tour of the home by the design consultant, Niko Geane of Evanston.

This three-bedroom, eight-bathroom home will have taken two years to complete by the time it is finished in November. It boasts of a cedar shake roof, walls of stone and a 41-foot high living room ceiling – a foot and a half shorter than a five story building. Featuring the best of both worlds, it is entirely custom designed and built, and, of course, includes a swimming pool and tennis courts nestled in acres and acres of land. When it is completed, I am certain that it will win many architectural awards for its unusual design, grace and beauty.

Later, 150 friends and relatives drove to the Olympia Fields Country Club where we dined and danced to the music of Perry Fotos and his orchestra, until the wee hours of the morning.

CONDOLENCES ARE……extended to a friend of many years and a fellow columnist, Jim Mezilson, on the death of his beloved mother, Dorothy, wife of the late Michael Mezilson, who died on May 5th. Death is no stranger to Jim who lost his young and lovely sister, Connie Alevizos of Minneapolis, and still another sister, Helen Pappas of Salt Lake City, all within a period of five years. We hope that this is the last of such occurrences for the Mezilson clan. Mrs. Mezilson is also survived by another son, Christ, and his wife, Shirley, and a daughter, Fay and her husband, Peter Machinis.

THE ELEGANT…..doors of the Governor's Suite of the Continental Plaza Hotel will swing open at 9 pm on May 25th when The Greek Women's University Club sponsors yet another annual cocktail party and dance. Hors d'oeuvres will be served at this swinging bash and music will be supplied by the George Delis Orchestra.

IMPECCABLE SCHOLAR……is Cassandra Flambouras who has been accepted in the school of political science and law at Georgetown University, where she will work towards her Master's Degree. Daughter of George and Frances Flambouras, this pretty miss graduates from Loyola University on June 7th.

QUOTE OF THE WEEK: "Immature love says, 'I love you because I need you.' Mature love says, 'I need you because I love you.'" – Eric Fromm

and [illegible] d'oeuvres will be served at this swinging bash and [illegible] will be supplied by the Georgia Tech [illegible].

[illegible] Cassandra [illegible] [illegible] in the [illegible] of [illegible] and [illegible] [illegible]

[illegible]

1980-89

"The pride of the Don Juan type of man might possibly be dampened if he ever reflected that if other men devoted as much time and energy to conquests as he does, they would be equally successful; for, if there is one thing that is sure, it is that the world is full of women waiting to be taken advantage of." – Harris

YOUNG IS.....beautiful and this year's crop of debs, scheduled to bow at the St. Helen's Debutante Cotillion, sponsored by the St. Helen Women's Club of Sts. Constantine and Helen Greek Orthodox Church in Chicago on June 15th at the Conrad Hilton Hotel, depict beauty in its most radiant and refreshing form – fresh, fragrant, breezy hair crackling with life and lights; clear, fresh, unwilting skin, innocent eyes that can move mountains.

This year's spring bouquet, all fresh and lovely like a Parisian April sky following a rain storm, first unfolded its petals at the Presentation Tea given by the St. Helen Women's Club on March 30th. Here, Mrs. Stephen Manta, cotillion chairman, introduced each deb and her mother. Frosting on the cake at this tea party was the fashion show at which lovely post-debs modeled gowns from past cotillions. Dee Tzakis, chairman of the first cotillion and presently executive advisor, moderated the fashion show.

This year's debs include: Mary Arsland of Chicago; Elaine Kathryn Caras of Des Plaines; Joy Elizabeth Childs of Northbrook; Cathy Elaine Costakis of Lake Forest; Stephanie Dakajos of Northbrook; Theodora Stephanie Furla of Glenview; Angela Gouvis of Chicago; Tasha Dena Kostantacos of Rockford; Marie Anthoula Mansour of Oak Park; Chrisanthe Joan McHale of Lake Forest; Susan Soultana Petas of Toledo, Ohio; Pamela Toscas of Chicago; Angela Vlachos of Oak Lawn.

"LET ME.......entertain you" was the theme song of Nike Giannakis who liberally sprinkled her guests with luscious food, an open bar, and a rhythmic combo at a party given in honor of her visiting granddaughter, Christa Cocoris of Boston, Massachusetts, who recently turned 21 years of age. The melody was sweet and the lyrics appropriate for Nike – one of Chicago's original Pearl Mesta's – who spread her very social wings on this special occasion, fluttering them over her family and friends who joined in to help celebrate the lovely Christa's 21st birthday. Her parents, Bill and Matia Cocoris had flown in with their son and Christa's paternal grandmother to wish her a happy birthday.

On hand to greet guests at this festive occasion was daughter number two, Sophia Giannakis Koretzky, who acted as second hostess for the evening.

QUOTE OF THE WEEK: "It requires a secure sense of maturity to accept the fact that what people say about us is always true – not our truth, perhaps, but theirs, and equally valid in the final equation of the personality."

"Any stranger will lend you a hand in distress, but it takes a real friend to forgive your success."

THIS WEEK.....one of our town's most illustrious scholars, Andrew T. Kopan, professor of education at DePaul University, recently contributed a chapter on the Greeks of Chicago in a new book, "Ethnic Chicago" published by William B. Erdman Publishing Company of Grand Rapids, Michigan. Entitled, "Greek Survival in Chicago: The Role of Ethnic Education, 1890-1980," the chapter is one among a collection of chapters structured around the continuing debate over cultural pluralism and the melting pot in Chicago. While the book focuses specifically on experiences of ethnic groups in Chicago, it also examines group values, social structures and lifestyles of each group.

An authority on the history of Greeks in Chicago, Andy brilliantly presents the story of Greek survival through education and the entrepreneurial aspect of the group, bringing into focus the humble, rural folk who came to America neither with urban skills nor education but who, nevertheless succeeded.

THE FAMILY.....of Gus Pappageorge is wearing its heart at half-mast since his death. The candle of Gus' life was snuffed out after traveling a difficult road but we are certain that his tremendous faith eased the pain of suffering that was a part of his illness. He is survived by his wife, Kathryn; two children, George and Vicki; two brothers, Chris and Elias Pappageorge.

It is also with sadness that I write about the death of a very valiant lady, Elaine Sedares Sarocco of Hinsdale. Elaine had an indomitable spirit which carried her to the end of the road with great courage. She is survived by four children: Kathie, Toni, Robert and Billy; her mother, Katherine Sedares; and two brothers, Billy Dare Sedares and Louis J. Sedares.

THIS TYPEWRITER.....is typing ribbons of raves about pretty and talented Cynthia Maniates, daughter of George and Eileen Maniates of Glenview. Cynthia designed all of the costumes for the musical production, "Zorba," currently at the Candlelight Dinner Playhouse. The zesty play got excellent reviews in both of our Chicago newspapers singling out Cynthia's costumes as exceptional.

Nominated for a Jeff Award for costume design two years in a row for both "Funny Girl" and "Follies," she heads a company called, "Cindy Makes Things" and has designed costumes for many theater productions.

Artistic talent runs in the Maniates family for Papa George is one of the most outstanding graphic designers in the country. Currently, he is associate creative director and vice-president of J. Walter Thompson, and an all time sweetie-pie.

AND ANOTHER.....one of our pretty talents, Elaine Markoutsas, has been caught in the tender trap. Elaine, well-known feature writer for the

Chicago Tribune, will middle-aisle it some time in the spring. Her heart is Charles Leroux, also a feature writer for the *Trib*. Best wishes to a gal that rates A+ in my books – both as a writer and as a friend.

THIS WEEK…..we point with pride to George Pappageorge, son of Chris and Gloria Pappageorge of Glenview, who was recently presented with the American Institute of Architects Award. This great guru of design, together with a fellow architect, David Haymes, took a chunk of a crumbling Chicago shoe factory and carved out award-winning condominiums at a price well below growing rates. Congrats are in order.

QUOTE OF THE WEEK: "To believe something, then not to believe it, and then to believe it again, is the best way to grasp a creed; for those who have never doubted, nor stood where their adversaries stand, have an incomplete hold on their beliefs."

"The art of living successfully consists largely in being able to hold two opposite ideas in tension at the same time: first, to make long-term plans as if we were going to live forever; second, to conduct ourselves daily as if we were going to die tomorrow."

AN ALBUM……of unprecedented importance to the Greek-Americans of Chicago will be published by the Greek Heritage'81 Committee of the United Hellenic American Congress in the spring of 1982. UHAC has long been aware of the importance of the Greek legacy. It has known that this legacy should be captured and documented so that generation after generation would have an accurate account of the growth of the Greek-American in Chicago in every facet of life. So the search began. As editor-in-chief of this book, I can honestly say that both Chris Pappageorge (general chairman and publisher) and I had a most difficult time finding contributors that met our standard for excellence in their fields. But our search bore fruit, and today we are happy to announce the names of our contributors and their areas of expertise: S.D. Soter, M.D. (medicine); Aris Angelopoulos (business); Ernest Panos, D.D.S. (television); William J. Russis (business); James Regas (law); Billy Dare Sedares (entertainment); Andrew T. Kopan, Ph.D. (Greek Community); Kathryn Adinamis (dress designers); Phil Bouzeas (sports); Stanley Fistedis, Ph.D. (research); Thomas Poulakidas, D.D.S. (dental); Elaine Markoutsas (Greek Heritage); Nicholas Philippidis (newspapers); Elena Savoy (television); Jean Fardulli (music); Angeline Caruso, Ph.D. (education); Hon. Nicholas J. Melas (government); Alex Karanikas, Ph.D. (writers); Fotios Litsas, Ph.D. (religion); Harry Mark Petrakis (foreword); Yiannis and Antigone Lambrou (radio); Leon Marinakos (UHAC); Nicholas Jannes (art); Katherine Valone (Greek schools); Harold Peponis (organizations); and James Mezilson (stellar Hellenes). Entitled, "Hellenism in Chicago," the album will run approximately 200 pages with a circulation of about 5,000.

A COSMOPOLITAN……collection of people extended extra-strength love to His Beatitude Diodoros, beloved Greek Orthodox Patriarch of Jerusalem, throughout his four-day pastoral visit to our town, giving him an opportunity to amass a plethora of glorious memories to share with his people on his retun to the Holy City. Special commendation to all of our Chicago Greek-American community leaders (whose names are impossible to list in the short space of this column) who worked long and arduous hours to make His Beatitude's visit an unforgettable experience.

I must type ribbons of raves over the civic luncheon hosted by Mayor Jane Byrne, and members of the Civic Welcoming Committee for it was a very classy event. Andrew A. Athens, co-chairman of the committee, opened the luncheon program with introductions. Then Mayor Byrne spoke to her luncheon guests in glowing terms about her visit to Jerusalem. His Beatitude presented her honor with gifts from the Holy City, while Nicholas Melas, co-chairman of the Civic Welcoming Committee, translated his words of gratitude. Archbishop Iakovos also addressed the luncheon group thanking Mayor Byrne for the delightful luncheon. It was a splendid afternoon.

Climaxing the visit of His Beatitude was the 60th anniversary banquet of the Greek Orthodox Archdiocese of North and South America. Held at the Conrad Hilton, the celebration was held under the auspices of the Diocese of Chicago, the Ecumenical Patriarchate, the National Ladies Philoptochos Society and the United Hellenic American Congress. Master of Ceremonies was Andy Athens, first vice-president of the Archdiocesan Council, who served as chairman of the 60th anniversary committee. His Beatitude was honored by the presence of 2,000 dinner guests.

QUOTE OF THE WEEK: "The world will get better only when we stop blaming, for blaming is always a paranoid projection of our own feelings of inadequacy, and allows us to be as bad as we want to be, while pointing the finger elsewhere."

"Those censorious persons who are so convinced that current literature is corrupting morality seem never to have considered the even more plausible possibility that current morality is corrupting literature; for it is one of the inevitable marks of a narrow and rigid mind that it mistakes a symptom for a cause." -Harris

THOSE WHO……attended the recent 25th anniversary festivities honoring Jim and Georgia Regas of Oakbrook are saying such terribly nice things about their three children – Suzanne, Dean and Allyson. Tall, handsome Dean, and his two beautiful blonde sisters, who hosted the event, chose the very chi-chi Toulouse Restaurant to celebrate the 25th wedding anniversary of their parents and their warmth and conviviality made the anniversary event one of the loveliest on record. From the very finest in French cuisine and French wines, to the festive decorations and the cake shaped like a wedding bell – the party was a smash. To me it seems utterly impossible that 25 years have gone by since the Gatziolis-Regas nuptials but gone with the wind they have.

You'd never know it by looking at Georgia and Jim. They still make a very handsome couple.

A NEW……assault has been made in the field of entertainment in Athens, Greece by Billy Dare Sedares who has been packing them in nightly at the Athenaeum Intercontinental Hotel, the ultra new luxury hotel that opened last spring on Syngrou. According to a hot-off-the-press copy of the September issue of *The Athenia*, Greece's English Monthly, Billy has been breaking attendance records in the Cava Cocktail Lounge since last April.

Billy, a refreshingly spirited entertainer who exhibits a riveting, distinctive style that has made him one of the enduring pleasures of the musical club scene in Athens, has a voice that is provocative, and his bright piano style has a measured sense of tempo, allowing him to give full value to his melody line and syncopation. Stop in and hear him at the Cava Lounge next time you're in Athens.

CUPID'S ARROW…….has struck again. Pretty Marcia Tzakis and Mathew Garoufales will middle aisle it. Marcia is the daughter of Dee and the late Sam Tzakis, and Mathew is the son of Byron and Irene Garoufales. Almost within a fortnight George Michaels and another beauty, Carrie Trivelas, announced that they would become one. Carrie, who is originally from Charleston, South Carolina, is the daughter of the Rev. and Mrs. Nicholas Trivelas (Father Travelas is the brother of Lou Hondras, who is the wife of the Rev. John Hondras, former pastor of St. Andrew's Church. George is the brother of Dee Tzakis whose daughter just announced her engagement). Now if you have all of that straight, we'll move on to other things.

THE WORLD…..is a lot sadder and poorer since the death of gracious and lovely Martha Russis, wife of William J. Russis; mother of James (Connie), the late Euthemia, and Katherine (Charles) Heard; grandmother of Martha and Vasili Russis, and Diana, the late Carla, and Chuckie Heard.

The epitome of classic culture, Aunt Martha gave much to those of us who were fortunate enough to have known and loved her. May the drops of spiritual sunshine she sprinkled on all of us in her lifetime stay with us forever.

ONE OF……the most beautiful mini-estates (just a little old summer place) is the one owned by Dr. Bill Kagianis in Grand Beach, Michigan. Bill had a carload of friends take the two-hour drive to Grand Beach recently. It was fun, food and swimming amid the most luxurious surroundings.

QUOTE OF THE WEEK: "Not to suggest that soft-voiced people cannot be stupid, but it is generally true that the louder the voice the lower the level of intellect."

"The same beauty that initially attracts a man eventually repels him if there is no strength of character beneath it; and the same strength that initially attracts a woman eventually repels her if there is no tenderness of character beneath it."

IMPECCABLE INSIGHT….was used by Chief Judge John Boyle in appointing Judge James Geocaris as supervising judge of the Housing Division for the Circuit Court of Cook County. Appointed judge of the Circuit Court of Cook County back in 1971, Jim presided over personal injury trials and served in the Housing Division, and in the Narcotic, Felony and Criminal courts. Nice news about an old friend who is one of the really great gurus of law.

AND ONE……of the greatest shockers was the death of one of the really nicest guys in our town – fellow columnist, Lou Nicholas of "Akousa" column fame. I don't think I know one person who ever said an unkind word about Lou for he abounded with real goodness. A man with an easy sense of humor, and genuine fair play, Lou was devoted to many causes and did much to further these causes in the best way he knew how. He will be sorely missed by those of us who circled his orbit for our world has become a lot sadder since his passing. My deepest condolences are extended to his family – particularly to his vivacious and charming wife, Vickie – for the real spark has been snuffed out of her life.

WE POINT.....with pride to Dr. Angeline Caruso, Area Associate Superintendent of Area C of the Chicago Board of Education, who recently became the recipient of an Honorary Doctor of Humane Letters degree from DePaul University. Angeline is the only woman involved in the operation of nearly 200 elementary and high schools on the north, northwest and west sides of Chicago. She joined the Chicago Public Schools as an elementary school teacher in 1944. The recipient of many awards, among those she treasures most is that presented by the Puerto Rican Congress.

ATTORNEYS CHRIS......and George Karafotias are wearing their hearts at half-mast over the death of their beloved father, Nicholas, who succumbed recently. A widower for 25 years, Mr. Karafotias was a well-known retired businessman, who served the Greek community with devotion during his lifetime. His sons have followed in his footsteps.

TWO VERY.....special people recently celebrated their 25th wedding anniversary – George and Connie Chrones of Glenview. You'd have to look long and hard to find two people who complement each other as much as these two do – attorney George with his unbelievable wit, and Connie with her warmth and sincerity.

QUOTE OF THE WEEK: "There is as much healing power in a Mozart quartet as in a box of aspirins. But people find it easier to swallow than to listen."

"Why do we say 'I wasn't myself' when we are provoked by anger or vanity or greed into disclosing what we really are?"

IT'S BEEN.....quite awhile since I've written this column, but between a physical move made by my company to different quarters, a change in my job status to managing editor, and the additional time spent on UHAC's album, "Hellenism in Chicago," I felt I owed myself a respite from all journalistic efforts. Now that this period is over, I would like to target some of this white space with black type to acknowledge some very special people: to three wonderful friends who served as associate editors on this album – Leon Marinakos, Andy Kopan and fellow columnist, Jimmy Mezilson; to another special friend, Chris Pappageorge, project chairman, who seems to always get me involved in special projects; to Jimmy Regas, whose efforts on behalf of this album brought us some much needed revenue; to Andy Athens, national chairman; to Estelle Kanakis, secretary of UHAC; and to all of the contributors who researched and wrote such informative articles, A GREAT BIG THANK YOU.

In the year it took us to put this album together, we went through a process of learning. We found out about our forefathers, their travails, their hopes, their dedication to family, church and to their motherland. We found out "who's who" among our Chicago Greek-Americans. We walked through the past, the present, and we looked into the future, and our trip made us rich in knowledge about our heritage and our accomplishments.

"Hellenism in Chicago" is now perched proudly on the shelves of a great majority of our educational institutions, in the offices of our Chicago executives, our mayor and our governor; the Library of Congress, all of our churches and in the homes of the majority of our Chicago Greek-Americans.

To those of you who were kind enough to call and write telling us how much you enjoyed reading, "Hellenism in Chicago," we are deeply grateful. To those of you who have not yet been able to obtain a copy, I suggest you call the United Hellenic American Congress office and order a copy. Perusing its pages is a nostalgic trip worth taking.

SINGULAR HONOR.......was recently bestowed on our very own, Nicholas J. Melas, president of the Metropolitan Sanitary District of Greater Chicago. Nick, who has become a household word with all of his achievements, recently had a new and large recreational facility in the village of Mount Prospect named after him: Melas Park. The dedication ceremonies were impressive – as well they should have been – for, to my knowledge, this is the first time that a recreational facility has been named in honor of a Chicago Greek-American. The park has approximately 70 acres, and it is located at Busse Highway and Central Road in Mount Prospect. We point with pride to Nick who has raised the Greek image high in the city of Chicago.

ONE OF.......the most fun parties on record was the one hosted by pretty and petite, Irene Manus Singh, for her vivacious mom, Maria Manus. Held at Deni's Den – the occasion was Maria's birthday – and it was a knock-out in food, drinks, music and home-made entertainment. Some of the personalities who participated in this wing-ding were, of course, Irene, and her handsome son, George; Helen Anthony, Maria's niece; and John Adinamis who presented Maria with a Funeral Director's Award for her superb handling of all funereal arrangements (original caskets, lighting, floral decorations). It was a knock-out delivery.

QUOTE OF THE WEEK: "There will be no rest, and no release, for the human spirit as long as we stubbornly keep confusing the pursuit of pleasure with the pursuit of happiness."

"No person has room for more than one major theme in his emotional life; for example, if someone has remarried and still bears active hate and resentment for the former partner, the new marriage is not a happy one-if it were, the happiness would drive out the ancient grudge."-Harris

LONG STEMMED.......roses to pretty and talented violinist, Jennifer Marlas. The recent musical performance of the 12-year-old daughter of Dennis and Connie Marlas awed all of those who attended her Advance Student Recital held in the palatial home of Don and Demi Dadas of Lake Forest. Never have I heard such beautiful music. Jennifer's performance was pure rapture as she elicited melodic tones from her violin. A student of Almita and Roland Vamos at the Music Center of the North Shore, Jennifer wowed us all for her violin had soul and her body moved to the passion of her music. This young lady bears watching for a talent such as hers cannot be ignored. Thank you, Jennifer, for giving us two hours of pure unadulterated musical bliss.

INTERESTING FEATURE.......story on Mike Stefanos, the 40-year old owner of Dove Candies and Ice Cream recently appeared in *Crain's Chicago.* It told how he began making his Valentine's Day candy way back in August. in the heat of summer. It went on to say that Christmas, Easter, Mother's Day, Sweetest Day and February 14th account for more than 60% of the old-fashioned stores' annual candy sales – 1.2 million pieces of candy with $500,000 at the register.

AND THE.......charming Vasils ladies certainly get around: Theodora Vasils recently translated, "Alexander the Great," by Nikos Kazantzakis and the new novel is being published this month by Ohio University Press, coinciding with the "Arch for Alexander" exhibit now touring the United States. The work was originally published in Greece in serial form in 1940, and republished in a complete volume in 1979 following the discovery of the royal Macedonian tomb at Vergina in northern Greece where Alexander's father, King Philip II, is believed to have been buried. The brilliant Theodora has translated and published several books by the famous Greek author. She was awarded an honorary Doctor of Letters degree from Rosary College. As for Themi, she has announced that NBC will present a program highlighting Easter in the Eastern Orthodox Church on Easter Sunday. Themi will interview the Rt. Rev. Athanasios Emmert, pastor of St. George Eastern Orthodox Church in Oak Park.

KEEP YOUR......eyes on a brilliant and engaging young man whose name I predict, will soon become well-known in the automotive world. His name is Dennis Melas, and he is the son of Danny and Dorothy Melas. A top student at IIT, Dennis recently was named a General Motors scholar after an extremely intensive selection process. Translated that means that for the next two years, Dennis' tuition will be fully paid. In addition to the two year scholarship he was awarded, Dennis was guaranteed an internship with a GM division during both this summer and the summer of 1984. The awarding of this scholarship makes him the top electrical engineering student in his class at IIT, with a GPA of 3.8.

QUOTE OF THE WEEK: "I don't want to scare you," the precocious seven-year-old informed his teacher, "but my daddy says if I don't get better grades, somebody's going to get spanked."

"Any man who thinks he has lived up to his own ideal of himself had a very low ideal to begin with."

ALL SENIOR.......citizens please take note and hang your head in shame if your bones are aching and the feeling of being old just won't leave you alone. The proven formula for staying young – both in body and in spirit – has been concocted by a handsome and distinguished gentleman by the name of Anthony Matsoukas who lived in Chicago – way back when – and who has lived in Los Angeles for a great many years.

Uncle Tony recently was honored at a 90th birthday party by his beautiful daughter, Euthemia, and her affable husband, Lambros Karkazis, MD, and their three children, Frank, Anthony and Georgene, in their Deerfield home. Cuz Euthemia, and her hubby wined and dined approximately 90 guests in barbecue style – with the lamb going round and round on the spit, and the tables and chairs all set up on the banks of Lake Eleanor – which just happens to be their backyard. All the ladies in the arthritic set sang hearts and flowers to Uncle Tony for there is no doubt about it, he is the most charming and eligible senior citizen bachelor to hit our own in a long time.

THIS WEEK.....we point with pride to Dr. Andrew T. Kopan, professor of education at DePaul University, for writing to the National Broadcasting Company to protest the recent portrayal of an Orthodox priest, in the television series, "Taxi," who advised a communicant to commit adultery. In his letter to Grant Tinker, chairman and chief executive officer of NBC, Andy said, "As an Orthodox Christian, I denounce this episode as an insult to the Orthodox Church and as a compromise of the religious belief of millions of Orthodox Christians in the U.S. Andy continued, "I cannot comprehend with what mentality and naivete a major network such as NBC would approve of such a gross and crude sitcom based on blatant falsehood. It is a complete disregard of the sensibilities and cherished beliefs of moral people everywhere. I trust that your network will have the decency to make an apology for this unfortunate situation."

AND THEN......we have the talented and creative Bilder family. Color them successful, enthusiastic and imbued with the high energy level it takes to do a good job. From January 30-February 17, Dorothea Bilder, a teacher at Northern Illinois University, will have a one-woman art show at The Gallery, College of DuPage, Glen Ellyn.

Another creative member of the Bilder family, Chryssie Bilder Tavrides, also saturated with talent, recently won first prize for a portrait she painted entitled, "Dolly." The award-winning Chryssie currently makes her home in Lakeland, Florida.

While supposedly retired, gracious Angelo K. Bilder, patriarch of the triumvirate, still paints constantly in his LaGrange home, working in all media – oil, watercolor, pastel, and pen and ink. W.Clement Stone recently purchased many of his paintings at a recent one-man show.

ONE OF......our town's talented graphic artists, who possesses the business acumen of a Rockefeller, has purchased the Wrigley mansion, a

Chicago landmark. Title of the 1890s mansion was recently transferred to Nick Jannes, from the estate of Helen A. Wrigley, wife of Philip Wrigley, the late chewing gum magnate. The 40-room house has been vacant since 1931.

QUOTE OF THE WEEK: "Young people know less than we do, but they understand more; their perception has not yet been blunted by compromise, fatigue, rationalization, and the mistaking of mere respectability."

"Each inanimate object in the world seems to reach out and rub up against an injured finger; and so it is with an injured psyche, which cannot see that the sensitivity resides within itself, not in the objects it encounters."

INTELLECTUAL GIANT.......Alexander Karanikas, Ph.D., has put a lot of work into his new and fascinating book, "Hellenes and Hellions," published by the University of Illinois Press. The book, which has been highly researched, is a monumental account of the presence in American literature of modern Greek character and is an outgrowth of parallel lifelong interests of Dr. Karanikas' heritage and his interest in literature. An honor graduate of Harvard University, the author received his doctorate degree from Northwestern University. His poems, articles and stories have appeared in many journals. One of his books, "Tillers of a Myth," won a Friends of Literature award.

PEOPLE ARE.......still talking about the talented children of John and Theo Bartholomew who once again entertained their guests at the family's annual Christmas Musicale held in the Bartholomew Lincolnwood home. Amelia and Georgette, both attractive and talented teenagers, and their younger brother, Michael, he of the adorable full and rosy cheeks, play the piano, the violin and the flute. Theo, a talented musician in her own right, accompanied her children on the piano during the Christmas Carol Session.

Amelia, daughter number one, was guest soloist with the Metropolitan Youth Symphony at a concert held at Orchestra Hall last May.

THE EVER.......active, Beatrice Marks, who has performed many philanthropic deeds for the Greek Orthodox Church, was honored at a luncheon which took place in the Grand Ballroom of the Knickerbocker Hotel. His Grace Bishop Iakovos of the Greek Orthodox Diocese of Chicago, and the Diocesan Ladies Philoptochos Council honored Bea for the services she has performed as past president of the Chicago Diocese Philoptochos.

Currently vice-president of the National Ladies Philoptochos Board, Bea received the title of Archondesa from the late Patriarch Athenagoras, and she received a cross and an award from the late Patriarch Beneditos of Jerusalem. She is the first life member of the National Ladies Philoptochos Board, as well as the Chicago Ladies Philoptochos Board. Bea recently received a proclamation from the State of Illinois naming her Church Woman of Chicago. Married to the late George Marks, she has served as president of the St. Andrew's Women's Club and is currently serving on the parish council.

WONDERFUL TO......know that some of our up and coming young adults are bright enough to finish college in a span of three years. One of those is handsome Kevin Price, son of Bill and Holly, who received his Bachelor's degree in chemistry and physics from Purdue University in a span of three years. Mama Holly is the immediate outgoing president of the St. Demetrios (Chicago) Philoptochos.

QUOTE OF THE WEEK: "Whenever we have an argument with ourselves, the side that usually loses is the one that shouts, 'You shouldn't!' and the side that usually wins is the one that whispers, 'You deserve it.'"

"Few things are more disconcerting than being utterly agreed with by a person whose general views you find revolting." – Harris

WITH A.....sparkle in her dazzling brown eyes, a blush in her cheeks, and a sensational fresh, young smile, Elaine Bakakos, daughter of Judge Peter and Kiki Bakakos, was married to one of our town's most eligible bachelors, Gregory Papas, son of Dina Papas Bacaintan, and the late Spiro J. Papas on December 4th, at Sts. Peter and Paul Greek Orthodox Church, with both the Reverend George J. Scoulas and the Reverend John Kutulas officiating. Elaine wore an exquisite peau de soie wedding gown setting off the tiniest of waists and spilling out into full and gracious folds. Her fragile fingertip veil was caught by a jeweled head band worn on her forhead in the newest and most avant-garde looks.

The shiny-tressed picture-pretty bridesmaids looked delicious in their super rich, deep blue velvet skirts and white waist length Victorian styled blouses with balloon sleeves and high necks. The outfits were topped off with white gloves and small blue velvet cocktail hats on which poufs jauntily perched giving the entire outfit a flirtatiously Victorian sophistication.

The cocktail dinner reception at the Ritz Carlton was a pull-out-all-the-stops production that exceeded the most ambitious fantasies of even a Perle Mesta. It was a four-star event. Then there was dancing, dancing, and more dancing to the music of Perry Fotos. The handsome couple will honeymoon throughout Europe.

AND TODAY......the world suddenly became very sad as I learned of the untimely death of a very dear family friend, Curt Lulias, whom most of us knew from the days he had a concession at No-Man's Land – where posh and elegant hi-rises now stand. Curt was Mr. No-Man's Land himself as we were growing up, and there is no one that did not know him. He cut a beautiful figure in his perennial tan and crew-cut – a guy who looked like a model in a pair of shorts – as every girl could attest to.

Beloved Curt died on December 8th, just four days following the marriage of his niece, Elaine Bakakos to Greg Papas. Everyone at the wedding knew that Curt had been hospitalized and that he was critical – but none of us realized how critical until we heard of his death. Curt was a lifelong resident of Wilmette where his parents ran the family restaurant – the former Curt's Resturant at 601 Green Bay Road for more than 50 years. He is survived by his lovely wife, Helen; a son, Curt Jr.; three daughters, Cheryl, Jennifer and Allison; and a sister and brother-in-law, Kiki and Judge Peter Bakakos.

CUPID'S ARROW.....HAS STRUCK AGAIN. This time it aimed at the hearts of the offspring of two of our best known celebrities – Bud and Georgia Photopoulos. Son Jim and his love, Ellen Neubauer, will middle-aisle it in April; daughter, Kerry will become one with Andrew Simerman of Ft. Wayne, Indiana, in September.

QUOTE OF THE WEEK: "Money and time are the heaviest burdens of life, and the unhappiest of all mortals are those who have more of either than they know how to use." - Johnson

"Hearing a lie told about ourself is never as painful as hearing the truth; a lie merely fills us with healthy indignation. The truth can paralyze us with dismay."

ONE OF........our town's most powerful forces, Nicholas J.Melas, former president of the Metropolitan Water Reclamation District of Greater Chicago, was honored recently when the Centennial Fountain was dedicated and named the Nicholas J.Melas Water Reclamation District of Greater Chicago Centennial Fountain at ceremonies held at the river front. This was a well-deserved honor for a man who has served the district, the city of Chicago and the Greek-American community in a manner unlike any other individual.

Bursting with energy throughout his tenure, Nick's performance at the district will never be matched by any other force. Friends, relatives, those in high office in Illinois and two of our pastors, Reverend Byron Papanikolaou and Reverend Chris Kerhulas, held the torch up high for Nick as they spoke of him in glowing terms. Introduction of distinguished guests was made by Commissioner Gloria Alitto Majewski.

A few weeks later, Nick and his family took the big bird to Baltimore where, on behalf of the Association of Metropolitan Sewerage Agencies, the Awards Committee of that powerful body had selected Nicholas to receive its Public Service Award – an award given annually to a public official who has exhibited a particular awareness of the challenges faced by municipal waste matter treatment agencies.

AND A……fun evening was enjoyed by all those attending the graduation party of Harold Pavlakos, son of Dino and Jean Pavlakos of Oak Brook. Held on Sunday, May 23rd at the Carlisle in Lombard, Harold rode the magic carpet of happiness the whole night through.

Loving words about Harold were uttered by proud papa, Dino, and by Harold's godfather, Chris Kalogeras. Talented Harold, who graduated from the University of Illinois in Champaign, majored in psychology and was his own DJ at the party.

A CELEBRATION…..of laughter, love and intense happiness permeated the village of Leonidion on May 23rd, when a cuddley bunch of femininity was given the baptismal name of Avra, in memory of her late and beloved young aunt, Avra, who died a few years ago. First-born child of Dena and Iakovos Platis, she is the granddaughter of two well-known Chicagoans, Soto and Phyllis Colovos. A bevy of friends and relatives took the big bird out of O'Hare to attend this once-in-a-lifetime event. Among them were her parents and grandparents, Dena Colovos, Peter Colovos, Angeline and Tina Chiropulos and Jennifer Rochester. It was a love-in when paternal grandfather, Panagioti Platis, first met his granddaughter.

Following a stay in Leonidion and then Athens, Soto and Phyllis flew to Cairo, Egypt, where they embarked on the luxurious Presidential World Tour and Cruise. Then the peripatetic Colovos' connected with yet another tour to the Holy Lands – then back to Greece and home.

"PIN A.......Medal on Me Daddy" was the theme song of State Representative Samuel Maragos of our town who recently received a medal from the Illinois Optometric Association during the group's annual conclave held at the Peoria Hilton in Peoria.

QUOTE OF THE WEEK: "There is no way to know yourself except to allow yourself to be known to another, fully and freely; this is why introspection as a means of self-knowledge or self-fulfillment is a dead end."

"The hardest way for a man to earn money is by marrying it." – West

SLATED TO....open at the Royal-George Theater, 1641 N. Halsted, for an open-ended run is the exciting play, "Steel Magnolias," a play written by Robert Harling that proved to be a smash broadway hit. The Hellenic Professional Society of Illinois has picked up on this hit. On November 12th, the HPSI has planned an exciting evening which will include attending this hit and dining at the adjacent Café Royal. The evening will include a pre-show buffet dinner at 6:30pm, a theater ticket for the 8pm show, and pastries during intermission.

THE WORLD.......is a great deal sadder since the death of one of the most charming senior citizens in our town, 94-year-old Charles Limpert of Lincolnwood. Our family has known this most affable man since I was a moppet – and a more dapper and debonair gentleman did not exist. He is survived by his widow, Diana, his daughter and son-in-law, Tula and Gus Mazarakis and two grandchildren Tom and Daphne.

AN UNUSUAL.....Memorial Day was spent by all those invited to an outing by dear friend, Sophia Koretzky. What with inclement weather – and so forth – everyone ended up in Sophia's high-rise apartment giving her an "A" for being able to handle such a big crowd on such short notice.

THIS WEEK......we point with pride to Andrew A. Athens, national chairman of United Hellenic American Congress, who was lauded in the October 10th issue of *Crain's Chicago Business.* The article on Andy, entitled, "A Quiet Man Raises Big Bucks for the Duke," pointed him out as one of the biggest fund-raisers nationally for the democratic presidential nominee reversing a democratic tradition of lagging fund-raising efforts for presidential campaigns in Illinois. Early last year, he had raised $20,000 for a George Bush fund-raiser. The article pointed out that Andy has always remained politically neutral. A Dukakis fund-raising event in Chicago late last month brought in about $2 million, far more than any democratic presidential nominee has raised in the state.

TWO OF....our town's greatest scholars, Andrew and Alice Kopan, recently had a private audience with His Holiness Patriarch Demetrios at the Ecumenical Patriarchate in Istanbul. His Holiness received Professsor and Mrs. Kopan at his office in the Phanar. The audience took place during the 14th Annual DePaul University tour to Europe.

IN CELEBRATION....of its 60th anniversary, the St. Demetrios Greek Orthodox Church of Chicago will hold its Diamond Jubilee Ball, November 5th at the O'Hare Marriott Hotel. According to Paul Stamos, Alex Kopsian and George Atsaves, co-chairmen, the ball will highlight 60 years of Christian service to the community.

QUOTE OF THE WEEK: "In times of misfortune, we are prone to reflect that we do not deserve such unhappiness, but in times of felicity, it rarely occurs to us that we are equally undeserving of such happiness."

"A marriage vow is a blank check, written in a fit of hysteria, filled in for an impossible sum, and when subsequently presented for cashing returned for 'insufficient funds.'"- Harris

THIS TYPEWRITER…….is typing rave reviews on Andrew T. Kopan, professor of education, who was lauded and applauded at his recent retirement party hosted by the DePaul University School of Education on September 16th. Held in the Commons Building on campus, Andrew received accolades for his distinguished career. He was applauded for his academic work by students and friends alike (including colleague, Dr. John P. Graven), all of whom had nothing but praise for him. Eleven professors spoke about his achievements in glowing terms giving those present a picture of Andrew the scholar; Andrew the teacher; Andrew the friend.

Always an academic achiever, his colleagues also spoke of him as an originator – an originator of organizations all formed under his direction. Author of several books, "The School in Modern Society, Rethinking Educational Equality and Education and Greek Immigrants in Chicago, 1802-1973," and the co-author of another, "Rethinking Urban Education: A Sourcebook of Contemporary Issues." His most recent achievement is, "The Greeks of Chicago, the Role of Education in the Americanization Process," published by the University of Illinois Press.

Andrew's research has concentrated on educational foundations, particularly urban education, equality of educational opportunity, academic standards and ethnicity and education. His work has been recognized internationally, and he has served as consultant in England, Greece and Israel. He is the recipient of numerous awards – including special citations from the University of Texas and Yeshiva University in New York.

AND THE…….dream that many Greek-Americans have held for many years will soon become a reality. The Greek American Nursing Home project is now underway – but it needs your help to become a reality. Under the terms of the contract, the balance of $385,000.00 is due by November 10 (1994) in order to take off. Earnest money in the amount of $40,000.00 has been paid. Now the committee needs everybody's help in order for the project to begin. Site for the home is Wheeling, Illinois, and it will be built on eight rustic acres. The home will be a full service state-of-the-art facility and will accept both Medicaid and

Medicare. Dr. and Mrs. Theodosis Kioutas invite each and every one of you to support this much-needed project.

AND THERE.....will soon be another pretty bride walking down the aisle. The date will be December 30th and the forthcoming nuptials those of Sia Demeros, daughter of Arthur and Athena Demeros, to Anthony Karkazis, son of Dr. Lambros and Euthemia Karkazis. Vivacious Sia is a school marm with lots of smarts, while Anthony is the owner of North Shore Turf.

AND A.......happy, happy birthday to Scorpios all over the country – particularly to the three very special people whose natal day – November 18 – I share: James Corolis, Daisy Farmakis and Dee Tzakis. This year's Scorpio bash will be hosted by yours truly. The usual Scorpio entourage will attend – Helen Anthony, Dr. William Kagianis, John Graven and Nicholas Contos – all part and parcel of our Scorpio world.

THIS WEEK.....we point with pride to handsome bachelor, Vasili Russis, son of Jim and Connie Russis of Glenview, who not only passed his CPA exam a few years back, but also passed his bar exam last week making him one of the youngest CPA/lawyers in our community.

QUOTE OF THE WEEK: "An old man complaining that 'things aren't the way they used to be' rarely includes himself in that appraisal."

"It is easier to forgive someone who injures us than someone who does us no harm but regards us with polite contempt; we can grudgingly respect power, but we can only resent the cool assumption of superiority."

BE ON.....the lookout for a tall, slim, fair-haired young man, who goes under the name of Brian Smenos, for he bears the mark of explosive happiness. He captured the heart of a tall-stemmed beauty, known in certain circles as Ginie Seno, while sharing a classroom together at Bradley University in Peoria. They are armed with plans for a February 2nd wedding.

ONE OF.......our town's artistically inclined, Dena Anastos of Morton Grove, recently held a grand opening of her "Dena's Flowers." The shop features original designs of fresh, silk and dried flower creations that would add a touch of class to any home. It is located at 4350 W. Touhy in Lincolnwood.

OUR HEART......goes out to two very wonderful people, Evelyn and Andrew Demetrius of Glenview, over the death of their son, Mark. Evelyn, who is one of Sts. Peter and Paul's sunniest personalities, and her Andrew, have a multitude of friends who are trying to help ease the pain and grief of losing a son.

IN CLASS.....and a grand sweeping style, A.T. Tsoumas and his lovely wife, recently hosted a cocktail party honoring Governor and Mrs. Dan Walker at Sage's East. While I had to send my regrets, my special wire tap service tapped out.....HUGE SUCCESS.

VERSATILE AND.....talented Nick Poulos, *Chicago Tribune* staff writer and former president of the Chicago Press Club, has left the *Chicago Trib* to join the First National Bank of Chicago as vice-president in charge of domestic and international press relations. Nick's stint at the *Trib* has included services as assistant financial editor, financial editor and financial columnist.

GREAT TO.....see an article in the Tempo/Food-Health Section of the *Chicago Tribune* on Helen Kavathas of Wilmette. Wife of attorney Sam and mother of five, Helen has decided to share her Greek cooking tricks with other women by coming into their home, morning or afternoon, to help them prepare a Greek meal.

MY THANKS......to Georgia Mitchell of Glenview, president of the Choir Federation, for sending me a complimentary copy of a most beautiful liturgy recording sung by the members of the Federation. The record features selections from the Holy Liturgy of St. John Chrysostom set to music and conducted by Professor Michael Petrovich. The cover of the album is a photograph of the Madonna and Child Mosaic which adorns the apse in the Holy Sanctuary of Sts. Peter and Paul.

QUOTE OF THE WEEK: "The only true wisdom is in knowing you know nothing." - Socrates

"Hearing a lie told about ourself is never as painful as hearing the truth; a lie merely fills us with healthy indignation; the truth can paralyze us with dismay."

YOUNG BEAUTY...in its most radiant and refreshing form – fresh, fragrant, with breezy hair crackling with life and lights; clear, unwilting skin and innocent eyes capable of moving mountains – was in abundance at the recent St. Helen's Celestial Soiree and Debutante Cotillion. Sponsored by the St. Helen Women's Club, auxiliary of Sts. Constantine and Helen Church, Palos Hills, the annual event was held in the Grand Ballroom of the Conrad Hilton Hotel on June 11th.

This year's spring bouquet of debs consisted of the following rosebuds: Chrystyan Akathiotis, Debbie Lynn Alles, Maryanne Andreakis, Mary Lee Becharas, Holly Eloise Brotsos, Maribeth Brown, Maria Gina Chakos, Angela Koconis, Deanne Marie Liaros, Kathleen Pappas, Margo Lynn Rigas, Cynthia Dine Sampalis, Colleen Demetra Stamos, Marcia Anthe Tzakis, Christina Maria Vusikas, Constance Yiannas. Their escorts – 32 in number – included such handsome young men as Gary Pappas, Steve Betzelos, Alex Childs, Nick Tzakis and Lee Bakakos – to name a few.

The cotillion, which had the very good looking and talented John Drury of Channel 7 TV as its master of ceremonies, was first presented in 1965 under the chairmanship of Dee Tzakis.

As we were leaving the cotillion we saw George and Helen Assimos of Wilmette smiling from ear-to-ear so happy and proud were they. They had just attended the commencement exercises of the Loyola Stritch School of Medicine (held at the Hilton) at which their super bright son, Dean, had received his M.D. degree. Accompanying this proud trio were his grandparents, Gus and Angeline Assimos, Mrs. Manos (Helen's mom) and Dean's younger brother, Steve.

IT'S THAT.....time again – for the annual picnic antipasto parade of souvlakia, Greek cheese, red tomatoes, slabs of cucumbers, hard rolls, baklava, hot loukoumades drenched in honey and sprinkled with cinnamon, steaming hot black coffee, ice cold beer, chilled red wine, mosquitos, a few flies, sun, rain, clouds, clear skies, cold weather, warm weather, hot weather, romances with nice Greek girls, romances with bad Greek girls, romances with some not-so-nice Greek boys, romances with some very nice Greek boys, Greek dancing, fun and games, aching feet, dusty feet, etc. But what would the summer be without these little ole Greek picnics. According to Jim Bartholomew, chairman, and Nick Dennis, president of the parish council, Sts. Peter and Paul's picnic special will take place on the church grounds on July 15, 16 and 17. They invite you all to attend this three-day ring-a-ding-ding event.

AND THE.......love bug has bitten Sophia Chiganos and Michael Stefanos whose wedding bells will chime oh so merrily on June 4th. Sophia, the daughter of the Reverend and Mrs. William Chiganos, is a student at Elmhurst College, majoring in speech. Michael, son of Mrs. Sophia Stefanos and the late Leo Stefanos, founder of Dove Candies, graduated from Northern Illinois, Magna Cum Laude. A certified public accountant, he is currently attending the University of Chicago working towards a Master's in Business Administration.

WE POINT........with pride to our dear friend, vivacious Elaine Markoutsas, who did a super special job once again in the writing of, "Are Men Afraid of You?" which appeared in the Lifestyle Section of the March 20th issue of the *Chicago Tribune.*

QUOTE OF THE WEEK: "The hinge of the future is on the door of the present. Keep men of honor and integrity in places of trust and you will not fear the future." –Martin De Vries

"When we repress a thought or feeling, we do not thereby get rid of it; for it inevitably takes its revenge by returning, far stronger, in a form that shocks us with its unexpected intensity."

SIZZLING ON.......the legal entertainment platter is our very own John H.Secaras of Kenilworth, who will be feted on February 27th at a luncheon to be held in the Empire Room of the Palmer House. A lawyer who is retiring after 42 years of federal service, John is being honored by the staff of the Chicago Regional Office of the Solicitor, U.S. Department of Labor.

The Secaras family is a family with lots of smarts. Wife, Mary, is an educator with many years of meritorious service both in the city and in the burbs; son, Harry, is a lawyer and his wife, Maria, is an audiologist; daughter, Katina, who holds a master's degree, is currently working as an occupational therapist at Evanston Hospital; and the baby of the family, Evangeline, is at theUniversity of Illinois working towards her PhD.

WHO COULD.....ever forget the adorable curley-headed moppet in the bib overalls who sang the Oscar Mayer ditty, "My bologna has a first name, it's O S C A R...." Well, the *Chicago Tribune* recently had an item on this little kid who is now a big kid. When the commercial began, Andrew Lambros was four-years-old and the commercial ran for 18 years – the biggest run for any commercial according to the *Trib.*

What is Andy doing today and what does he think of all of this? Well, he is now 25 years of age and the owner of the WM Adventures exotic pet store in Woodland Hills, California. Andy said, "I've been told that the commercial is one of the longest running in existence. It helped me through college. I did it once again on the Sally Jessy Raphael show, but I usually try not to," he added. Andy's dad is former Chicagoan, Ted Lambros and when he married the former Jeannie Lambros of California many years ago, they made California their home.

WHAT A.....way to begin the new year: On the mend following a nasty spill is cuz, Dina Gregory Bacaintan. Houseguest of her sister and brother-in-law, Aliki and Bill Bryant of MacLean, Virginia, Dina inadvertently mistepped her footing in the dark – landing on concrete – a fall of three feet. She is currently recuperating at the home of her daughter and son-in-law, Maria and George Cantonis of Bellaire, Florida.

CRUISING ON ......the high seas aboard Cunard's "Dynasty" are Helen and Alice Anthony, Peter and Daisy Farmakis and Chris and Marianthe Korbakis – all neighbors at their summer homes in Grand Beach, Michigan. Back from their cruise aboard Royal Caribbean's, "Monarch of the Seas" are Nick and Aggie Kafkis, Dino and Marie Leventis and Peter and Stephanie Anton. Back from Cancun. Mexico, after lapping in the luxury of the sun is the Nicholas Contos family from Brookfield – Nick, Stella, Marianne, Michael and Christopher. While doing the Orient scene were Gus and Joan Pappas, formerly of Chicago and currently residing in Naples, Florida.

QUOTE OF THE WEEK: "What most people fail to learn until too late, if ever, was tersely expressed by Freya Stark: 'There can be no happiness if the things we believe in are different from the things we do.'"

"The pathos in life is not that people have to suffer in order to grow, but that so many persist in suffering without growing."

A DELICATE.......floral array of tender, refreshingly sweet pink blossoms beautified the altar, while other blushing flowers, tied together by large pink satin ribbons and plucked at their fleeting moment of perfection, adorned the aisle pews at the wedding of Joy Elizabeth (Gigi) Childs to George P. Iliopoulos. The day was Sunday, October 9th, the time was four in the afternoon, and the place was Sts. Peter and Paul Greek Orthodox Church.

Daughter of Peter and Helen Childs of Northbrook, Gigi was given away in marriage by her father who was visibly moved as he held both his daughter's hands while escorting her down the aisle. Following the ceremony, guests stood in the receiving line outside of the Grand Ballroom at Marriott's Lincolnshire Resort to wish the newlyweds a lifetime of happiness together. Standing alongside Gigi and George were the groom's charming parents, Mr. and Mrs. Peter G. Iliopoulos, who had taken the big bird in from Tripoli to attend the nuptials and the events preceding them.

Among the out of town guests were the bride's aunt, Mrs. Nick Koukis (the former Mimi Tsioutsias) who had flown in from California to attend the nuptials.

WE BOW....our heads and let the tears flow freely over the death of beloved, Christine Bacouris, a most delightful lady who sucumbed a short time ago following a brief illness. I remember Christine when she wore her happiness on her sleeve – in the days when her father, Tom Andrianakos; her husband, John; and her handsome and talented architect son, Tommy – were all alive and well. And then – as fate would have it – within a brief span of time Christine lost all three of her loved ones making life a lot more difficult to endure. But endure she did, handling herself like a Trojan, with the love and devotion of her sister-in-law and her husband, Glykeria and Alex Lamperis.

AND IT......was smooth landing for Lou Malevites and some business associates who recently took a three-week trip to the Orient on business making stops in Tokyo, Taiwan, Hong Kong, and Singapore. Ryookoo wa tanoshi katta ds ka, Lou?

SMASHING TIME......was had by all those attending the recent cocktail party hosted by bachelor Bill Kagianis, DDS, in his Park

Ridge home. Bill gave us all a taste of "heaven" with his succulent hors d'oeuvres, wickedly concocted cocktails, and a lovely lady who provided the background music by strumming on her harp.

AND OUR ……..very own Dena Anastos of Morton Grove, wife of Attorney Themis, was recently appointed Republican committee woman of Niles Township. From what I can ascertain, I believe Dena is the first Greek committee woman to be so appointed.

QUOTE OF THE WEEK: "You will find, as you look back upon your life, that the moments that stand out, the moments when you have really lived, are the moments when you have done things in the spirit of love." – Henry Drummond

"When a person says with great finality, 'I know my own mind,' what he commonly means is that his feelings have ordered his mind to stop thinking on the subject."

TOTALLY AFFECTIONATE…..group of people, numbering over 70, gathered together at an ingeniously shower-dinner party with a 50's-60's dance theme – to honor pretty Melanie Corolis and her fiancée, Dr. Nick Chionis. Hosted by Debra Price Prodromos, cousin of the bride, and Holly Price, Melanie's aunt, it was held at the 50's-60's place in Glenview – P.J. Moondoggies.

Everyone present attacked the succulent platters of hors d'oeuvres with gusto – again and again and again – so delicious were they. Dinner was followed by dancing. Highlight of the evening was the giant three level cake fit for a wedding.

THIS WEEK…….we point with pride to our very own, Nicholas J. Melas, president, Metropolitan Water Reclamation District of Greater Chicago, for master-minding and executing the dedication of the

Centennial Fountain. The event was one of the most impressive that I have ever attended and our Nick was lauded and applauded by many who took the podium – especially Neil Hartigan, attorney general of the state of Illinois.

Mayor Richard M. Daley gave the welcome and Nick was master of ceremonies. The activation of the fountain and water arc was accomplished by all of the board of commissioners. The Metropolitan Water Reclamation District's Centennial Fountain and its water are over the Chicago River. The event commemorated the district's 100 years of protecting the water supply of Lake Michigan and the health of the people of Chicago and suburban Cook County. Clean water is the Metropolitan Water Reclamation District's commitment to future generations.

THE WORLD......is a great deal sadder since the death of super terrific aunt, Toula Fotopoulos, who succumbed recently at Evanston Hospital following a brief illness. She had a legion of friends – among them the ladies at the Hollywood House – where she resided the last nine years of her life. Wife of the late and beloved, Gus, she is survived by her daughter, Elayne (Chris) Pappas; a son, Perry (Connie) Fotos; four grandchildren – John (Judy) and Gary Pappas; Dana (Peter)Nikoloulis; Curt Fotos; two great grandchildren, Katie and Christopher.

A COUPLE.......formerly hooked on education and currently hooked on travel, John and Ann Graven, were in London during the recent "weather blitz" and can now attest to the fact that Chicago is not the Windy City – but London is. The Gravens took a sojourn to London and were caught in that city's schizophrenic weather pattern. Even though planes were cancelled and the airport was pandemonium for two days, they got through it all with ease and grace and can now regale friends with fascinating tales.

THE TENDER.......trap has caught pretty Alyssa Kosner, who recently pledged her troth to handsome, George Kafkis, son of Nicholas and Aggie Kafkis. The coosome twosome will become one in July.

FUN FILLED……Acapulco was the winter playground for two handsome hunky bachelors from Deerfield – Dr. Frank Karkazis and Anthony Karkazis, who came back from across the border deliriously happy. Mexican fever is still running rampant in their veins.

QUOTE OF THE WEEK: "Ever since our love for machines replaced the love we used to have for our fellow man, catastrophes proceded to increase." Man Ray

"Everything we have, including life itself, is simply on loan to us; and the greatest mistake, creating the greatest misery, is to regard such as permanent possessions 'belonging' to us by right – for not even our children 'belong' to us, as possessive parents quickly discover."

BE SURE……to be glued to your boob tube on April 2nd, when our very own native son, young and spectacularly talented, Billy Zane, will appear on Channel 5's movie of the week, "The Hillside Strangler," along with veteran actor Richard Crenna and Chicago's Dennis Farina. Billy has appeared nationwide on TV in many outstanding movies, one of which was a major role in one of Angela Lansbury's, "Murder She Wrote" episodes a short time ago. Billy's latest movie, "Dead Calm," will open nationwide in theatres all over the country on April 7th. A thriller, it is about a married couple, just getting over a personal tragedy, encountering a stranger while cruising the Pacific. The movie also stars Sam Neill and Nicole Kidman.

MAKING HISTORY……for years for his good deeds and philanthropic causes is Andrew A. Athens, president of Metron Steel Corporation, and national chairman of the United Hellenic American Congress, who will once again be bestowed with honors in Washington, D. C. The Athens clan will take the big bird to the nation's capitol to see their beloved, Andy, hosted by Belgium Ambassador Dehennin at the

Belgium Embassy in Washington, where he will be presented with the Commander of King Leopold II Award. The first time he was honored by this government was back in 1979 when he was awarded the Order of the Belgium Crown for serving as chairman of the Midwest Chapter of the Belgium American Chamber of Commerce in Illinois. At the forthcoming luncheon he will be honored for playing a leading role in starting commerce between Belgium and America – in short – for serving as a liaison officer between the two governments. That same evening the Athens family will be transported to yet another embassy. This time the Greek Embassy – where a black tie dinner will be he held for him by Ambassador Papoulias.

ONE OF.......the most elegant social events on record was the recent gala dinner-dance benefiting The Judge James A. Geroulis Educational Foundation, held at the Westin Hotel. It featured an evening with comedienne, Phyllis Diller – and her show was great . From the nippy-tippy cocktail hour, to the delicious gourmet dinner and dancing to Franz Benteler and The Royal Strings, it was a magnificent evening and a love-in for the late and beloved Judge Geroulis. In attendance at this gala event were a gallery of personnages. Aside from the financial benefit that the Foundation received, it was an evening of fun.

ARTICLE WRITTEN.......by Pat Butler in a recent issue of *Sky Line* was all about Jean Fardulli, opera star, translator, entrepreneur, and a most dapper and refined gentleman. The article relates some of the antics and achievements of Jean who still wears the purple decoration he received from the French government more than 50 years ago for his contributions to the arts. Having visited the Fardulli family residence on Pearson Street, I can honestly say that it is loaded with fascinating mementos – ranging from an autographed photo of longtime friend, Maurice Chevalier, to a 14th century icon given to him by a Russian priest during a 1952 visit to Moscow.

QUOTE OF THE WEEK: "It requires a secure sense of maturity to accept the fact that what people say about us is always true-not our truth perhaps, but theirs, and equally valid in the final equation of the personalities." - Schiller

"Pretty clothes are like husbands. They should be easy to take care of.. They should be made out of the right fiber. And they shouldn't cost you a fortune." – Susan Rahn

PLAUDITS TO.......John P. Graven, PhD, educator, achiever and good friend of long standing, who recently was honored by his friends and colleagues at a retirement dinner given at the Martinique Restaurant. It was a love-in for John who was surrounded by luminaries in the field of education and devoted friends. Special recognition comments were made by Harry Mark Petrakis, illustrious author and lecturer, and well-known educator, Dr. Joseph E. Lee.

Distinguished scholar with an outstanding scholastic background, John's extensive teaching career reached its peak as principal of Taft High School. During his tenure there, he became one of the most popular high school principals in the city of Chicago. This was evidenced by the honors he received from both his teaching staff and his students at the time he left his position as principal of Taft to climb to yet another ladder as assistant superintendent of the Department of Operation Services, Board of Education.

Recognition has been given to John numerous times during his career. A few of the awards he received include: Service to Youth Award, Archer Road Kiwanis; Outstanding Principal's Award, Citizen's School Committee; Chicago Ambassador Award for service to youth; Outstanding Educator Award from the Hellenic Council on Education.

Married to the former Anastasia Peters (another educator), they have often been referred to as the Alfred Lunt and Lynn Fontaine of education.

BURSTING THEIR …buttons with pride are Jim and Bess Maros whose oldest daughter, Sandra, received her MBA from Georgetown University this weekend. Smart as a whip, Sandra, was guest speaker at the graduation ceremonies – along with Jean Kilpatrick, former U.S. representative to the United Nations.

ONE OF……the saddest moments of my life took place on February 20, when "bestest" friend, Harriet Lamperis Andrews, succumbed following a less than two month bout with acute leukemia. It was a devastating shocker to all of us for Harriet was radiant and full of life with not the slightest indication of ill health. She entered Northwestern Pavillion on December 28th and died six weeks later. Fun-loving, vivacious and quick on the draw, Harriet was a marvelous companion and her loyalty and devotion to her friends was unwavering. She is survived by her parents, Alex and Glykeria Lamperis, and her sister and brother-in-law, Maggie (Jim) Alexander.

GRIEF HAS…….clutched the hearts of everyone who knew handsome and, oh so charming, 24-year-old Craig Thomas Gallanis, who was recently killed in a tragic auto accident in North Carolina. A graduate of Northwestern University, he was an honor student and had served as rush chairman of his fraternity, Alpha Tau Omega. At the time of his death, he was in his third year at Bowman Gray School of Medicine, Wake Forest University, where he had been ranked as sixth scholastically in a class of 110 students. Besides his mother, Helen and his father, Dr. Gallanis, he leaves his sister, Kathy, two grandmothers, aunts and uncles, and many first cousins.

QUOTE OF THE WEEK: "Human nature, as a whole, is somewhat manic-depressive, for things are never quite as good or quite as bad as we think they are."

"What the essential difference between the wise man and the ignorant man boils down to is that the wise man will often know without judging; the ignorant man will judge without knowing." – Harris

SHOWCASE FOR.....the new breed of big beautiful dolls with freshly laundered hair and shining eyes, who will make their debut at the forthcoming St. Helen's Annual Debutante Cotillion, was the recent presentation luncheon given under the auspices of the St. Helen Women's Club at the Westin O'Hare Hotel in Rosemont. About 375 ladies of assorted sizes and shapes came to wine and dine while sneaking peaks at the new crop of pretties who will be presented on July 1st.

Frosting on this afternoon tea cake was the bevy of lovely post-debs – some from last year – some from the first cotillion of 25 years ago – who returned to the runway displaying a beautiful collection of sensational white floor length gowns. Dee Tzakis, 25th cotillion chairwoman, gave a short biographical sketch of each new deb as she and her mother approached the podium. Mrs. Spiro Chionis, president of St. Helen's, presented each deb with a floral remembrance.

WE POINT......with pride to Jennifer Marlas, talented violinist, who has stirred the musical world with her extraordinary talent. Pretty 18-year -old, Jennifer, a recent graduate of New Trier High School in Winnetka, has credentials that are amazing for one so young. Certainly, in the past year her name has become a household word in the Chicago Greek-American talent world.

She began studying the violin at the age of six. Currently, she is a student of two greats, Almita and Roland Vamos at The Music Center of the North Shore in Winnetka. In 1988, Jennifer was a finalist in the National Arts Recognition and talent Search Competition. In 1987, she was a finalist in the Seventeen Magazine/General Motors National Concerto and Chicago Symphony/Illinois Bell Young Performers Competition. First prize Placements included the 1985 Junior Division of the Fischoff National Chamber Music Competition, the 1987 Union League Musical Art Competition and the St. Paul Federal Musical Arts Competition.

Her performances are far too numerous to mention in this short space. Suffice it to say that she has been lauded, applauded and 'bravoed' by the finest impresarios in the country. The award-winning violinist recently performed in a Master Class for the Suzuki Teachers of America Convention. This summer, Jennifer will return to Musicorda Music Festival in Massachusetts and, in the fall, she will attend Indiana University where she will be a student of violin master, Joseph Gingold, who taught Isaac Stern.

TIME DID.......not permit me to attend the recent press luncheon held on September 8th, in honor of the Minister of Culture for Greece, Madam Melina Mercouri, at the residence of His Eminence, Archbishop Iakovos. At this luncheon Madame Mercouri announced the national launch of the exhibition, Holy Image, Holy Space:Icons and Frescoes from Greece, on display at the Walters Art Gallery in Baltimore, Maryland. The exhibition's curator, Dr. Gary Vikan, gave a slide presentation and discussed the important exhibition which actually comprises 70 Byzantine icons and frescoes from the 10th to the 16th centuries, including early works by El Greco.

QUOTE OF THE WEEK: "We try to make our children become more like us, instead of trying to become more like them-with the result that we pick up none of their good traits, and they pick up most of our bad ones."-Harris

"Blessed are those who give without remembering and take without forgetting." Elizabeth Biobesco

FELT A......great surge of sadness when I learned of the death of Father John Hondras of Clearwater, Florida. My mind went back in time to the years he was parish priest at St. Andrew, and I fondly recalled cherished memories of this unique priest who served his flock long and well. A no-

nonsense man, there was no hypocrisy in his character. Father John always told it like it was – a rare and admirable trait. He had an abundance of sarcastic wit that kept us all on our toes; a brilliant mind that exercised our thinking process every time he gave a sermon. He was respected as a priest and adored as a human being who understood human foibles. Our sincere condolences to his wife, Lou, and to his three children.

WE EXTEND….our sympathy to the family of yet another warm and mellow senior citizen, Alex Lamperis, who succumbed on September 4th. His family – his beloved widow, Glykeria, and his lovely daughter, Maggie, and her husband, Jim Alexander – are wearing their hearts at half-mast for the second time this year. First to go was the Lamperis' oldest daughter, Harriet Andrews, who died in February.

MEMBERSHIP DRIVE….is being conducted by The Greek Women's University Club. Qualifications include the following: prospective applicants must be Greek or of Greek descent and graduates of a four year college or university accredited by the North Central Association of Colleges and Secondary Schools. Applicants must submit a xeroxed copy of their diploma. All applications and necessary papers must be submitted before October 15, 1988.

IT'S THAT…….time again – so mark your calendar for Friday, October 7th. On that day, the Hellenic Interlude Radio Show, "The Voice of the Greek Americans," Yiannis and Antigone Lambros will celebrate 27 years on the air. The cocktail-dinner-dance celebration will be held at the Fountain Blue of Des Plaines.

THIS WEEK…..we point with pride to Joanna Collias, daughter of Nick and Jane Collias of Burr Ridge, a 17-year old volleyball super-star on the Mother McAuley varsity volleyball team. Joanna was featured in the October 24th issue of the *Chicago Tribune* for her athletic prowess. A second-string player on the team, she made it to captain within the short span of a year. An honor student, Joanna has kept up a 3.58 grade point average.

ONE OF…….our town's most prominent architects, George Pappageorge, was recently lauded and applauded by an audience of 600 crème de la crème guests as he stood at the podium and accepted the Residential Interior Architecture Award. The occasion was the Design Ball held at the Chicago Hilton and Towers. Son of Chris and Gloria Pappageorge, talented George has been consistently honored by his peers for excellence in residential design.

QUOTE OF THE WEEK: "Woman is like a private fortress, and men who regard her like a public building are always shocked and surprised, after they have successfully gone past the 'No Entrance' sign, to find on the other side an even more implacable sign reading 'No Exit.'"

"I really had a rough childhood. Even my rocking horse died." Anonymous

OUR TOWN…….recently suffered a devastating loss with the death of one of the most beloved gals in our town – good friend, Connie Geocaris Chrones, wife of Judge George Z. Chrones (Polychrones) and mother of Jeffrey. I don't think I know one person who ever said an unkind word about Connie for she abounded with real goodness. She had an easy sense of humor, a delightful laugh, and genuine fair play. Actually, you'd have to look long and hard to find two people who complemented each other as much as Connie and her George did – he with his unbelievable wit, and she with her warmth and sincerity. Connie fought the good fight with all of her might, and for those who knew and loved her – the world will now be a lot emptier without her. My deepest condolences to George, Jeffrey, her many brothers and sisters (Anastasia, Angelo, Bob, Carol, Jim, Becky and Sandy) and to her brother-in-law, Jim – for a real spark has been snuffed out of their lives.

THIS WEEK……we point with pride to Georgia and Bud Photopoulos for sharing their lives with all of us through their newly published inspiring book, "Of Tears and Triumph." We will all get a chance to purchase and receive autographed copies of this book at an autographing party which will take place at Kroch's and Brentano's, Water Tower Place, September 15th from 5:30pm to 7pm.

SUPER BEAUTIFUL......bash – attended by the veddy socially elite of McLean, Virginia – as well as out-of-town guests – was hosted by Bill Bryant of McLean – in honor of his wife's 50th birthday. And Aliki Gregory Bryant, formerly of Chicago, was indeed surprised when she returned home after a three-day holiday –to face greetings by over 300 guests. Bill's theme was the 1950's and all of those in attendance were dressed in accordance with the dress code of the '50's. It was great party time.

STRONG BONES......and a well-developed physique best describe Chris Brown, senior at Northern Illinois University, who entered the Collegiate Mr. Illinois Physique Championship contest at Southern Illinois University placing third in the state as Collegiate Mr. Illinois. Still going strong, he then entered the body building contest at Northern Illinois University, winning the title of Mr. University Plaza. Mr. Body Beautiful is the son of Peter and Helen Brown of Northbrook.

GONE LIKE.....the wind is another beloved and respected citizen, Peter Gust Theodore. The candle of Peter's life was snuffed out on May 15th, leaving his family and friends a lot sadder. A man filled with the spirit of fun and with a delightful sense of humor, Peter was a very devoted Christian who not only served his church, Sts. Peter and Paul, in many capacities during his lifetime, but also as its president. Our sympathy is extended to his children, Connie (Michael) Teska and Peter Theodore.

QUOTE OF THEWEEK: "Nobody realizes that some people expend tremendous energy merely trying to be normal." – Albert Camus

"The most obnoxious affectation is the affectation of blunt candor when it is only malice masquerading as honesty."

THE FAMILY……of Julia Stevens is wearing its heart at half-mast since her recent death following a lingering illness. She was the wife of the late and beloved, Basil E. Stevens, M.D., by far the greatest benefactor of St. Andrew's Greek Orthodox Church (the parish's Greek School was named after him). A devoted Christian who had been honored by the Red Cross following World War II for her organization of volunteers to make bandages, she was soft spoken,, charming, and one of the most elegant ladies of her era. Active in the parish of St. Andrew, she had served as president of the woman's club from 1944-46. She was preceded in death by her three sisters: Mrs. S.J. (Rita) Gregory, Mrs. Thomas (Bessie) Tubekis, and Mrs. Angelos (Tasia) Sofianopoulos.

I UNDERSTAND…….that a totally affectionate group of people, still filled with pazzaz and that fiery GOYA spirit, gathered together in Boston to have their reunion – after a lapse of ??????? years. It was a super reunion with much back-slapping, hugging and kissing. As a matter of fact – a very close friend of mine – Tasia Koutroulakis Argiris, formerly of Birmingham, Alabama, and now living in Lancaster, Pennsylvania, with her neurosurgeon hubby, Dr. James Argiris, stopped by our town following the reunion to break bread with some of her old time friends. And it was nostalgia time for many of us seeing that lovely Southern belle – the epitome of the South – still lovely and still with a thimble-size waist – despite three grown children.

BACHELORS ALL…..over the country could take lessons from Bill Kagianis, DDS, host of this year's gathering for the Scorpio in-clan birthday celebration for, as parties go, this one was strictly the top of the line. As guests slipped in from the cold into the nippy-tippy cocktail hour, their temperatures rose matching the warm hospitality of the host. From the elegant dinner held at the Courtier Club in Park Ridge, to the danceable music of the Demos Orchestra – it was a super happy event at which smiles were prolific and nimble feet were the hit of the evening.

SO VERY……happy to learn that good friend Billy Dare (Sedares) is currently starring at the Lake Point Tower Club in our town. The internationally known pianist/singer/comic has appeared in clubs in the U.S. and abroad and has received rave reviews. When Billy appeared at the Hilton Hotel in Nicosia, Cyprus, a columnist wrote, "Billy Dare is causing a problem at the Paddock Bar. His nightly non-stop combination of piano playing, patter and singing is packing the place so full, there is standing room only – and the Hilton management has run out of space. Early in the evening, Billy plays background music, but at 10 o'clock, Billy begins to swing. Judging by their reactions, the customers love it."

AND ONE…..of our most beloved priests, the Reverend Byron Papanikolaou, will be honored by his parish on December 4th at a testimonial dinner marking his 20 years as pastor of Sts. Constantine and Helen Greek Orthodox Church. One of the finest priests I have ever had the pleasure of knowing – Father Byron's great compassion and understanding of people has given him a legion of admirers who will be on hand to honor him. Chairman of the event is Mark Frank Manta.

QUOTE OF THE WEEK: "Not merely what we do, but what we try to do and why, are the true interpreters of what we are." - Woodward

"Parents who think they love their own children, but find other people's children annoying or deficient or blameworthy, don't really love their own, except as possessions or as extensions of their ego; for a person who genuinely loves trees might especially favor a tree growing on his front lawn, but would find all trees interesting and attractive, no matter where they grow."

IT IS……with a heavy heart that I write about the death of a 16-year-old angel, Nina Philippidis, daughter of Nick and Yvonne Phillipidis, who left our midst on October 29th following a bout with cancer. A love of a little girl, who had just turned 16 on September 29th, Nina was indeed the apple of her parents' eye for she was special in so many ways. No words I write will ease the pain in the hearts of the Philippidis family. I can only bow my head in prayer, along with the rest of their friends and relatives, and hope that God, in his infinite mercy, will ease the anguish in the hearts of Nick, Yvonne and their two sons.

PLAUDITS TO.....the United Hellenic American Congress and the Hellenic Council on Education. The two groups will honor Dr. Angeline Caruso, interim general superintendent of Chicago Public Schools, in a special award ceremony to be conducted on January 12th at the Illinois Athletic Club. Dr. Caruso will receive the "Socratic Award for Excellence in Education," which is being presented to her for her extraordinary ability in restoring the public schools of Chicago to economic solvency while maintaining educational quality. Her expertise in educational concerns that plagued the Chicago Schools during the recent financial crisis has earned her the respect and admiration of educators throughout the nation.

Dr. Caruso is the recipient of numerous recognitions and awards among which have been: Kellogg Foundation Fellowship (Harvard University); Educator of the Year, Kappa Delta Pi; Community Leader of America Award; Woman of the Year, National Council of Administrative Women in Education; Doctor of Humane Letters, DePaul University; Distinguished Alumna Award, Chicago State University, and many others which space precludes my mentioning.

ORCHIDS TO.....Themi Vasils, Theodora Vasils and Leon Marinakos for weaving together an outstanding program in observance of the 100th anniversary of the birth of Nikos Kazantzakis. The event, sponsored by the United Hellenic American Congress, was presented in conjunction with the Chicago Public Library Cultural Center on November 8th at the Center. The observance was highlighted by the appearance of Mrs. Helen Kazantzakis – wife of the late author – who has written, "Nikos Kazantzakis – A Biography" – as well as other works including a book on the life of Mahatma Gandhi. In addition to Mrs. Kazantzakis, three other authors graced the program: Harry Mark Petrakis, award-winning author of numerous novels and short stories; Studs Terkel, who has a daily program on Chicago's fine arts station WFMT; and Dr. George Anastaplo, professor of constitutional law and jurisprudence at Loyola University, School of Law.

MERRY TUNES....were crooned by Nick Tzakis, Helen Vaselopulos, Bess Wilson and Jim Stamos, who split the grand prize of $4,000 at the recent Smoker sponsored by The Women's Philoptochos of St. Andrew's Greek Orthodox Church. Each went home $1,000 richer. But we all had fun and ate a dinner catered by Patrick Papas whose cooking has been making history for quite some time now. He is the Guru of Cookdom on the North Shore.

QUOTE OF THE WEEK: "Lovers' quarrels are a way of testing their love, not repudiating it; they are a means of renewing love from the doubts, the apprehensions, and the fears that are attendant upon passion; and unless quarrels are too frequent or too fierce, they possess a self-healing quality."-Harris

"To act without impulsiveness, and to wait without anxiety, are the two surest signs of maturity; for neither of these can be done, at the proper time, by the neurotic personality."

VERY GENEROUS.....endowment was recently presented to Northwestern University by John N. Nicholson, M.D. at ceremonies conducted at Northwestern's Scott Hall. The ceremonies followed a luncheon for approximately 25 of Dr. Nicholson's closet friends. Many renowned names on the Northwestern roster were present at the ceremonies including our very own Dr. Charles Moskos and Dr. George Thodos.

Dr. Nicholson will present a yearly gift of $12,500 beginning in 1984, to support one fellowship for any one graduate student, in either the Evanston or Chicago campus of Northwestern, pursuing an M.A.or a PhD degree in basic science and/or engineering only, excluding the humanities and social services. The recipient of this fellowship must be a citizen of the U.S. preferably of Greek extraction. While the fellowship will begin in 1984, upon his death, Northwestern will receive the income of his gift to support seven or eight fellowships, preferably to those students of Greek extraction, annually forever, every year in perpetuity.

CONGRATULATIONS TO.....Alexandra Scoulas, daughter of the Reverend George and Presbytera Scoulas of Glenview, who recently graduated from the University of Chicago. A girl with lots of smarts, and with big, beautiful aquamarine eyes, Alexandra took the big bird to Greece this week for a well-earned vacation.

INTERESTING SPREAD.....on the Ethnic Kitchen/Greek appeared in the March 18th issue of the Graphic Section, *Chicago Tribune*. The article focused in on Mary Koulogeorge (Mrs. James) of Northbrook, who generously contributed her succulent recipes on Greek pastries. (I really got a kick out of the translations of these pastries: diples – honey curls; saragli – baklava pinwheels; galopita – custard pudding cake.)

Written by Joanne Will, the recipes in the Graphic Section looked tasty and the four-color one-page pastry spread, photographed from Mary's home, was especially outstanding. Taken by John Austad, the tsoureki – not to mention the other delectables – really looked mouth-watering.

EXCITING WEEKEND... was recently spent by Jim and Maggie Alexander. Jim, who planned and executed the Annual Midwest Meeting of the Frozen Food Association (of which he is executive director) invited President Gerald Ford to be the guest speaker. The Alexanders wined and dined with the former President who got rave reviews from both of them.

GREAT GURU……of broadcasting, George Collias, has announced that Century Broadcasting Company has acquired its first AM station, WAIT. Handsome bachelor, George, is chairman of the board of Century Broadcasting. Let's color George successful.

BETTER LATE…..than never to congratulate Bea Marks for executing a most memorable reception in honor of our new and beloved Bishop Iakovos, who now presides over 56 parishes in the Midwest. Held at the Continental Plaza following the enthronement, it boasted of an attendance that included everyone, at least that I know, in the city and its environs.

QUOTE OF THE WEEK: "The animosity between two persons who don't like each other and know it is negligible compared to the tension between two persons who don't like each other and won't admit it to themselves."

"The man who does things makes many mistakes, but he never makes the biggest mistake of all – doing nothing."

ONE OF…….the biggest shockers in the month of January was the sudden death of a beloved friend whom I had known since childhood. Peter G. Koconis of Whitewater, Wisconsin, died suddenly leaving his family and friends with a large void in their hearts. He had gone upstairs to change his shirt on Sunday afternoon, January 20th when he collapsed. His sudden and untimely death took the starch out of all of us who knew and loved him.

Pike, as we affectionately called him – even as children – was a "Gargle" and, in case you don't know what that is, it means that his parents hailed from Gargaliani, Greece. Most of our parents grew up together and migrated to America around the same time. That made us all a tightly knit family.

As teenagers we formed the Gargle Club which included friends and relatives alike – names familiar to everyone in the Chicago scene: Pike, his brother, Jimmy, Ann Pappas Smenos, Chris Pappas, Elayne Fotoplay Pappas, Perry Fotos, my sister, Irene, Bess Maros, Gus Pappas, Ann Savoy Zoros, Harriet Diacos Becharas, Nick and Danny Melas, Dorothy Lewis Melas, Dr. Harry Lithas, Katie Lithas Xeros, Penny Savoy Nielsen, Niko Geane, etc. Indeed, we had happy days together. We went to each others homes, we went on outings, we participated in plays, musicals, etc. Our greatest event was the hosting of a dinner for Vice-President Spiro Agnew. For all intents and purposes, he was one of us. Well – Pike was a charter member of that group – and one of its first leaders.

A native Chicagoan and a fellow Scorpio, he was married to the former Mary Assimos. We shall miss our good friend, Pike. He is survived by his wife, Mary; his children – Pam (Dean) Boosalis; his daughter, Angela; his son, George; his mother, Tula; and his brother, Jim (Helen).

A GAL…..with lots of creativity running through her veins, Teddie Vasils, recently had her translation of Nikos Kazantzakis' "Serpent and Lily" published. An autographing party for Teddie is scheduled to take place on March 26th at 4:30 pm at Lake Point Tower.

AND OH……yes – Jackie O made one of her rare appearances on Sunday afternoon last month at the Astoria Manor Restaurant, a mirrored and chandeliered banquet hall in New York. Nice Greek boys and girls who attended the event said that this was the first appearance of the reigning Regina, on behalf of her brother-in-law, Senator Ted Kennedy. Those in attendance said she wore a frozen countenance and a bewildered smile – for she was doing what she hates most – campaigning among the masses. But an appreciative audience of 1,200 Greek-Americans applauded her frantically and gave their hard-earned cash to Teddie's campaign. The draw was unmistakingly Jackie.

ACCORDING TO……a recent press piece in the *Chicago Tribune*, Chicago fashion designer, Becky Bisoulis, has been discovered by singing star, Natalie Cole, who wore one of her dresses on the Johnny Carson show. I also understand that Crystal Gale and her famous sister, Loretta Lynn, both own many of Bisoulis' lacey fashions.

QUOTE OF THE WEEK: "For every one person ruled by thought, a hundred are ruled by appetite; for every hundred ruled by appetite, a thousand are ruled by custom, fear and inertia."

"It is the free man who must win freedom for the slave; it is the wise man who must think for the fool; it is the happy who must serve the unhappy."

THE ENTIRE……..Greek community is buzzing about one of its most well-known celebrities, Georgia Photopulos – who recently received the coveted *Sun-Times* Thomas Jefferson Award. Valiant Georgia is one of 11 people chosen for the Jefferson Award for community service out of hundreds of names submitted by the public. Georgia's nomination letter was written by someone who knows her best – her husband of 22 years – handsome and amicable Bud, ABC-TV news correspondent. The loving tribute he wrote stated:

"Georgia is a cancer patient who has surmounted the pain, fear and anxiety created by the disease. Despite the fact that she bears unremitting pain from her own illness, and the after-effects of her treatment, she shows no outward indication that she suffers. She is, in fact, an inspiration to countless numbers of patients while working without respite to help them adjust to living after suffering man's most dreaded disease."

Georgia was honored by the *Sun-Times* at a luncheon held on March 21st with a bronze medallion bearing the Great Seal of the United States. The award winners will be considered for one of five $1,000 national Jefferson Awards to be presented in Washington, D.C. in July by the American Institute of Public Service.

DON'T FORGET ....to remember to attend the forthcoming 24th Festival of Leadership Awards Scholarship Banquet to be sponsored by the Little Flower Lay Board. The event is scheduled to take place on Saturday, May 17th, in the International Ballroom of the Conrad Hilton Hotel, and our very own Engie Gouletas has been named general chairlady of this year's festival. Engie was awarded the coveted "Business Woman of the Year" award at last year's banquet.

This year – as in past years – the greatest leaders in the Chicago area will be honored on that night. Among them is the spiritual leader of the Greek Orthodox Church in the Midwest – our beloved Bishop Iakovos. Honored alongside our revered bishop will be: Mayor Jane Byrne, Maria Talchief Paschen, DePaul's Coach Ray Meyer, Mrs. Len O'Connor, Ron Laurent and Mrs. Jewel LaFontant.

INTERESTING PIECE.......written by Jerry C. Davis in the June 10 issue of the *Chicago Sun-Times* tells about John Annes' new restaurant which opened at 161 E. Huron Street. According to John, his new restaurant will be known simply as "Johnny's," rather than the "Johnny's Steakhouse" name that was a loop institution for 25 years. John believes the restaurant business and the dining customer have changed so much that he will be launching an entirely different type of restaurant – nothing like the old steakhouse. He will retain only the steak items from his own menu, and balance the selection with at least six seafood items, and such exotic dishes as grilled breast of goose, salmon tournedos and steamed sea bass with fennel.

The sleek $1.1 million restaurant includes a series of five foot high booths with controlled lighting, a mezzanine, a separate bar with a piano, and considerable window expanse. His son, George, will manage the restaurant, marking the third generation of the family in the business.

QUOTE OF THE WEEK: "We are more ourselves when playing than when doing anything we deem serious, for the way in which we play reveals a deeper stratum of our personality than the careful postures of our adult activities."

"It's always the semi-cad who is the most careful to be proper about the little amenities, for he wants to preserve his reputation by concealing his character. It's only the man who is sure of his decent instincts who can afford to dispense with the amenities when necessary."

THE FIRST......rosebud was recently planted in the St. Haralambos Ladies Society garden of achievements when the society hosted its first annual luncheon-fashion show in the Guildhall of the Ambassador West Hotel. The neophyte group did everything they should have done to make their first event a smashing success – and a success it was from the warm reception accorded to the guests present – down to a menu chock full of goodies and fashions that reeked with glamour.

The showing moved with staccato-like precision beginning with Chicago designer – Babacho's originals – hand-painted silk creations that really made statements. Guests then feasted their eyes on daytime suits that sprung into action with their zip and zest. Frosting on this cake were some very special Bisoulis gowns modeled by pretties who practically shimmied down the runway. And while we ogled designer fashions with our ravenous eyes – our ears were turned into music from the '50's giving the showing an exciting upbeat mood. Congratulations to Helen Kanellos, president, and Linda Bilissis and Popi Vaselopoulos, chairladies.

TWO OF.......the most affable people in the world of communications are celebrating 19 years on the air – John and Antigone Lambros – who have filled us with news and, with their special charisma, have captured the hearts of their listeners. On October 18th, the Lambros' are sponsoring, "Interludes 1980," an annual dinner-dance and show spectacular hosted once a year in order to give John and Antigone an opportunity to meet their legion of admirers – their listeners. A fun-filled event.

AMERICAN INVSCO........has been making history for a decade now – and the company's 1980 Annual Awards Banquet, held in the

International Ballroom of the Conrad Hilton Hotel on October 24th, added yet another chapter to its success story. In attendance at this gala event were a gallery of personnages numbering well over 1,000 – some of whom had taken the big bird into our town to participate in the excitement of annual awards presented to those who – like spacecrafts had zoomed into the magical land of successful condominium selling.

Our hosts – Nick, Vic and Engie – who have become the real estate giants of the country in the last decade and who now reign majestically over Condominium Land – were on the podium welcoming their guests and passing out awards to those who made it. With the theme of, "Beginning our Second Decade," the awards banquet offered its guests a plethora of goodies: a nippy-tippy cocktail hour, a great dinner, the music of Franz Benteler and his Royal Strings, the talented voice of Jimmy Damon, and the frolicking humor of Joey Bishop, who served as master of ceremonies.

QUOTE OF THE WEEK: "There are two kinds of men who fear women: one kind holds them off at a distance so they cannot strike; the other kind clasps them so closely that they cannot strike. Thus both the misogynist and the Don Juan are displaying the same fear in directly opposite ways."

"We feel nothing but scorn for the husband who runs off and deserts his wife, but many a wife has deserted her husband in spirit and service and the world hears nothing of, so long as she continues to inhabit the same house." -Harris

AND A........whoop-de-doo time was had by all the beautiful people who attended the recent namesday party given by Aggie Kafkis for her husband, Nick, and her brother, Nick Jannes. The over 80 friends and relatives in attendance drank frothy cocktails, dined and danced till the wee hours of the morning. Son number two, handsome George Kafkis, came in from the University of Wisconsin for the occasion, and son number one, another gorgeous hunk, brought in all of his buddies to tend bar. Phyllis (Mrs. Soto) Colovos stole the show with her cake that measured about five feet across and spelled out NICHOLAS. Strictly a labor of love, it took three days to bake, cut, frost, mount, etc. Each initial was a cake and the base which carried the name NICHOLAS was also made of cakes. How the Colovos' got that concoction into their Caddie had to be the trick of the week. My "Baker of the Week" award to the talented Phyllis.

THIS WEEK……we point with pride to a pretty miss – Diana Heard by name – who is a contestant in the Miss Iowa USA contest. Diana is the daughter of Chuck and Katherine Heard and the granddaughter of Bill and Martha Russis. Diana – indeed a beauty – is a freshman at Iowa State University. Special aside: modest Diana is still recovering from the shock of being chosen as one of the contestants.

WATCH OUT……..Chris Evert! A pretty young lady by the name of Daria Smenos, a freshman at Morton College, swings a mean tennis racket! Daria had an 11-1 record for the season. She came in fourth in the tennis state tournament at LaSalle-Peru, winning two medals: she downed her singles rival and then won in a doubles challenge, taking a fourth place win for both. This year the women's tennis team at Morton College capped its best year ever. And get this – they're called the Lady Panthers. Daria is the daughter of Ann Smenos of Berwyn.

"EVERYTHING'S COMING…….up roses" is the tune being crooned by two singularly charming gentlemen, Nick Skountzos and Nick Verveniotis, about their latest hit, Nikos' Grecian Inn, 5000 West 95th and Cicero. If you remember, their first hurrah was Nikos, 7600 South Harlem Avenue, Bridgeview, an outstanding eatery featuring gourmet dining and nightly entertainment.

A triumph both from a visual and a taste standpoint, Nikos' Grecian Inn creates two diversified moods. One of its dining rooms is reminiscent of a Greek Island. Nikos' two other dining areas are more discreet, secretive – the place for a rendezvous. In cozy tones of toast, their main attraction is the plethora of unusual Greek vases.

AND TALKING.......about fashions – what about our own Andrew Athens of Metron Steel fame? According to a recent issue of the *Sun-Times* – Andy is right in there with Egypt's Anwar Sadat and *Sun-Times* columnist, Kup, as one of "the ten best-dressed men in the free world." The report came from the Men's Fashion Guild of America.

QUOTE OF THE WEEK: "Wealth is like a viper, which is harmless if a man knows how to take hold of it; but if he does not, it will twine around his hand and bite him." – St. Clement

"A well-adjusted person is one who can play golf and bridge as if they were merely games."

IMPECCABLE INSIGHT.........was used by members of The United Hellenic Voters of America in its selection of the five "Most Distinguished Greek Americans of 1981": His Grace Bishop Iakovos, Angeline P, Caruso, PhD ; Stanley H. Fistedis, PhD; Evangeline Gouletas and Nicholas J. Melas. The five were honored at the group's second annual awards dinner held at Nikos in Bridgeview, with a turnout of about 700 guests. With Dr. D.G. Kyriazopoulos serving as honorary chairman, Dr. Lambis Anagnostopoulos as honorary co-chairman, and Nonda Harris as general chairman, it turned out to be a star studded evening with such luminaries as Mayor Jane Byrne of Chicago and Governor Hugh Carey of New York in attendance.

Since His Grace Bishop Iakovos, who was selected as humanitarian of the year, was unable to attend the awards dinner, the Very Rev. Isaiah Chronopoulos, chancellor of the Greek Orthodox Diocese in Chicago, took the podium and spoke for him. He was followed by Dr. Andrew T. Kopan, professor of education at DePaul University, who prefaced remarks about Angeline Caruso, PhD, interim general superintendent of schools, who was named educator of the year.

Martin Butler of the city of Park Ridge, then spoke about the third honoree, Stanley H. Fistedis, PhD., manager of the Engineering Mechanics Program, Reactor Analysis and Safety Division, Argonne National Laboratory, who was named scientist of the year. Evangeline Gouletas, chairman of the board of American Invsco Development, had two charming gentlemen at the podium extol her expertise as business woman of the year. Governor of New York Hugh Carey, and Alex Gianaris, president of Transformer Manufacturers Inc. The fifth honoree was the Honorable Nicholas J. Melas, president of the Metropolitan Sanitary District, who was named government man of the year. The Honorable Senator Samuel G. Maragos (retired) spoke for him.

GRIEF HAS……clutched the hearts of everyone who knew handsome and, oh so charming, 33-year- old Peter G. Porikos, who died recently following a brief bout with cancer. Peter was the son of Georgia Porikos, one of our town's most gracious ladies, and the late attorney, George S. Porikos. He was a partner in the law firm of Porikos and Rodes. A graduate of the University of Illinois College of Law, Peter was a member of the Chicago Bar Association, a captain in the U.S.Army Reserve, and a faculty member in the Paralegal Studies Program at Harper College. He is survived by his mother and a sister, Katherine Koopmans of New York City.

THE KNICKERBOCKER……Chicago officially reopened on March 20th when Mayor Jane M. Byrne and Carol Channing of "Hello Dolly" fame pushed the button which simultaneously raised the chandelier in the Grand Ballroom and lighted dance floor at the hotel, formerly the Playboy Towers. The ceremony was followed by a gala reopening party for 700, featuring a grand buffet in the ballroom, music and champagne in all of the public rooms. Greeting guests was the owner of the newly refurbished Knickerbocker, Tony Antoniou, and his lovely wife, Irene, and president of the firm, George Marks and his charming wife, Niki.

When the Knickerbocker was purchased five million dollars was spent returning the famous ballroom to its original state and renovating the other public and private rooms. Today the new Knickerbocker will offer a standard of service and personal attention which is rare.

QUOTE OF THE WEEK: "It is fallacious to believe that having children can save a marriage; children make a good marriage better, but a bad marriage worse."

"Many parents never learn the fundamental lesson that sometimes the best way to convince a child he is wrong is to let him have his own way."

AMID SUNBURSTS,........of smiles, flashing cameras, dignitaries of both church and state, celebrities from all walks of life, relatives, friends, a heavenly choir, an archbishop, a bishop and five priests, Evangeline Gouletas, looking radiant in her short, pale pink wedding gown was united in marriage to Governor Hugh Carey of New York. The scene was the interior of New York's Holy Trinity Greek Archdiocesan Cathedral – and the enthusiasm and contentment that the buddingly beautiful celebration that the Carey-Gouletas wedding elicited, stretched like an elastic band from Manhattan to Albany.

As we arrived at the church for the 10:30 am wedding ceremony, a caravan of 18 shiny black limousines were parked on the cathedral block, which had been cut off to all traffic. People stood riveted together allowing no standing room for a newcomer anxious to see the celebrities; in direct contrast the residents of the area dangled outside their windows craning their necks for a glimpse of their Governor and his lady. New York City police motorcycle escorts stood outside of the church and state troopers waited patiently in a fine drizzle of rain.

All of Governor Carey's children were in the bridal party. His pretty daughters, with shining hair and faces brightly lit with happiness, walked slowly down the cathedral aisle in their pink flutter of skirts brushing past pews tied with flowers warmed to their peak of fragrance and perfection. They were followed by two junior bridesmaids, Engie's two very young nieces, Andrea and Victoria Gouletas; the bride's sister, Irene D'Agnese; her daughter, Maria Kallas Stamelos, and her daughter, a 2 ½ year old fluff of femininity, who, when the ritual began, returned to the isle to pick up the rose petals she had already strewn and began to strew them all over again – drawing both attention and affection from all the guests.

When it was over, and the bride and groom started to walk outside of the cathedral, a crowd of about 600 people, all behind police barricades, began to cheer, and when the Governor turned to kiss his bride – the crowd went wild. It was like a movie scenario.

The wedding reception was held in the elegant St. Regis-Sheraton Hotel. After unabashedly shaking hands with hundreds of onlookers standing outside the hotel, the Governor and his new First Lady were escorted by a group of bagpipers, a color guard and a guard dog into the first reception room. Then, as they stood in front of their 11 tiered wedding cake, the Governor and Engie energetically received the warm wishes of those in attendance.

Later the couple fled to the second reception which took place in the penthouse of the hotel. Here, champagne flowed like a fountain – and cracked crab, strawberries, tasty little tidbits of cheeses, and many other delicious goodies were in abundance. Then Peter Duchin's band struck up, "How About You."

Later in the afternoon, when the bride and groom had departed for Albany, 150 guests were whisked off by chartered buses and planes to the Governor's Mansion in Albany. Here they were treated to an unforgettable evening of cocktails, dinner and entertainment. It was, indeed, the frosting on the Carey-Gouletas' wedding cake.

Some of the celebrities we spotted at the reception included: Bess Myerson, Robert Goulet, Kitty Carlisle Hart, Mayor Jane Byrne of Chicago, Governor and Mrs. Thompson of Illinois, Cicely Tyson and George Stavropoulos, famed dress designer, who did a smashing job on the gowns of the entire bridal entourage.

QUOTE OF THE WEEK: "There is an optimum point of compassion:it is a sentiment rarely felt by those who have not suffered at all, and never felt by those who have suffered too much. The absence of suffering makes men think they are gods, and the excess of it turns them into beasts."

"For most people, 'getting along with others' means pretending to agree with them even when you don't; but really getting along means being able to disagree without damaging their self-esteem, which is a much harder and more comfortable feat." – Harris

THIS WEEK.....we point with pride to Nicholas J. Melas, former head of the Metropolitan Water Reclamation District of Greater Chicago. Nick, an achiever, has been making history for years as a leader in our town – having received a multitude of honors and awards in his time. Well, he's done it again.

Each year, The Bright New City honors outstanding individuals and organizations for contributions that brighten our city. The Bright New City, Inc., a not-for-profit coalition of business, civic and government leaders, architects, historians, and urban planners dedicated to improving the quality of life in Chicago, recently selected Nick as one of its City Brighteners in recognition of his leadership in improvement of Chicago River aeration plants and installation and development of recreational facilities. This year's awards were presented by Mayor Daley in a ceremony held in the beautiful new DePaul Center, 1 East Jackson on March 8th.

WE ALL....remember her from the period in which she lived in Chicago – a tall, statuesque head-turner with a warm, vivacious personality. Her name: Karitas Sigurdsson-Mitrogos, wife of Alexander Mitrogos, senior Greek trade commissioner, currently residing in New York City. Well, the Big Apple has spurred Karitas into carving a jewel of a culinary career for herself. But then – her background in the field of culinary arts is impeccable. Her new culinary concept, "My Way – Easy, Fun and Simple" is a unique international cooking club that brings the entire world of fine cuisine into your home.

On her recent trip to Chicago, Karitas appeared on her third live segment, "What's Cooking," and she was 40 minutes live on the Danny Bonaduce evening show. All of this took place on Friday. On Saturday, she did a stint on WBBM radio, "In the Kitchen" with Sherman Kaplan, plus a cooking demo and showcase of Greek products in the Market Place.

Back home in New York, Karitas was on prime time on the latest food network channel. Hosts of the show were Donna Giuliani (wife of the Mayor of New York) and David Rosengartern – one of the most respected food show hosts who also writes for the *New York Times*. While there is not enough space to write all about her appearances, Chicagoans would be interested in knowing about the special Greek television Easter show in which she shall demonstrate how to prepare all of our Greek easter goodies. Karitas has taught gourmet classes throughout the world, most recently at the renowned Culinary Institute of America in Hyde Park.

In "My Way," she offers a unique interpretation of international cuisine illustrating her belief that home cooking has to be easy, fun and simple. Further information on her cooking club can be obtained by calling 1-800-424-9095.

QUOTE OF THE WEEK: "We can never understand someone until we are able to hear what he is not saying."

"The most brilliant, witty and intellectual man in the world still finds it difficult to make talk with his own relatives, for, usually, we have the most to say to those we have the least to do with."

ALL THOSE.......in the chic and beautiful people set attended the recent christening of one of our town's newest members of the mush and pablum set – pretty, dark-eyed Renee Michelle Tzakis, daughter of Nick and Jeannie Tzakis; granddaughter of Andrew and Irene Tzakis and

Stratte and the late Helen Coorlas. And what a scrumptious christening that was. From the moment Renee made her debut in church, cuddled in the arms of her grandmother, Irene, to the end of the christening service, Renee's eyes darted around the church – taking in everything and everyone. She was totally aware that this was a special day and that she was the guest of honor. As she came out following the service, Renee looked utterly smashing in her "designer's" white gown squirming in the arms of her handsome godfather, Dr. Michael N. Mastoris.

During a most delightful two-hour cocktail reception guests mingled together as they munched on delicious hors d'oeuvres. Dinner was tastefully executed at tables of ten which boasted of yet another assortment of floral pieces set in the center of the table. It was obvious that guests were being indulged in beauty, good taste and luxury. Later, guests danced to the music of Perry Fotos and his orchestra, and feasted from the abundant table of sweets -some of which were baked by Jeannie and Irene Tzakis.

HOLLOW CHEEKED.....beauties with lean and moving hipbones will model an exquisite collection of trousseau clothes – kept under deep secrecy and designed especially for St. Andrew's forthcoming event – THE WEDDING. An annual luncheon –fashion show, sponsored by the prestigious St. Andrew's Women's Philoptochos Society on Saturday, September 27th at the Continental Plaza – it promises to make every woman in attendance wish she was about to take the plunge – for the first, the second, or the third time. The trousseau will feature the designs of internationally famous couturier, Becky Bisoulis, whom the parishioners of St. Andrew point to with pride. Becky grew up in that parish and she is still very much a part of it. The tall-stemmed beauty is the only non-New Yorker in a group of six designers to win the prestigious 1979 Prix de Cachet award – no small accomplishment. Highlighting elegance and unlikely fabric and texture combination – she boasts of clients way up in the six figure bracket.

TEN OF......our most distinguished jurists were honored by the United Hellenic American Congress at the group's annual banquet which took place on October 31st at the Hyatt Regency Chicago Hotel. They included: U.S. District Judge Charles P. Kokoris; Illinois Appellate Court Judge John J. Stamos; Cook County Circuit Court Judges Peter Bakakos, Christy S. Berkos, James A. Geocaris, Peter Georgas, James A. Geroulis and James A. Zafiratos; and Associate Judges Arthur C. Perivolidis and John J. Limperis (retired). With a theme of "Hellenism in Greater Chicago Honoring Greek-American Jurists," the event had as its general chairman, Andrew A. Athens, national chairman of UHAC.

THE FAMILY……of the late Helen Stamos, wife of Appellate Court Judge John J. Stamos, is wearing its heart at half-mast since her death. Beloved Helen, well-known in our town, was an active member of the Philoptochos of Sts. Peter and Paul. Prior to the Stamos' move to Northbrook, she worked diligently for the parish of Sts. Constantine and Helen. She is survived by her husband, four children – James, Theo, Colleen and Jana – and by her mom, Fannie Voutiritsas.

QUOTE OF THE WEEK: "Hating someone is like burning down your own house to get rid of a rat." - Fosdick

"We think that our opinion of someone depends on what we see in him; it does not – in most cases, it depends on what he makes us see in ourselves."

CLOUD SPUN…..flourishes of lace; curving peplums and puffed shoulders; seductive plays of sheerness and shimmer; spills of gold and silver on silk chiffon; sheerness with mega watt dazzle; imaginative textures; bare backs; petal-hemmed skirts; Mykonos white cut linen; hand-painted velours; touches of bareness; narrow waists; cuddles of feathers; clothes for playful days and daring dark nights; eclectic elegance and opulent fashions – all of these and much more opened up the soul of every woman who sat in awe ravenously devouring the stunning collection of designs created by Becky Bisoulis especially for the fashion-luncheon show, "The Wedding."

Sponsored by the St. Andrew's Women's Philoptochos Society, it was held in the Wellington Room of the Continental Hotel on Saturday, September 27th.

The Bisoulis showing climbed mountains and scaled walls and far surpassed the showings I have seen from such remarkably talented designers – the Greek boys – James Galanos and George Stavropoulos. The 1979 Prix de Cachet award winning Bisoulis is a super talent, and if you wore one of her designs once, you could create a legend. She works magic on suede; pours imagination into colors; and her evening entrance-makers fulfill every woman's fashion fantasy. Her clothes don't talk – they shout, they dance, they sing, and the mood she sets with the energy provided by her background music is unsurpassed.

Congratulations to Ms. Bisoulis whose designs should fill the pages of *Vogue*, *Harper's Bazaar*, *W* and *Women's Wear* for every woman to feast upon for she wears her creativity like a second skin and her great showmanship is apparent in every gesture of her models.

Orchids to St. Andrew's delightful chairlady, Helen Deligiannis and to its creative president, Yvonne Philippides for master-minding the biggest fashion coup in church-sponsored luncheon fashion show history. There will never be another like it.

WELL-KNOWN.......lecturer and TV personality, Arianna Stassinopoulos, will probably reap millions in sales on the biography she recently authored, "Maria Callas: The Woman Behind the Legend." Her English publisher, George Weidenfeld, suggested she write the biography shortly after Callas died. According to "W," Arianna was born in Athens, graduated with honors from Cambridge, where she was the first female president of the Cambridge Union. She wrote two books of ideas: "The Female Women," which is an appeal to feminists to avoid rhetorical extremism, and "Beyond Reason," a polemic urging intellectuals to explore mythical and spiritual rather than merely rational truth.

THE WORLD......is certainly a lot poorer and a lot sadder since the death of one of our town's most beloved and respected citizens, George Manus, who died recently, making a dent in the hearts of all of us who knew him. An astute business man, and a beloved humanitarian, George's generosity knew no bounds. A man with enduring qualities, George was a very devoted Christian who served the parish of Sts. Constantine and Helen in many capacities in his lifetime. We extend our sympathy to his widow, Maria; his daughter, Irene; and his grandson, George.

QUOTE OF THE WEEK: "Husbands who tend to be extremely critical of their wives in public are often quite dependent upon them in private, and the public treatment is simply a way of expressing resentment of the private dependence."

1990-96

"A man can fail many times, but he isn't a failure until he begins to blame somebody else." –John Burroughs

AND ALL.....of those who heard the incredibly sweet tones emanating from the violin of Jennifer Marlas were enthralled with her immense talent. The technically deft Jennifer was presented in concert by The Chicago Fine Arts Society on January 25th in the Skyroom Atrium Gallery in the Water Tower Bank Building and underwritten by Mr. and Mrs. Nicholas A. Karras.

Jennifer's youthful energy and intense emotion were evident in her outstanding performance. Her violin ached with richness of tone and the jam-packed audience listened with rapture as she went from one number to another.

A native of Chicago, she is the daughter of Dennis Marlas and Connie Lewis, and the granddaughter of Helen Marlas. In her young life she has won numerous awards, including first prize in the Fischoff National Chamber Music Competition, the Arts Recognition and Talent Search and the Talman Classical Music Competition. She was a finalist in the Julius Stulberg National Competition, the Seventeen Magazine and General Motors Competition and the Chicago Symphony Young Performers Competition. She is currently concertmaster and soloist with the Bach Ensemble of Baltimore.

CONDOLENCES ARE.....extended to the family of Maria Marinakos, wife of the late and beloved Constantine, who succumbed recently following a lengthy illnesss. She was the mother of Leon Marinakos, cultural attaché; Presvytera Panayiota (the late Rev. Theodore Thalassinos), and the loving grandmother of two.

THIS TYPEWRITER.....is typing rave reviews about James Z. Chrones, St. Andrew's Greek Orthodox Church's "good will ambassador." A revealing article about him was written by Angelo Leventis in the St. Andrew's Anchor. Entitled, "Someone You Should Know," the article gives details on Jim's professional background and is chock full of all the good deeds he has accomplished – both professionally and personally – throughout his lifetime. Leventis refers to him as St. Andrew's "good will ambassador" – a title that Jimmy has earned throughout his years in the parish.

A DELICATE.....floral array of tender, refreshingly sweet coral blossoms adorned the altar at the wedding of Dina Gregory Papas of Wilmette to Nicolai Bacaintan of Cleveland, Ohio. The event, which took place on December 29, was held at St. Andrew's. The bride, daughter of Mr. and Mrs. S.J. Gregory and the widow of the late Spiro J. Papas, wore a dazzling coral silk chiffon gown embroidered with showers of shimmering gold. Her only attendant was her daughter, Maria Papas Gleason, who wore a chocolate long, whirly-swirly silk organza gown flounced with an off the shoulder ruffle. Best man was Mrs. Bacaintan's brother-in-law, William Bryant of McLean, Virginia. A small intimate group of friends and relatives attended the cocktail-dinner reception held at the Ambassador West Hotel.

POSTCARD PENNINGS........from Eva Polydoris of Lake Forest from the Theatre Restaurant Imperial in Tokyo: "Stu and I spent one week in Tokyo last week after which we needed a second week's rest at our favorite spot, the island of Hawaii. Tokyo has one Greek restaurant called the Double Ox, however, we were being entertained by Stuart's clients to such a degree that we didn't get a chance to go there." Beautiful Eva always manages to find a Greek church or a Greek restaurant in her many travels with Stu.

QUOTE OF THE WEEK: "Reflect upon your present blessings, of which every man has many; not on your past misfortunes, of which all men have some." – Dickens

"Smile, if only for the lift it gives to another person." Edna Kaehele

WHAT A.....magnificent coup for the United Hellenic American Congress to have as its honored guest one of the Greek-American legends of our time – the talented Olympia Dukakis. The award-winning actress will be the guest of honor at the forthcoming 20th annual UHAC dinner-dance scheduled to take place at the Sheraton Chicago Hotel on November 11th. The announcement was made by Andrew A. Athens, national chairman of UHAC. The talented actress is a woman who has had a lifetime love affair with the theater – her credentials are outstanding – her experience voluminous – and she has the stuff that keeps great audiences glued to their seat. UHAC has honored many outstanding citizens – but to have the winner of the coveted Academy Academy for Best Supporting Actress in our midst for an evening – has stirred excitement among all of us. So I suggest that you get your reservations in quickly for this very special evening.

IN THIS.....column I offer a special prayer for the recuperation of beloved Kosta Zografopoulos who met with a tragic accident a few weeks ago. A very handsome, young entrepeneur, with one of the finest catering businesses in our town, all of his friends and relatives are praying for his recovery. On Monday, December 18th, the parish of St. Andrew's held a blood drive for Kosta. They are also setting up a trust fund that will assist in his rehabilitation. Further information on this will emanate from the parish sometime in January. In the meantime, we all offer our prayers for this valiant young man.

WHO SAYS.....romance is dead? For all of you ladies who have a lack luster relationship or perhaps a marriage that lost its sparkle a long time ago – eat your heart out. There are men out there who are romantic, adoring, chivalrous and loving. Case in point is good looking bachelor, Tony Athans, owner of the Lincoln Restaurant and Knicker's in the burbs. Tony recently became engaged to his squeeze, and do you know how he proposed? He rented Tony Difiglio's, "Anita D" for two hours. As they cruised the blue waters of Lake Michigan – all coosome and lovey on this ship – Tony popped the question. Who could resist this irresistible guy! Tony is the son of Mr. and Mrs. John Athans of Lincolnwood and Mary is the daughter of Mr. and Mrs. Peter Liapis of Niles.

GLOBE TROTTING……Mary Gatsis and Georgia Kotsiopoulos recently toured Germany, Austria, Hungary and the Czech Republic. Ditto Nick and Stella Contos of Brookfield, Wisconsin, Peter and Helen Childs of Northbrook and Gus and Tula Mazarakis of Lincolnwood who drove through parts of Europe. My sister, Irene, and I, with good friends, John and Ann Graven, took the big bird over to Italy. We toured Rome, Florence, Venice, Sienna, Assisi and Copenhagen, Denmark and had one heck of a good time. Legal beagles Peter Regas and Peter Kamberos also took the big bird over to Italy where they rented a car and toured that country.

QUOTE OF THE WEEK: "We might not find the chronic drinker so intolerable when drunk, if we realized how intolerable he finds himself when sober; I have never yet met a lush whose self-esteem was not drenched in self-contempt."

"Every person has a lifestyle best suited to his temperament, and only those who find it, and accept it, can rest comfortably within themselves, regardless of the buffeting of the external circumstances."

WE POINT…..with pride to Lane Tech High School senior, Bart Brotsos, son of Jim and Adeline Brotsos, who recently won a Nationwide Scholastic Aptitude Test. Rated one of the top two percent in the nation, Bart's biography will appear in "Who's Who Among High School Students." Bart has already been accepted at Northwestern University.

A HEARTWARMING.....community expression of love and appreciation to a dedicated priest and his lifelong service and devotion to the Greek Orthodox Church was recently extended to the Rev. Father Joseph Xanthopoulos when the community of St. John the Baptist Greek Orthodox Church in Des Plaines, held a dinner honoring him. Father Xanthopoulos has given 61 years of pastoral service in behalf of the church, and was honored because of this on Sunday March 11th.

A BEAUTIFUL......collection of over 300 people, all bedecked and bejeweled in their finery, waited in line at the Orrington Hotel in Evanston to wish pretty Melanie Corolis and her handsome bridegroom, Nicholas D. Chionis, DDS, a lifetime of happiness together. The couple had just arrived at the Orrington after being married at Sts. Peter and Paul in Glenview where His Grace Bishop Iakovos officiated at the ceremony, along with Father George Scoulas and Father George Zervos.

Charismatic Melanie was radiant in an ivory antique lace gown, an exact duplicate of the wedding gown worn by Fallon on TV's "Dynasty." Her sister, Joanna , was maid of honor, and Frank Karkazis, DDS, was best man. The bridesmaids wore ivory tea-length dresses and carried bouquets of orchids and red roses. Melanie's parents, Jim and Lee Corolis of Glenview, hosted the elegant dinner reception which was followed by dancing until the wee hours of the morning.

THE STORK......dropped a bundle of sheer femininity at the home of Tom and Marianne Leibrandt of Broadview whose first little tax exemption was born on October 26th. Named Sara, she weighed in at 6 lbs 3 ozs. Proud grandparents are Gus and Amphie Presvelos.

MEMBERS OF......the Gladys Trigoureas family are wearing their hearts at half-mast since the death of this beloved lady following a lengthy illness. Indeed, she was one of our town's most loving and affable human beings – always eager and ready to aid and assist in anyway she could. An active member of the parish of St. Andrew's Greek Orthodox Church, she is survived by three sisters: Pauline (Chris) Kalogeras; Mary and Bessie Trigoureas; and a brother, Sam (Kiki) Trigoureas. She was preceded in death by her sister, Esther.

CONGRATULATIONS TO........Lou Canellis, son of George and Nancy Canellis, for being selected winner of the Chicago Headline Club's 1988 Peter Lisagor Awards for Exemplary Journalism in the category of "Journalism – Sports – Radio." The award was presented to him at The Chicago Headline Club's annual awards banquet which took place last month in the Guildhall of the Ambassador West Hotel. The Chicago Headline Club is the Chicago Professional Chapter of the Society of Professional Journalists, Sigma Delta Chi.

"All women's dresses are merely variations on the eternal struggle between the admitted desire to dress and the unadmitted desire to undress." – Lin Yutang

SO MANY......wonderful good people passed on in the last 30 days – many of whom suffered extensively before their candle of life was finally snuffed out. They were all civic leaders in their time – known to all of us for their good deeds; some were brilliant business people; some were homemakers. But all of them were very well known in our community.

The first to go was our beloved James Maros – a good family friend – whose business acumen was legion. He was one of 50 original operators of McDonald's restaurants. He and his wife, Bess, owned and operated ten of the franchises in Chicago Heights, Matteson, Homewood, Sauk Village and Park Forest. Jim was credited with creating the original Ronald McDonald doll. The awards he received were endless. Among them were being named McDonald's Operator of the Year, receiving the Ronald award in 1972; receiving the Prime Minister of Israel Medal for his commitment to making the future of Israel better; and being honored with a lifetime membership by the DuSable Museum. A kind, gentleman who was loved by his employees and by all of us who knew him well, he is survived by his wife, Bess, and his two daughters, Alexandra and Frances.

Another dear friend who succumbed recently was Danae Collias Kornaros who fought the good fight with all of her might. A very devout Greek Orthodox Christian, she had worked on many causes during her lifetime and had given of herself to many philoptochos groups. A wonderful homemaker, she was the mother of Nikolas of New York City, Aristotle and Achilles, and the beloved sister of Nicholas, George and Jean Collias.

Dear, dear friend, Jim Bartholomew, fought valiantly for his life for two years. As a matter of fact, he was to have received an honorary plaque from the parish council of Sts. Peter and Paul in Glenview at that parish's vesper service for all the many good deeds he had done in that parish. But, as fate would have it, the plaque was presented to his widow, Pat, following the vesper service, which turned out to be the day following Jim's burial. Beloved Jim was a dedicated Christian who had served on the parish council for a very long time. General Chairman of the Sts. Peter and Paul picnic for many years, he was first vice-president of the council at the time of his death. He is survived by his wife, Pat, his three children, Mary, George and Theresa; his sister, Irene Tzakis, and his brother, John.

AND THE....exquisitely beautiful Empire Room of the Palmer House will be the setting of the forthcoming scrumptious Christmas Scholarship Brunch to be sponsored by The Greek Women's University Club on Sunday, December 26th – making the Christmas weekend full of food, fun and social games. Held in honor of the 1982 scholarship recipients, the event promises to be saturated with beauty – the GWUC lovelies – and the majestic Empire Room setting. Handling the event will be Diane Golemis, general chairman, and Bess Smyrniotis, scholarship chairman.

CONGRATULATIONS TO.........Dr. Kevin C. Price, son of Holly and the late Attorney William Price, who recently was awarded his

PhD degree from the University of Illinois School of Medicine in the College of Pharmacy.

QUOTE OF THE WEEK: "Many people when they fall in love, look for a haven of refuge from the world, where they can be sure of being admired when they are not admirable, and praised when they are not praiseworthy." - Russell

"The best way to win an argument is to concede as much as can possibly be conceded to your opponent's view without sacrificing anything essential to your own; success in argument is a direct opposite to success in bargaining."

AND ANOTHER.....personality-plus young lady pledged her troth during the holidays. She is vivacious and pretty, Frances Maros, daughter of Jim and Bess Maros of Chicago. Fran, who has been living in Hawaii for the past few years, will tie the knot with Craig Hill of Maui.

Handsome bachelor, Nikolas Kornaros, formerly of Chicago and now residing in New York City, popped the question during the holiday season. He will wed Pauline DeLaslo, a dazzler who is a resident of the big apple, but who hails from Windsor, England.

And yet another wedding in the Kornaros family. Achilles Kornaros married Snezana Mircic, daughter of Stogisas Mircic of Belgrade, Yugoslavia on February 11th at Alexander Navsky Church in Belgrade.

Nikolas and Achilles are the sons of Danae Collias Kornaros of Chicago and Dr. Christopher Kornaros of Lisle.

LOVE ONCE.......again bloomed like the proverbial rose during the holiday season. Lovely Georgia Lithas, daughter of Dr. Harry and Helen Lithas of Elmhurst, became engaged to Gregory Contos, son of James and Katherine Contos of Niles.

AN ILLUSTRATED.....lecture entitled, "Christ Portrayals in Byzantine Art" will be presented by the master of all illustrated lectures in our town, Leon Marinakos, cultural attaché (honorary), Consulate General of Chicago, at the Art Institute of Chicago on Tuesday, April 2nd at 6 pm. No one – but no one – has been able to capture beauty on slides the way Leon has, and his generosity in giving to the Art Institute and to other organizations the benefit of his talent, has certainly been admirable.

A CRÈME DE LA....creme extravaganza that promises to exceed the most ambitious fantasies of even the late Perle Mesta, has been organized by the Greek American jet-setters of Manhattan. It is the 5th Annual Hellenic Times Scholarship Dinner Dance scheduled to take place on May 10th at the New York Hilton. This year's honorees will be Chicago's pride and joy, the charmingly gracious Billy Zane and his lovely sister, Lisa, both of whom are cresting the waves in Hollywood's ocean of acting talent.. The Hellenic Times Scholarship Fund has named them, "The Humanitarians of the Year."

Many luminaries will grace the podium at this star-studded event. Honorary committee consists of Michael Chiklis, "The Comish." TV's Bob Costas, lovely actress Melina Kanakaredes, Costas Mandylor of "Picket Fences," and Mr. and Mrs. Ernie Anastos (Ernie had his own radio show in Evanston awhile back).

QUOTE OF THE WEEK: "Friendship that flows from the heart cannot be frozen by adversity, as water that flows from the spring cannot congeal in winter."

"Most people mistakenly believe that to be 'free' is to be able to do what you want to do; when in truth, to be free is to be able to do what is best for yourself- and learning what is best for yourself is the only way to get rid of the slavery of self-indulgence."

DEATH TAKES……..no holiday. Sometimes it comes quickly and without warning – taking our loved ones under its wings, then soaring like an eagle quickly and painlessly into the air. Other times the journey is incredibly long with no end in sight – like a coast to coast ride in an uncomfortable bus that makes endless stops along the way. Our destinies unfold in various ways – but the end result is the same.

The young life of lovely, Elaine Bakakos Papas, was one of those that was snuffed out without warning – leaving a great big void in the hearts and minds of those who knew and loved her – her husband, her three small children, her parents, her brother and her legion of friends.

Tall and slender, Elaine had an individuality all her own. She was an innovative, artistic and musically talented woman involved in the activities of her parish and in the community in which her young children went to school. She was adored by her husband, Gregory; cherished by 9-year-old Gregory, 6-year-old Bradley, and 3-year-old Curt. She was the nourishment of her parents, the Honorable Peter and his wife, Kiki, and her brother, Lee; she was the pride of her mother-in-law, Dina Bacaintan. Her death left all of those who loved her in shock. May she rest in peace and may her memory be eternal.

And yet another dear friend of many years standing died on April 4th following a lingering illness whose relentless fury was unbelievable. But our beloved, Helen Anthony, fought for life valiantly, without self-pity, but with strength and tenacity. The devoted daughter of the late Theodore and Angeline Anthony, she will be sorely missed by her loving sister, Alice Anthony, for they were constant companions. Astute in business, prior to her retirement she was trust manager of the First Chicago Bank; a past president of The Greek Women's University Club; a board member of the Annunciation Cathedral Philoptochos; and a board member of the Foundation for Fighting Blindness.

IF YOU'VE……been asked to dine with a Duke, rub elbows with an Earl, attend a garden party for Princess Anne, or splash around the Mediterranean on Onassis' ocean pad on the third weekend of July –just forget it – for a friendly flock of nice Greek boys and girls are extending an invitation to you to attend their annual picnic festivities where you will be able to watch the antics of an uninterrupted stream of perfectly fascinating people while gorging yourself on gastronomical tidbits guaranteed to contribute to your jello-flab-pot.

The invitation is being extended to you by the parishioners of Sts. Peter and Paul Greek Orthodox Church in Glenview who will host their picnic on July 20-22. This year's event promises to be a product of impeccable Greek workmanship which will please everyone – from the nice Greek boy lawyer set to the nice Greek girl teacher set. A great deal of thought has even been given to those whose taxes will be due in July. With a keen eye toward the financial future of all Greek property owners, the committee crew is raffling off $3,000 in cash or a 21-day trip to Europe, the biggest first prize in this royal flush raffle. More details on this later.

QUOTE OF THE WEEK: "No man is free who is not master of himself." – Epictetus

"Running water cleanses itself, and so does an active mind; we should distrust as possibly poisonous all those ideas we have held for a decade or more without continually re-examining their source and the degree of their stagnation." – Harris

RECIPIENT OF....the Hewlett Packard Award for outstanding leadership and contributions to Northwestern University is tall, stemmed rose, Daphne Mazarakis, daughter of Gus and Tula Mazarakis of Lincolnwood, who will be graduating from Northwestern's School of Engineering shortly. A member of Tau Beta Phi, honorary engineering society, she will be joining the firm of Deloitte and Touche this summer as an assistant analyst. Beauty and brains – all in the same package.

Brother Tom Mazarakis, a graduate of Northwestern School of Engineering, is an environmental engineer with Rust International. He will be on location in Louisville until fall. Apparently, both offspring have followed in the engineering footsteps of good old dad, Gus Mazarakis.

HANDSOME AND….very, very talented Billy Zane is not the only thespian in his family (not counting sis, Lisa, who we know is also a talent). His stunning Australian wife of six years, Lisa Collins, recently appeared on NBC's TV movie, "Deception," as a woman obsessed with a married psychiatrist. A look alike for Sharon Stone, Lisa is not only a beauty – but a genuinely super nice person.

PRAISING THE……work of George Pappageorge, architect at the Chicago-based firm Pappageorge Haynes Ltd., was a recent article in the *Chicago Tribune*. Pappageorge drafted a solution to a client's need for adding a second level to his loft.

ANOTHER NEW…..member of Tau Beta Phi, honorary engineering society, is George Manus Singh, a sophomore at the University of Illinois. Next fall he will serve as student director of the Illinois Tutoring Program for the Champaign School System.

BOUNCY AND……bubbly Georgia Photopulos and her special TV news anchor husband, Bud - or as she calls him, "Socrates" - recently took the big bird to Alaska for a five-day jaunt. After an overnight in Anchorage, they took a "much smaller bird" to Dead Horse, Alaska, 250 miles north of the Arctic Circle (an awesome and adventuresome journey) then on to Prudhoe Bay – the beginning of the Alaska pipeline. For posterity's sake, they were smart enough to take their camcorder with them.

WE EXTEND……a warm welcome to pretty Mia Shanley, who recently made her debut into the world of wee little people. Named after her maternal grandmother, Euthemia Karkazis, she is a potential heart-breaker. Mia is the daughter of Larry and Georgene Shanley of Palatine.

CONDOLENCES TO…the family of Sam Angelopoulos who succumbed recently. A member of the St. Andrew's Church parish council; secretary and past president of the North Shore Chapter 94 of the Order of Ahepa, Sam was supervisor with the Cook County Assessor's office for 20 years. He is survived by his wife, Renee; his mother, Katina; his brother, Peter; and two daughters.

QUOTE OF THE WEEK: "Nothing done to make us angry is as harmful to us as what we do as a result of such anger; and the instinct for revenge has not only ruined individuals, it has toppled whole empires."

"The open-hearted and open-minded people are the strong ones. They have the most power because they give instead of take. They give and gain while the takers lose."- Susan Trott

THE BIG……fashion swing to the 1950's – glamour, sophistication, femininity, spike heels, and lips that are slicked in fire engine red, are back with us again and all of this good stuff will be unfurled at the forthcoming luncheon and fashion show to be sponsored by the Sts. Peter and Paul Philoptochos Society. Here – models with lean and moving hipbones and hair full of sensual energy – will slouch across the runway modeling body hugging clothes. This spectacular will take place at the Hyatt Regency O'Hare in Rosemont on April 29th. Most of the proceeds have been earmarked for the Children's Memorial Hospital Hellenic Heart Program, while a smaller portion of the proceeds will benefit the many philanthropic activities to which the philoptochos commits its efforts during the year. Attendees can imbibe in nippy-tippy cocktails beginning at 11:30am and those with a hunger for good food can satisfy their palates an hour later when lunch begins. For reservations call Helen Gallanis or Georgia Klovens.

AND THE……restlessness that always seems to accompany the onslaught of spring has attacked everyone I know – and travel plans for the month of March have escalated: the Andrew Tzakis family did the Palm Springs scene. Hitting the slopes in Vail were Rose Linardos who joined forces with her good friends – the Karkazis clan – Euthemia, Dr. Lambros, Dr. Frank, Georgene Karkazis Shanley with her hubby, Larry, and baby Mia; Matina Theodore, Helen and Kathy Gallanis, and the Teska family – Mike, Connie, Bethany and Laynie. Nick and Achilles Kornaros also joined their uncle, George Collias on the slopes in Vail. Ann and John Graven returned from Hawaii looking fit and tan.

THIS WEEK.......we point with pride to the award-winning Perry Fotos big band that recently recorded its first stereo cassette, "Perry Fotos Big Band – Live." For all the Perry Fotos fans – and he has many – the new stereo cassette may be obtained by mailing a check to Perry, Perry Fotos Big Band, 6300 Pelican Bay Blvd., Suite A-303, Naples, Florida 33963-811. One tape is $12.50; two copies, $24.00 and three copies $33.00 (this includes the cost of mailing). The music is great stuff so buy a cassette, flip it in your player, grab your squeeze and dance away the nite to tender tunes – a treat for the ears and a bonanza for your dancing feet.

THE WORLD....of wee little people recently welcomed a bouncing baby girl, weighing in at 6 lbs. 5 oz. Named Alexandra Nicole, this cuddly little powder puff is the daughter of Dr. Nicholas and Melanie Chionis of Palos Heights and the granddaughter of Jim and Lee Corolis and Angelo and Connie Chionis. Alexandra Nicole was born on January 26th.

AND WE......certainly were so happy to learn that handsome and bright bachelor, Nicholas Angelopoulos, M.D., and his parents, Tassos and Helen, are on the mend following a nasty car accident in Indiana. The Angelopoulos' were on their way to Florida when a car hit them head on. Currently, they are all recuperating at Methodist Hospital in Indianapolis. Nick is an anesthesiologist at Mercy Hospital. We wish them all a speedy recovery.

QUOTE OF THE WEEK: "All genuine love comes from strength, and is a kind of surplus energy in living; false love comes from weakness, and tries to suck vitality out of its object."

"There is a sort of 'magnetic attraction' between lovers; but, just as often as not, it is simply the unconscious call of one neurosis crying for its mate, and time alone can tell if the attraction is based on real needs or self-punishing drives."

HOW VERY.....flattering for the Cite Lake Point Tower Restaurant and Lounge to be chosen by royalty as the site of a get-together following the investiture of the Hospitalier Order of St. Lazarus of Jerusalem held at the St. James Cathedral. Celebrated every 15 years in the United States, this time Chicago was selected as the site. Among those attending the soiree were: Princess Elizabeth of Ysenburg, fifth in line to the Danish throne and eldest daughter of Prince Friedrich Ferdinand and Duchess Anastasia; her son, Prince Hans-George; Sheik Mubarach of Kenya, Marquis Bernard Alexis P. Demenars of France, and military guests in uniform, together with their ladies, who came to see 15 international members of the order knighted. Hostess was glamorous Evangeline Gouletas, sparkling in beaded ivory, and her brother, Nicholas Gouletas, real estate pro, who gave the winning bid at the night's auction for the only remaining cup plate set that once belonged to Pope John XXIII.

AND A......fun time was had by all of us who attended the July 3rd fireworks party given by Bill and Thalia Zane in their gorgeous LSD apartment. I have seen many exquisite pads in my lifetime – but none to match this luxury apartment that reeks of contemporary dash, elegant sophistication and impeccable flare. The Zanes have brought their passion for beauty right into their highly polished home. It is a brilliant jewel in the Lake Point Tower Condominium Apartments. And, besides that, we had one hell of a good time.

PARISH FESTIVALS......are going off rapidly like time bombs this summer. Among those ready to be detonated is the 33rd Annual Greek Festival to be sponsored by the parish of St. Andrew's which will take place on July 24th on the church grounds. The great gurus of picnicology, who have been making history for years on their yummy festival fare, have put bachelor and man-about-town, Ernest Stavropoulos, one of the parish's most cherished trophies, in this year's driver's seat, and Ernie is doing his utmost to make this the biggest and the best festival ever.We suggest you red circle July 24th on your calendar for you will meet and break bread with an uninterrupted stream of perfectly fascinating people who will be on hand to take care of your every gastronomical need.

ACCORDED THE........DePaul University's highest faculty honor, the Via Sapientiae Award, at its commencement ceremonies held at the Rosemont Horizon on June 12th was Dr. Andrew T. Kopan, professor of education in the School of Education. During his tenure at the university he has served as: chairman of the Department of Educational Foundations, director of Educational Policy Studies and Services and, director of Graduate Programs, all in the School of Education. In addition, Andy served on the old Faculty Advisory Council and in the now extinct University Senate, representing the School of Education.

THIS WEEK.....we point with pride to Nicholas C. Tapas, son of John and Connie Tapas of Glenview, who graduated from the Stritch School of Medicine, Loyola University. A brilliant student, Nicholas will specialize in pediatrics. He will do his three year residency at Lutheran General Hospital.

QUOTE OF THE WEEK: "Failure to respect a child's privacy – of spirit, as well as of material existence – is responsible for more estrangement between parents and children than any other single cause."

"When you run into someone who is disagreeable to others, you may be sure he is uncomfortable with himself; the amount of pain we inflict upon others is directly proportional to the amount we feel within us."

WHILE THE……*Greek Press* was on holiday for a month – death was not and, in that period of time, our community lost some very important personages. Our world will certainly be a lot sadder without our beloved, Nick Philippidis, editor of *The Greek Star*; elegantly beautiful Becky Bisoulis, and yet, another glamorous beauty, Mary Ellen Kotsos. While we could write reams about all these outstanding individuals – the way they have graced our community is etched into our hearts and minds and their contributions to our world are legion. To one of the kindest and most loving individuals I have ever had the privilege of knowing, I say a fond farewell to Nick – a good friend and fellow journalist, who, with his charm and grace, was loved by everyone who ever came in contact with him. To Becky Bisoulis – whose accolades are too numerous to mention in this small space – we can only add that this beautiful woman was graced with talent that comes only once in a lifetime. Who could ever forget the fashion production she planned and executed for St. Andrew's showing all of her designs. It was phenomenal! As to Mary Ellen Kotsos, whom I had the good fortune of meeting during my GWUC days, she was a lady who shone as a beacon in the world of education and as a wife and mother. May they all rest in the peace they so richly deserve.

A VERY…..important social event looming up into the horizon, is "Greek Odyssey," a cocktail-dinner-dance event which is being sponsored by The Judge James A. Geroulis Educational Foundation on September 25th at the Chicago Yacht Club. Guest speaker will be Justice Robert Chapman Buckley, Illinois Appellate Court. The formation of the foundation many years ago is another reminder of all the good works that were accomplished by the late and beloved, Judge James Geroulis.

BEST WISHES…..to newlyweds Esther Spiropoulos and Peter J. Contos who tied the knot this summer at St. John the Baptist Greek Orthodox Church. Officiating at the ceremony was the Rev. Manousos Lionikis, brother-in-law of the bride. Nicholas Contos of Brookfield, Wisconsin, was the best man for his brother. Esther is a retired teacher in the Park Ridge School System and Pete was chief electrical engineer, city of Chicago, before his retirement.

AND YET……another member of the pablum set was officially christened and given the name of Constantine (Dean) Thomas Murphy – after his maternal grandfather, Constantine (Dino) Tubekis of Wilmette. Son of Daniel Murphy and Susan Tubekis, the baptismal ceremony took place on September 17th at St. Andrew's. The luncheon following the christening was held at the Michigan Shores Club. Dina Gregory Bacaintan, aunt and godmother to Susie, also became the godmother of Susie's son.

CONGRATULATIONS TO…….Maria Vastis who recently purchased Flowers by Dena Inc., formerly owned by Dena Anastos. We wish Maria a great deal of success in her new venture. From a personal standpoint, I can say that we have used this elite flower shop for many occasions and their flower arrangements are unique.

QUOTE OF THE WEEK: "The worst form of disappointment often consists in getting exactly what you wanted."

"The truest test of independent judgment is being able to dislike someone who admires us and to admire someone who dislikes us."

A CHRISTIAN DIOR……white silk shantung off-the-shoulder wedding gown – adorned with white signature roses on the off-the-shoulder slope and the bustle back, showed off the thimble-sized waist of Lisa Panton, OD, to perfection when she became the bride of one of our town's most eligible bachelors, Frank Karkazis, DDS. The event took place on June 19th at the Assumption Church.

Glamorous bridesmaids, wearing long, white cotton faille gowns with pale lavender roses adorning their off- the-shoulder slopes included:

Helen Chronis, maid of honor; Kathy Gallanis, Lori Hague, Dee Obstfeld and Georgene Karkazis Shanley, sister of the groom. Best man was Anthony Karkazis, brother of the groom. Groomsmen included: Drs. Peter and Robert Panton, Evan Panton and Larry Shanley. The world of wee little people was represented by Christina Panton, flower girl; and Master Jesse Narens, ring bearer.

All the chic and beautiful people – numbering 400 – enjoyed a lengthy nippy-tippy cocktail hour – followed by an unbelievable continental gourmet dinner. The event, held at the prestigious Four Seasons Hotel, exceeded even the most ambitious fantasies of a Perle Mesta. Flawlessly executed, it will be among the evenings that will long be remembered by all those attending.

Parents of the couple are Dr. and Mrs. John Panton and Dr. and Mrs. Lambros Karkazis. The couple is honeymooning in the island of Mykonos and will be at home at the John Hancock apartments.

IT'S THAT.......time again, for the annual picnic antipasto parade of souvlakia, Greek cheese, red tomatoes, slabs of cucumbers, hard rolls, baklava, hot loukoumades drenched in honey and sprinkled with cinnamon, steaming black coffee, ice cold coke, mosquitos, a few flies, sun, rain, clouds, clear skies, cold weather, warm weather, hot weather, romances with nice Greek girls, romances with bad Greek girls, romances with not so nice Greek boys, romances with some very nice Greek boys, Greek dancing, fun and games, aching feet, dusty feet, etc.etc.etc. But what would the summer be without these little ole picnics? Two of these specials will be served within a very short period of time- the St. John's Greek Orthodox festival and the St. Andrew's Greek Orthodox Church picnic.

On Sunday, July 8th, the 12th Annual One-Day Picnic of St. Andrew's will take place and on June 22-24, the three-day festival sponsored by St. John's will be held. Your St. Andrew hosts will be Andrew Tzakis and John Bartholomew and the affable Chris Bazos will be your host at St. John's.

CONDOLENCES ARE.......extended to Fay Machinis, widow of Peter, who succumbed recently. The 81-year-old World War II veteran who had retired as Lt. Col. of the US Army and as civil engineer, was the father of Cathy (James) Economos and Alexander (Lea). Fay, a former Mezilson, is the sister of columnist, Jimmy.

QUOTE OF THE WEEK: "Nothing else in the world can make man unhappy but fear. The misfortune we suffer is seldom, if ever, as bad as that which we fear." - Schiller

"Every discontented person I have ever met has been discontented because, at bottom, he has been trying to be someone he is not; self-acceptance is the indispensable prerequisite of all mental health." – Harris

GLOBETROTTING: These people did not canoe across the Sahara or walk backward through the Andes – but jumbo-jetted around a portion of our globe. September was the heaviest month of European travel among Greek-Americans in our town. Biggest destination: Greece. Second biggest: Paris. While traveling across time zones can wreck biological clocks – those who already returned home are none the worse for wear. Doing the Greece/Paris stint were: Nick and Aggie Kafkis of Skokie; Dino and Marie Leventis of Lincolnwood; Alex Jianas and George Kapsimalis of Kansas City; Peter and Helen Childs of Northbrook; Helen Gallanis of Kenilworth and her "tres jolie" attorney daughter, Kathryn; Matina Theodore of Glenview, and her brother and sister-in-law, George and Helen Karkazis of Northbrook.

Lounging around in the sun in glamorous Glyfada and Vouliagmeni were Michael and Callie Panagiotou of Northbrook and Bill and Valerie Valos – also from the northern burbs.

Dr. Lambros and Euthemia Karkazis of Deerfield took the big bird to Greece where they met up with their lovely daughter, Georgene, and her hubby, Larry Shanley of Palatine. Bess (Wilson) Geanakoplos and her West Coast sis, Lillian Cavin, took off for London and Paris for a holiday. And Tina Treantafeles of Oak Lawn took the big bird to Greece to join her mom.

WE WILL.......certainly all miss delightful Lillian Skoules, formerly of Evanston and currently of Chicago, who succumbed recently. Preceded in death by her husband, Steve, by many years, she was the mother of two charmers, Floraine (Frank) DuMez and Ethel (Ion) Caloger; grandmother of five and great grandmother of one. One of our town's most attractive senior citizens, Lillian gave much to our community in her lifetime.

AND IT.....was a deep loss to our community when Evon Kontos of Wilmette died following a lengthy illness. A World War II veteran, US Navy, he was a kind, gentleman who brought many happy moments to all those he came in contact with. He is survived by his devoted wife, Diana; his children, Stephanie (Steven) Michols, DDS, and Christine (William) Tarant; two grandchildren and two sisters, Helen Fanaras and Hope (Robert) Kennedy.

WITH HIS.....energies fully percolating, Charlie Moskos, military sociologist, was recently headlined in an article which appeared in the Tempo Section of the *Chicago Tribune.* Entitled, "Political Firepower," it was written by Paul Galloway.

In the proliferating business of politics, Charlie has played a momentous role behind the political scene with brilliance, grace, knowledge and common sense. With nonchalance, he has exuded the air of a poker player keeping a straight face when he's had a handful of wild intellectual cards. According to the article, Charlie was behind the bill that Clinton signed into law on September 21st – the National Service Act. It was his baby and so is the gays in the military compromise. He is the author of "Greek Americans, Struggle and Success," "Peace Soldiers," "The New Conscientious Objections," and "Resolving the American Dilemma." We point with pride to Charlie and all of his accomplishments.

QUOTE OF THE WEEK: "People who live rigidly by the 'rule of reason' eventually drive themselves into a fanatical excess of reasonableness, failing to recall Santayana's gentle reminder that 'reason is only a harmony among irrational impulses.'"

"The people with the clearest insights are not necessarily those with the finest minds, but those who were least damaged by their environment while growing up."

THIS YEAR'S……honorees at the 19th annual dinner-dance of the United Hellenic American Congress will number four: The Honorable Lee Hamilton, The Honorable Adeline Geo Karis, Louis Mitchell and Paul Vallas. The announcement was made by Andrew Athens, industrialist, civic leader and UHAC's national chairman. This year's banquet chairmen are Tom Athens, Frank Kamberos, Michael Halikias and Jack Mitsakopoulos. The event is scheduled to take place on November 19th at the Sheraton Chicago Hotel and Towers For further information on purchasing tickets to this event please call the UHAC office.

THOSE WHO…..will be attending the forthcoming Seventh Annual meeting of the Orthodox Christian Laity will be happy to learn that the group has nabbed Evanston's distinguished Charlie Moskos, PhD, professor of sociology at Northwestern University, to be the keynote speaker at its luncheon scheduled to take place on the last day of the OCL's conference at the Skokie Hilton Hotel on October 30th. The weekend meeting will be hosted by the OCL Council of Metropolitan Chicago, according to Nicholas Karakas, president, and Nicholas Nicholaou, general chairman. The workshops, the annual meeting and elections, and the church services will be held at Sts. Peter and Paul in Glenview.

AFTER THE …..initial shock wore off, pretty Melanie Chionis regained her composure and had a barrel of fun at her surprise 30th birthday party. Planned and executed by her sister, Joanna Corolis, and her husband, Dr. Nick Chionis, the bash was held at Joanna's Chestnut Street condo. About 60 friends and relatives attended this delightful party.

TIM ALLEN…..is not the only new Santa Claus on the horizon. There is Thomas Veikos, a unique and non-serving gent, who is going to donate fully cooked dinners for a fundraiser in honor of selfless, bouncy, energetic Georgia Photopulos. It seems that Georgia has been counseling cancer patients and their families at Sts. Peter and Paul for quite some time. Then the Cancer Support Group, led by Georgia, was opened to parishioners from St. Haralambos, St. Andrew and St. John the Baptist. Well – Santa Veikos, a member of St. Haralambos and a long-time admirer of Georgia's selfless efforts, decided he wanted to do something in return to help Georgia continue providing such beneficial service to the community. So, he offered to donate fully cooked dinners for a fund-raiser in her honor. Dinner proceeds will be used to establish the Sts. Peter and Paul Cancer Ministry Fund and to sustain Georgia's valuable work.

In addition to Mr. Veikos' contribution, Spyros and George Vaselopoulos are donating wine for the dinner and Jerry Minetos is donating his music.

OUR WORLD…..is a lot sadder since the death of our beloved, Angelyn Adinamis Poulos of Wilmette, wife of the late Gus Poulos, founder of Homer's Ice Cream in Wilmette. Gus, along with his two brothers, Jim and Pete, founded the Sweet Shop in Winnetka, another well-known North Shore confectionary, before opening Homer's – which is now run by the Poulos sons. Survivors include three sons – Stephen (Priscilla), John (Rose) of Palm Beach, and Dean (Jeanne) Poulos; six grandchildren; two brothers and two sisters.

QUOTE OF THE WEEK: "There will be no rest, and no release, for the human spirit as long as we stubbornly keep confusing the pursuit of pleasure with the pursuit of happiness." - Harris

"Some women go through life in such a state of chronic complaint that if, in the next life, the doors of heaven were flung open to them, they would demand to see the manager."

AND A....happy, happy birthday to Scorpios all over the country – particularly to the three very special people whose natal day I share – November 18th – Daisy Farmakis, Dee Tzakis and James Corolis. This year's Scorpio bash was dynamite. Hosted by Nick and Stella Contos, native Chicagoans now living in Brookfield, Wisconsin, it took place at the Greek Islands. Nick and Stella have since then taken the big bird, along with Gus and Tula Mazarakis of Lincolnwood, to the far off Orient. Their 21-day tour is all encompassing and the reason for such a bonus trip is a celebration of 25 years of marital bliss for both couples.

AS COOL.....as new sheets on hot, dry sunburned skin will be the forthcoming Christmas bazaar scheduled to take place on November 20th from 10am to 10pm making it easy for everyone to put in an appearance. Sponsored by the chic ladies in the North Shore parish of Sts. Peter and Paul Greek Orthodox Church in Glenview, the bazaar promises to inject fresh adrenaline into the tired-blood existence of any and all attending, for it will feature impeccable originality. Some of the world's greatest homemakers will be on hand to greet you at the Country Christmas Bazaar. This is an adventure in wonderful stuff – so do plan to attend.

AND ONE.......of our town's prettiest, Sia Demeros, daughter of Arthur and Athena Demeros, became the bride of one of our town's most eligible bachelors, Anthony Karkazis, son of Dr. Lambros and Euthemia Karkazis of Deerfield, on December 30th at St. Haralambos Greek Orthodox Church. It was a beautiful celebration of commitment between two people. The cocktail-dinner reception was held at the Chateau Ritz where guests sipped, supped and danced the night away.

The couple honeymooned in the island of Maui and are now living in their Deerfield home.

ALL THE.....chic and beautiful people will be swinging over to the InterContinental Hotel to sip and sup and to admire each other in their beautiful finery on December 4th, when the prestigious St. Andrew's Women's Club will once again open its doors to its fabulous dinner-dance. Wickedly concocted cocktails will precede the scrumptious dinner at which handsome devil-may-care guys will gush over sophisticatedly gowned ladies. The whole glorious night will be filled with splendor and romance. If you want to share in this fun-in, jolly over to your ring-a-ding phone and dial 334-4615.

AND OUR.......beloved senior citizen, Nicholas D. Markos, finally succumbed at the age of 101. One of the last of an outstanding generation who taught us right from wrong, he was indeed a delight to all those who knew him. Former owner of the ever-popular Sheridan Restaurant in days gone by, he was preceded in death both by his wife, Georgia and his son, Socky. He is survived by his lovely daughter, Kiki, his daughter-in-law, Georgia, and two charming grandsons, Nicholas and Christopher Markos.

THE DOOR.....has opened and closed to so many events at the St. Demetrios Greek Orthodox Church of Chicago. According to a recent press release, over the past 65 years, this parish has performed 9,500 liturgies, 6,285 baptisms, 2,549 weddings, and 2,629 funerals. This year, St. Demetrios' 65th anniversary will be observed at a gala dinner dance to be held on November 20th at the Rosemont Convention Center, Donald E .Stephens Ballroom. Co-chairmen of the event are Manny Giannakakos and Alex Kopsian.

QUOTE OF THE WEEK: "My favorite sensible answer to a stupid question was given to a reporter visiting a nudist camp who asked one of the campers, 'How did you get to be a nudist?' and the camper replied, 'I was born that way.'"

"What many persons want is not to be happy, but to be envied; they will endure the most private misery as long as they feel that they are publicly enviable." – Harris

IT'S NOT.....often that I have the pleasure of writing a rave review, but this is one such happy occasion. In general, big bands were a 50's phenomenon – the magical music of Glenn Miller, Tommy Dorsey, Harry James – to name a few – real dance music – real listening music – big band sounds that made you forget all the rest. If you liked the sounds, the rhythms of this era, take the next plane to Naples, Florida.

AND WE.....took the big bird to Naples recently for some much needed R and R. After landing into this oasis of manicured lawns and tranquil beauty, my sister, Irene and I, together with our close buddies, John and Ann Graven, made our temporary home away from home at the posh Registry Resort.

We contacted favorite cuz, Perry Fotos and his wife, Connie, who have been living the perfect life in Naples for the past six years. It was great to see them again – and even greater to discover that the great guru of big bands in southwestern Florida is Perry. He is the new Golden Boy of big bands and people flock in droves to hear and to dance to his music. *Gulf Coast Magazine* voted the Perry Fotos Big Band the "Best Big Band in Southwest Florida." His concert for the Muscular Dystrophy Telethon was a smashing success; his weekly big band dining at the Naples Beach Hotel and Golf Club packs them in.

AND OUR......town is a lot sadder since the death of our beloved, Nicolae Bacaintan, devoted husband of Dina Gregory Bacaintan, who succumbed December 1st at Evanston Hospital. Nicolae was a one- of-a-kind gentleman – warm, compassionate and very understated for a man of his credentials. A chemical engineer, he worked for more than 20 years for the CIA, receiving the Intelligence Medal of Merit when he retired from the CIA in 1973. Born in St. Paul, Minnesota of Roumanian descent, he spent 13 years in Roumania while growing up. Nicolae was recruited by the CIA because of his command of the Roumanian language. Other survivors include a stepson Gregory Papas, a stepdaughter Maria (George) Cantonis, five grandchildren and two sisters.

AND ONE…..of our town's loveliest, Laura Lampros, daughter of Louis and Ann Lampros of Oakbrook, became the bride of Daniel J.Pepke, Jr. on November 21st at HolyApostles Greek Orthodox Church. It was a beautiful celebration of commitment between two so-in-love people. The dinner reception was held at The Empress in Addison, where guests sipped, supped and danced the night away.

HIGH VOLTAGE…..energizer – cuz Harriet Diacos Becharas – recently Lufthansad her way to Germany to attend the nuptials of nephew, Jonathan Moss, to Silke Grim of Answeiller, Germany. Bridegroom Jonathan, is the son of Frank and Dee Moss (she is the former Dee Diacos of Chicago). Brian Becharas, son of Harriet Becharas of Evanston and George Becharas of Chicago (who also attended his cousin's wedding) has quietly unfolded his tent in Prague, Czech Republic, where he is making giant strides in a business venture.

QUOTE OF THE WEEK: "We must recognize that when we are made happy with a little praise, we are then vulnerable to being made morose with a little censure; and it is not worth the price, for generally praise does not please us as long as censure wounds us."

"The wise only possess ideas; the greater part of mankind is possessed by them." –Coleridge

SWEETIE-PIE……Ritsa Angelos was certainly stunned when she strolled into Sassi's Restaurant in Mt. Prospect and found herself drowning in a sea of smiling faces. When she came up for air – it became apparent that a surprise birthday dinner party in her honor was in full swing. Her two daughters and their husbands – Jeannie and Don Manhard of Deerfield, and Ann and Jimmy Manta of the east coast (who had taken the big bird in to host this gala) had pulled a fast one on mom. Grandchildren and wee little toddler great grandchildren grouped together on stage to sing-song their rendition of "happy birthday." Blooming like the proverbial rose was the 80-year-old honoree. In attendance with his pretty wife, the former Katie Manhard, was Don Pall, pitcher for the White Sox.

AND WHAT…..an honor it was to meet Bill Lefakinis, owner of Valef Yachts with international headquarters in Greece and USA headquarters in Pennsylvania. The ever-charming international entrepreneur formed his company in 1969 with only one yacht. But with hard work and persistence, he now owns 150 forming the largest fleet of yachts for charter in Europe. The delightful Lefakinis, who has been featured on Robin Leach's, "Lifestyles of the Rich and Famous," convinced me that chartering yachts in Greece is the way to go for it is easy, inexpensive and an enchanting way to spend a vacation. So if you enjoy the tranquility of the water, the exclusivity of the Greek Islands (and there are 4,000 to choose from), the privacy of remote beaches and secluded bays, and if you have from six to 30 friends you would like to share the yachting experience with, give me a buzz for I have it all together.

ONE OF……the most innovative invitations on record was the one sent out by the Karkazis family of Deerfield, inviting us to a surprise birthday bash honoring Euthemia "Babsey" Karkazis at the Seven Hills on January 8th. It was a photo of Babsey, taken in her high school heydays when she was crowned beauty queen in Los Angeles – wearing her long, flowing Venetian rich coronation robe, carrying her scepter, her lovely face shining as brightly as the dazzling crown perched on her head . Here she comes – Miss America!

The cocktail dinner bash was attended by over 100 people. While Babsey thought she had planned a surprise birthday party for daughter, Georgene Shanley, Georgene had skillfully planned a surprise party for her mom's birthday. The only one privy to the real plans of honoring both ladies were the remaining members of the Dr. Lambros Karkazis family: Dr. Frank and Lisa Karkazis – and handsome Anthony Karkazis. It was a double whammy. Both Babsey and Georgene were calling in menus to the manager of the Seven Hills – while the real menu was being executed by the other members of the family.

Balloons, magicians, mouthwatering food, congeniality, laughter, and a real sense of accomplishment by the other three hits and a miss – for having fooled the honorees – brought gales of laughter to all of us. Highlighting the event was the appearance of George Matsukas of Santa Inez, California, Babsey's handsome brother.

QUOTE OF THE WEEK: "Love is of all passions the strongest for it attacks simultaneously the head, the heart and the senses." Voltaire

"The trouble with advice is that you don't know whose to take; and if you know whose to take, you don't need advice."

THE WHOLE.....town is buzzing with excitement over the forthcoming opening night dinner gala at which the spectacular new exhibit, "Threads of Tradition – Greek Costumes from the Dora Stratou Collection" will be unveiled. Sponsored by the Hellenic Museum and Cultural Center, the gala will take place on March 11th at the Chicago Historical Society. According to Roula Alakiotou and Elizabeth Melas, co-chairwomen, the event will be one of the most elegant on record for it will encompass an evening of tastefully prepared dining and divine entertainment for those attending. Cocktails and hors d'oeuvres will be offered in the Portrait Gallery prior to the serving of dinner. Classical Greek music will be provided by the Linardakis Band both during and after dinner.

Never before exhibited in the United States, the unveiling of the Dora Stratou Collection, with its elaborate craftsmanship, is certainly a coup for the sponsors. The evening's festivities will include a ribbon-cutting ceremony, and traditional Greek folk dances performed by the Orpheus and Apollo Dance Troupe. The Dora Stratou Collection, which consists of over 2,500 complete costumes, will premiere in the Chicago Historical Society's Cudahy Gallery from March 11-25. The exhibit will then be displayed at the Hellenic Museum and Cultural Center from April 1 through June 1.

GLOBETROTTING IN…….and around the country are the following peripatetic friends: Pretty bachelorette Kim Chelos took a Princess cruise to Australia and New Zealand and wowed them with her glamour; Ion Caloger paused in Athens – then took the big bird on to Kuwait, Jeddah, Dhahran and Riyadh; in Los Angeles at the time of the quake, playing in the sun, was Anthony Karkazis who said that suddenly everything shook, rattled and rolled; Frank and Lisa Karkazis off to the most picturesque spot of all – the sun-drenched skies of Los Cabos; Phyllis Colovos and her daughters on holiday in St. John for some girl talk; Bill and Thalia Zane off to the exclusive Caneel Bay Resort – also in St. John; Ann Zoros – off to Denver to help plan her daughter Melissa's forthcoming wedding.

While February is the month for hearts and flowers – it is also the month for traveling to Florida as did Michael and Callie Panagiotou, Gus and Tula Mazarakis, Chris and Gloria Pappageorge, Helen and Alice Anthony; Nick, Aggie, Bob, Karen, George and Lisa Kafkis; Dino and Marie Leventis; Jaimie and Sophia Childs; George and Eileen Maniates. John and Ann Graven cruised the Caribbean aboard the Holland-American.

PROMINENT WASHINGTONIANS…will be in attendance at the 19th Anniversary Public Service Awards Dinner, scheduled to take place on March 5th at the Four Seasons in the nation's capitol. The black tie event will honor Arianna Stassinopulos Huffington, the Honorable Nicholas Petris, the Honorable Olympia Snowe, Michael Dennos,

Conrad Valanos and Linda Evans' squeeze, Yanni. Cuz Aliki Gregory Bryant, formerly of Chicago, is honorary chairlady; Ernie Anastos, well-known media anchor in New York, and formerly of Evanston, will be the master of ceremonies.

QUOTE OF THE WEEK: "When a great deal is expected of a child, he either rises to the expectation or is crushed by it; and this is why an expectation that is not realistic can cripple a child as much as depreciation does."

"Masculine vanity is so great that the only flaw in being a grandfather, which most men enjoy, is the uneasy realization that one is married to a grandmother."

THIS WEEK....we point with pride to a pretty young miss, with extra-strength smarts, Kathy Galanis of Kenilworth, who recently was assigned to one of Chicago's most publicized cases of child abuse. The assignment was made by Jack O'Malley, states attorney.

The media broke the case on February 1st when it was discovered that 19 children had been abused, neglected and abandoned by six mothers, at 219 N. Keystone Avenue. The children were taken to various area hospitals and examined. Two had signs of physical abuse; the other children made statements that they had not eaten. Only one of the six mothers came home at 11pm; another was at the hospital giving birth to her second cocaine baby. One mother was charged with cruelty to children; other mothers were charged with misdemeanors.

Being assigned to this mega case that reached international proportions publicity wise, was quite a coup for Kathy who has been in the states attorney's office for eight years. A trial specialist, she did her undergraduate work at Southern Methodist University, where she received a degree in business administration; she received her law degree at John Marshall Law School.

A PULL-OUT......all the stops production that exceeded the most ambitious fantasies of Perle Mesta was the recent Monte Carlo Benefit sponsored by the Hellenic Foundation. The elegant event took place at the Four Seasons in Chicago on January 28th. Over 200 staunch supporters raised over $60,000. Congratulations are in order to Paul Athens, general chairman; Maria Gebhaard, co-chairwoman, and to Anna Akrivos, silent auction chairwoman, for their untiring efforts in acquiring sponsorships and donated items for the Silent Auction. The entire evening was filled with the priceless ingredients of Monte Carlo style casino games, a silent auction which featured mega acquisitions, and music that made dancing a lot of fun.

THE WORLD.......of wee little people recently added another member to its roster. His name is Alexander Craig, son of Dr. Frank and Lisa Karkazis, who weighed in at 7 lbs 10 oz. He is the grandson of Dr. and Mrs. John Panton of River Forest and Dr. and Mrs. Lambros Karkazis of Deerfield.

ALL THE.....would be Picasso's will have their artistic wares on display at the forthcoming annual spring arts and crafts fair to be sponsored by the St. Nicholas Ladies Philoptochos Society of Oak Lawn. The display will take place on March 19-20. Over 70 exhibitors have been carefully selected to ensure a show of varied and unusual crafts.

THOSE WHO....are interested in attending the forthcoming George Dalaras Concert would be wise to make their reservations immediately – for tickets are going fast. A major international singer from Greece, who is renowned for selling out concert halls worldwide, he will be performing at the Arie Crown Theater at McCormick Place on April 2nd. Sponsored by the Hellenic American Congress, the Pancyprian Association of America and the Cypriot Brotherhood of Greater Chicago – it will be a sellout performance. George Dalaras has sold more than seven million albums of his own works and those in which he collaborated with other artists like Mikis Theodorakis and Manos Hadjidakis.

QUOTE OF THE WEEK: "A husband who doesn't look at other women generally doesn't look at his own very much either."

"We seek advice when we feel weak, rather than when we feel strong; yet the insolence of strength is often much more in need of counseling than the flutterings of weakness."

THE WORD...."farewell" always triggers off feelings of sadness in me for it means the end of the road and not the beginning. Its finality is quite sobering. These feelings of sadness came upon me when I received the notification that the United Hellenic American Congress, the Greek Orthodox Church Communities of the Chicago Diocese, and the Greek Orthodox Ladies Philoptochos Society were organizing the Midwest Farewell Testimonial Dinner Dance for our beloved Consul General of Greece, the Honorable Spyridon Dokianos, and his lovely wife, Maria Lisa.

I believe this dinner dance is the first of its kind, and I heartily congratulate those who came up with the idea – for while we have always been blessed with outstanding consuls, our Mr. Dokianos is, in my opinion, the finest man who has ever graced the portals of the Midwest consulate. With his warmth and compassion he has touched the hearts of all of us since his arrival in Chicago in 1976 for he has responded to people and to causes with attention, sensitivity and dignity – never slighting even the slightest among us.

In the past four years Mr. Dokianos has brought us admirable leadership. And so we honor this unique man who is being recalled to Athens for a new assignment in the Central Service of the Ministry of Foreign Affairs.

The dinner dance honoring him will take place at the Continental Plaza on July 18th and it will begin at 7pm with cocktails and hors d'oeuvres, accompanied by Franz Benteler and his Royal Strings. An outstanding dinner has been planned by general chairman Tony

Antoniou – a charismatic individual with oodles of admirers. Serving as toastmaster will be one of our town's greatest humanitarians – a man we can all point to with pride both nationally and internationally – Andrew A. Athens, national chairman of UHAC. A special commemorative program book has been planned which shall list all of the guests present.

BOO-HOO'S……are in abundance since it was announced that one of our town's most elegantly charming gentlemen, Alexander Mitrogos, Commercial Attache of Greece in Chicago, was being transferred to Stockholm, Sweden. The announcement of the transfer did not give any of us the opportunity to tell this marvelously cultured gentleman how much his presence did for our Chicago scene. So – with a melancholy typing ribbon we bid both he and his beautiful Icelandic wife – a tearful goodbye.

AND YET… another round of applause to Tom Kapsalis who was recently made Commissioner, Department of Aviation, Chicago. The appointment was made by Her Honor Mayor Jane Byrne – and she could not have picked a more capable guy. Tommy had taken over operations at O'Hare – giving the then Aviation Commissioner Pat Dunne an assist. Now he is the main player at O'Hare. Let's color him hard-working, bright, and successful.

QUOTE OF THE WEEK: "It is fruitless to look back upon our parents and grandparents and exclaim that they got along better in marriage than the majority of people do today. They got along better because they expected less, and we, unfortunately, live in an era of rising expectations, not only economically, but emotionally as well."

"How many travelers would bother to take trips if they were bound to a vow of silence about the venture upon their return?"

IN THIS.......chaotic and sometimes overwhelming world – some really surprising things do occur: One Thursday night, while watching people's blood and guts spill out on TV's most successful show, "ER," the faces of the handsome Zanes (Bill and Thalia) flashed across the screen in an "ER" elevator scene. I looked again and there they were big as life. It seems that Bill and Thalia had been invited to daughter Lisa's birthday party – so they had taken the big bird to Los Angeles for the occasion. At the time, Lisa was filming the episode in which she played the girlfriend of handsome hunk, George Clooney. She invited her parents to come on the set to meet her co-workers. After being introduced to the famous and the wanna-be-famous, somebody on the set called out that extras were needed for the elevator scene. Bill and Thalia were selected. Showtime for the senior Zanes.

In the meantime, son Billy, is busy in South Africa filming the adventure flik, "Danger Zone" with Robert Downey, Jr. On June 6th, the handsome Billy and the not-so-handsome Downey appeared on "Entertainment Tonight," and clips from their filming were shown. Aside from Billy's outstanding talent as an actor, he has the most magnificently dulcet voice. Next time you see him on screen, close your eyes and just listen. You'll see or rather hear what I mean.

HER CAPACITY...for delight was refreshing, her energy was boundless, and her graciousness was legendary. Athena Youtsos died on May 20th in her Evanston home, leaving a void in the hearts and minds of those of us who knew and loved her. One of our town's prettiest seniors, she was the wife of the late Nicholas Diacos and the late Gust Youtsos; the loving mother of Dee (Frank) Moss of San Francisco and Harriet Becharas of Evanston. So beloved was she by her family that all of her grandchildren and their families took the big bird in from San Francisco (Geoffrey, Dr. Gregory and Jonathan Moss); and from Boston (Tina Moran) to see their yia yia prior to her death and they all returned a second time to pay their last respects at her funeral. Her other two grandchildren, Stephanie Domark and Brian Becharas, reside in Evanston.

THE WORLD.....of wee little people was enriched in July by the addition of two potential femme fatales –Cynthia Elizabeth and Julia Christine – the Tsaoussis twins born to Solon and Patty. And, of course, the most loving tribute was the printing of cards by Themis and Frances Tsaoussis, grandparents, announcing their birth. Nice news about nice people.

IN THE.....inimitable gracious entertainment style of Larry and Georgene (Karkazis) Shanley all guests were pampered with delectable food – a la Georgene – following the christening of their daughter, Mia Marie, on August 27th at Sts. Peter and Paul. The reception was held at their Palatine home. Mia was named after her maternal grandmother, Euthemia Karkazis, and she is just as pretty, too. Godparents were Dr. and Mrs. John Tasiopoulos and Michael Cullen.

QUOTE OF THE WEEK: "Many people marry largely because they are afraid of loneliness; unaware that the loneliness within an ill-considered marriage is the most bleak and solitary of all."

THE STAFF OF THE GREEK PRESS IS WEARING ITS HEART AT HALF MAST SINCE THE DEATH OF ITS BELOVED EDITOR AND PUBLISHER, ARIS ANGELOPOULOS. ARIS HAD A LEGION OF FRIENDS, AND I WAS PROUD OF THE FACT THAT I WAS ONE OF THEM. HIS BRILLIANT MIND, HIS DISTINCTIVE PERSONALITY, AND HIS TALENT AS A JOURNALIST WILL ALWAYS BE REMEMBERED BY ME. IT WILL TAKE AWHILE TO ACCEPT THE FACT THAT THIS PERIPATETIC EDITOR WILL NO LONGER BE AROUND TO SHARE HIS THOUGHTS WITH ALL OF US.

INDEX

A

Adinamis, Kathy, 36, 41, 249
Adinamis, Michael, 45
Adinamis, John, 121, 233, 255
Adinamis, Peter J, 114, 205
Agnew, Spiro, 27, 32, 103, 138, 174
Akathiotis, Chrystyan, 269
Akrivos, Anna, 340
Alakiotou, Roula, 337
Alevizos,George , 18, 112
Alevizos, Connie, Bill, Timothy, Susan, Mary Jane, 125
Alexander, Magdaline, James, 28, 279, 282, 289
Alexander, George, Marina, 213
Alexander, Dean, Nicholas, Menda, 231
Alexandrakis, Menelos, 152
Alissandrato, Urania, 238
Allas,, Peter, Bill, Mary, 68
Alles, Debbie, 269
Anagnos, Marion, 152
Anagnost, Peter, 112
Anagnostopoulos, Chris, Stash, 43, 48
Anagnostopoulos, Kevin, 48
Anagnostopoulos, Dr. Lambis, 297
Anagnostopoulos, Nicholas, 141
Anargyros, Georgia, 15
Anast, Stanley, Gust, 41
Anastaplo, George, 288
Anastos, Dina, 33, 54, 65, 66, 83, 23, 268, 274
Anastos, Ernie, 339
Anastos, Nick, 131
Anastos, Ted, 274
Anderson, Martha, 130
Andonaides, Nina, Dimmy, 41
Andonaides, Nicholas, 199
Andreakis, Maryanne, 269
Andreakis, Tessie, 194
Andrews, Arthur, 195
Andrews, Christ, Marika, Theodora, 53
Andrews, George, Cleo, 24, 162, 214
Andrews, Harriet, 16, 28, 53, 279

Andrews, Peter, 16, 28, 53
Andrianakos, Tom, 273
Angelopoulos, Aris, 249
Angelopoulos, Sam, Renee, Katina, Peter, 320
Annes, Christine, 155, 211
Annes, George, 27, 198, 210, 293
Annes, John, 211, 293
Annes, Virginia, 211
Anton, Gus. 130
Anton, Mary, 210
Anthony, Alice, 10, 29, 158, 272, 318, 338
Anthony, Angela, 10, 29, 318
Anthony, Helen, 10, 16, 29, 158, 272, 318, 338
Anton, Stephanie, Peter, 272
Antoniou, Tony, 158, 206, 298, 312
Antoniou, Irene, 298
Apikos, Mrs. D, 101
Apostol, Dr. James, 64, 162, 214
Apostol, Mary, 64, 214
Apostol, Spiro, 64, 204, 214
Argiris, Bessie, Gust, Sam, 87
Argiris, Tasia, Dr. James, 285
Arsland, Mary, 245
Arvenitis, Clara, Vicky, 92
Arvenitis, Peter, 92, 102
Arvites, George, 198
Askounis, Thomas, Bessie, George, 13
Assimos, Angeline, George, Helen 205, 270
Assimos, Dean, Steven 270
Assimos, Gus, 199, 205, 270, 311
Athans, Tony, John, 311
Athens, Andrew, 36, 49, 146,148,150, 153, 163, 197, 200, 217, 219, 223, 249, 254, 265, 276, 297, 311, 330, 342
Athens, Aris, Irene, 147
Athens, Aristides, Dr. William, 146
Athens, Louise, 148
Athens, Paul, 340
Atsaves, George, 50, 265

B

Bacaintan, Dina, 145, 146, 199, 272, 310, 318, 326, 334
Bacaintan, Nicholas, 128, 334
Bacouris, Tom, Christine, John, 28, 273
Bafalis, Paul, 197
Bakakos, Elaine, 261
Bakakos, Kiki, 261, 262, 318
Bakakos, Lee, 269, 318
Bakakos, Peter, 151, 261, 262, 318, 304
Bakalis, Dr. Michael, 17, 39, 91
Balourdos, Steve, Mike, 89
Banis, Solon, 40
Bartholomew, Amelia, Georgette, Michael, 259
Bartholomew, George, Theresa, 315
Bartholomew, James, 30

Bartholomew, John, 30, 327
Bartholomew, Mary, Pat, 30, 315
Bartholomew, Theo, 30, 229, 259, 315
Basil, Joanne, 40
Batchos, Mrs. Louis, 101
Bazos, Chris, 327
Becharas, Brian, 335, 343
Becharas, George, 335
Becharas, Harriet, 291, 335, 343
Becharas, Mary Lee, 269
Besbekis, Gloria, 164
Betzelos, Angelo, Bessie, 91
Betzelos, A. Steve, 91, 134, 149
Betzelos, Irene, 66, 149
Betzelos, Jim, 16, 74, 88, 90, 91, 122, 134, 137, 166, 194, 210
Betzelos, Peggy, 91, 122
Betzelos, Persey, 16, 74, 88, 90, 91, 122, 166, 194
Betzelos, Peter, 193,
Betzelos, Steve, 91, 269
Bilder, Angelo, Chryssie, 258
Bilder, Dorothea, 40, 258
Bilissis, Linda, 294
Bisoulis, Becky, 164, 291, 304, 305
Blanas, Mary Ann, 120
Blasé, Faye, 78
Blasé, Nicholas, 25, 39, 204
Booras, Betty, 96
Booras, Sam, Georgia, 56, 133
Boosalis, Dean, John, Kay, 202
Boosalis, James, Bonnie, Sam, Connie, 48
Boosalis, Pam, 290
Boukidis, Calleroi, 151
Bourbules, Esther, 126
Bournakis, Rhea, Louis, 211
Bouzeas, Phil, 249
Boznos, Peter, 17
Brademas, John, 153, 163, 197
Brahos, Helen, 40
Brotsos, Adeline, 88, 312
Brotsos, Bart, 312
Brotsos, Holly, 269
Brotsos, Jim, 98, 106, 120, 312
Brown, Charlene, 80
Brown, , Chris, 221, 284
Brown, Gregory, 157
Brown, Helen, 82, 157, 221
Brown, Maribeth, 269
Brown, Peter, 82, 157, 204, 221
Bryant, Aliki, 31, 51, 128, 146, 272, 284, 310
Bryant, William, 31, 51, 128, 272, 284, 310
Bugelas, Cleopatra, 13
Bugelas, George, Kathryn, 13, 43, 221
Bymkos, Maria, 37, 42, 45
Bymkos, Nicholas, 37, 45
Byrne, Mayor, 249, 297, 298

C

Callas, Maria, 78
Caloger, Ethel, 92, 329
Caloger, Ion, 92, 329, 338

Canellis, George, Nancy, 68, 314
Canellis, George, Jr., 68
Canellis, Lou, 314
Cantonis, Ann, 145
Cantonis, George, 145
Cantonis, Maria, 272, 334
Cantonis, Michael, 27, 145, 198
Cappas, Peter, 36, 124, 272
Caras, Elaine, 226,245
Caras, Mrs. Louis, 226
Carres, Sophie, 16
Caruso, Angela, 124, 165, 213, 249, 253, 287, 297
Carvel, Tom, 58
Cavin, Lillian, 328
Chaimes, Nicholas, 200
Chakonas, Socrates Mrs., 78
Chakos, Maria, 269
Chandilis, George, 124
Chandris, Anthony, 53
Chelos, Kim, 338
Chiakulas, Dr. Peter, 89, 108
Chiganos, Becky, 209
Chiganos, Demetra, 195
Chiganos, Sophia, 270
Chiganos, Rev. William, 195, 270
Childs, Alex, 269
Childs, Gigi, 11, 62, 204, 243, 273
Childs, Helen, 11, 62, 101, 102, 273, 312, 328
Childs, Jaimie, Sophia, 338
Childs, Peter, 11, 62, 93, 101, 102, 124, 228, 273, 312, 328
Chimoures, Evie, Peter, 37, 43, 45
Chimouris, Pamela, 37, 44
Chimpoulis, Rosemary, 98
Chioles, Elizabeth, Ann, 102
Chioles, Constantine, 47, 102
Chionis, Connie, Angelo, 116
Chionis, Melanie, 322, 330
Chionis, Nicholas, 116, 274, 313, 322, 331
Chionis, Mrs. Spiro, 280
Chipain, Mrs. George, 209
Chirigos, E. M., 198
Chirigos, Nancy, 52
Chiropulos, Angeline, Tina, 263
Christopoulos, Mrs. Peter, 67
Christos, Roula, 52, 62
Christos, John, 75
Christy, Lorraine, 25
Chrones, James, 204, 310
Chrones, George, Connie, 253, 283
Chronopulos, Rev. Isaiah, 297
Cocallas, Tiana, 108
Cocoris Christa, 34, 246
Cocoris, William, Matia, 64, 134, 246
Colis, Peter, 93
Collias, George, 166, 207, 290, 315, 322
Collias, Jean, 146, 207, 315
Collias, Joanna, Jane, 282
Collias, Nick, 282, 315
Collins, Mrs. Nicholas, 78
Colovos, Dena, Peter, 263

Colovos, Jennie, 93, 144
Colovos, Phyllis, 166, 207, 290, 315, 322
Colovos, Soto, 105, 263
Colovos, Steve, 93, 141, 144
Colovos, Terri, 79, 93, 104
Condos, Paulette, 92
Coniaras, Rev. Anthony, 57
Conomikes, George, 156
Constandy, John,197
Constantinidis, Rev., 156
Contoguris, Christ, 41
Contos, Christopher, 272
Contos, Gregory, 316, 332
Contos, James, 316
Contos, Katherine, 272, 312
Contos, Rev. Leonidas, 56
Contos, Nick, 88, 267, 272, 312, 332
Contos, Peter, 325
Contos, Peter, 267, 272, 312, 332
Contos, Stella, 88, 316, 332
Coorlas, Eugenia, Stratte, 229
Coorlas, Helen, 229, 303
Coorlas, Peter, 267, 272, 312, 332
Corolis, James, 16, 71, 81, 95, 105, 116, 210, 267, 313, 322, 332
Corolis, Joanna, 313, 331
Corolis, Lee, 95, 100, 116, 210, 313
Corolis, Melanie, 116, 274, 313
Costakis, James, 133, 232
Costakis, Cathy, 245
Costopoulos, Tom, 133, 189
Costopoulos, Helen, Jane, 133
Cotsilis, Michael, 195
Cotseones, William, 198
Cotsirilos, George, 212, 217, 238
Cotsirilos, Theresa, Stephanie, John, George, 238
Cuser, Mrs. Andrew, 41
Cullen, Michael, 344

D

Dadas, Don, Demi, 221, 256
D'Agnese, Irene, 300
Dakajos, Stephanie, 245
Dalaras, George, 340
Damianos, John, 106
Dangles, Chris, 110
Dasaky, Florence, 9, 127
Dasaky, Chuck, John, 106
Daros, John, 137
Dedes, Bess, 108
Deligiannis, Antonia, 40
Deligiannis, Helen, 305
Demas, Angeline, Bill, Gust, 92
DeMet, Nick, 47
DeMet, Sophia, 102
DeMets, Pierre ,18, 90, 153
DeMets, Thula,153
Demeros, Sia, Arthur, Athena, 267, 332
Demes, Mrs. George., 40
Demetrios, Patriarch, 265
Demetriou,. Chris, 109

Demetrius, Andrew, Mark, 268
Demetrius, Evelyn, 234, 268
Demopoulos, Madeline, 13, 28
Demos, John, Paul,198
Dennis, Nick, Mary, 210
Dennos, Frank, 338
Deree, William, 16, 138
Diacos, Nicholas, 343
Diacou, Irene, 9, 29, 312, 333
Diacou, Stacy, 166, 174, 312, 333
Dinou, Christ, Helen, John, Kriton, Marina, 67
Diodoros, Patriarch, 249
Diveris, Mary, 146
Dokianos, Spyridon, Maria, 141, 152, 341
Domark. Stephanie, 343
Drakalovich, Fokas, 233
Dranias, Dean, 52
Dukakis, Olympia, 311
Dumas, Constance, 210
DuMez, Floraine, Frank, 329
Dunkas, Nicholas, 191
Duros, John, Kay, Constantine, 216

E

Economos, Cathy, James, 328
Economos, George, 105
Economou, George, 41
Ellis, Clara, 43
Ellis, Christ, Betty, 99
Esposito, Charles, 70
Ezekiel, Archbishop, 142

F

Fanaras, Helen, 329
Fardulli, Jean, 249, 277
Farmakis, Daisy, 10, 16, 71, 74, 98, 105, 167, 272, 332
Farmakis, Mary, 98
Farmakis, Peter, 10, 86, 98, 272
Fasseas, Kathy, 144
Fasseas, Milton, 127, 144
Fay, Alexander, Lea , 328
Fistedis. Stanley, 249, 297
Flambouras, Cassandra, George, Frances, 241
Flessor, Mrs.Gus, 88
Fotopoulos, John, 81, 93
Fotopoulos, Toula, Gus, 275
Fotos, Connie, 13, 98, 275
Fotos, Curt, 275
Fotos, Perry, 13, 87, 167, 275, 291, 322, 334
Frengou, Toula, 95
Furla, Theodora, 245

G

Gallanis, Craig, 279
Gallanis, Helen, 279, 321, 322, 328
Gallanis, Kathy, 279, 322, 328, 339

Gallios, Debbie, Pete, Sue, Jim, Vannie, 188
Gallios, Dr. John 195
Ganas, Irene, Terry, 129, 158
Ganas, Jim, 130
Ganas, Peter, 129
Gardeakos, Helen, 130
Garoufales, Mathew, Byron, Irene, 251
Gatsis, Mrs. George, 31, 38
Gatsis, Mary, 312
Geane, George, 62
Geane, Georgia, 112
Geane,Niko, 291
Geannopoulos, Harriet, Nicholas, 187
Gebhard, Maria, 340
Gehopolos, Mrs. Christine 16
Gelenianos, Michael, 141
Geocaris, James, 252, 304
Geokaris, Adeline, 330
Georgakakis, Rev. Peter, 212
Georgantas, James, 40
Georgas, Peter, 304
George, Peter, 93
George, Nicholas, Harry, Mary, 194
Georgeson, Tula, 146
Georgis, Mitzi, Ted, 68
Georgopulos, Violet, 60
Georgoules, Eugenia, Thomas, Vicki, 143
Georgouses, Phillip, 28
Geroulis, Judge James, 87, 277, 304,323
Gianacakos, James, 18
Gianaras, Alec, 71, 84, 124, 160, 168, 198, 230, 235
Gianaras, Alex, 168
Gianaras, Kay, 64
Gianaras, Vi, 97
Gianes, Thomas, 17
Giannakakos, Manny, 333
Giannakis, Nike, Dennis, 64
Gianopoulos, Debbie, 10
Gianukos, Denise, 120, 147
Gianukos, Peter, 114, 144, 147, 198
Gianukos, Pota, James, 147
Giatrakos, Constantine, 141
Gigios, Rev. Dean, 63
Gleason, John, 31, 43, 50
Gleason, John Sr., Mrs. John, 50
Gleason, Maria, 126, 128
Goetz, Mrs. Peter, 209
Golemis, Diane, 128, 315
Gordon, Mrs. G., 11
Gordon, Phyllis, 195
Gouletas, Evangeline, 75, 107, 114, 158, 169, 196, 224, 237, 295, 297, 299, 323
Gouletas, Nick, 75, 107, 114, 158, 169, 196, 224, 237, 295, 323
Gouletas, Victor, 75, 107, 114, 169, 196, 224, 237, 295
Gouletas, Steve, Maria, 169
Gouletas, Andrea, Victoria, 300
Gouvis, Angela, 245
Govostis, Costa, 86

Govostis, Dean, 225
Govostis, Dr. James, 170
Govostis, Dr. Mike, 170, 201
Gramas, John, 19
Graven, Anastasia, 74, 117, 124, 157, 160, 171, 175, 213, 312, 322, 334
Graven, John, 16, 74, 117, 124, 139, 171, 205, 213, 266, 267, 275, 278, 312, 322, 334
Gregory, S.J., 31, 51, 86, 128
Gregory, Rev. Basil, 38, 142
Gregory, Rita, 31, 128, 145, 285
Grigoropoulos, Sotirios, 17, 14, 198
Grim, Silke, 335

H

Hadjidakis, Manos, 340
Halikias, Michael, 330
Hannon, Joseph, 213
Harrington, Delphi, 159
Harris, Gus, Eugenia, Kay, 216
Hatsos, Michael, Anna, 200, 214
Heard, Chuck, Katherine, 40, 139, 251, 296
Heard, Diana,40, 251, 296
Heard, Carla, Charles, 40, 251
Hepburn, Katherine, 81
Heropoulos, Michael, 28
Hill, Craig, 316
Hondras, Rev. John, 118, 199
Hondras, Lou, 118, 123, 199, 281
Houpis, George, Maita, 210
Huffington, Arianna, 338

I

Iliopoulos, George, Peter, 273
Ioakimidis, Tony, Joan, Dr. Panos, Voula, Midas, 10

J

Jannes, Nicholas, 16, 63, 92, 249, 259, 293
Jianas, Alex, 328
Johnson, Mike, Kay, 24
Johnson, C.N., 198
Jones, Mrs. Joeffrey, 41

K

Kafkis, Aggie, 10, 30, 56, 86, 95, 171, 203, 216, 218, 272, 275, 295, 338
Kafkis, Bob, 48, 296, 338
Kafkis, George, 86, 214, 275, 295, 228
Kafkis, Karen, 338
Kafkis, Lisa, 338
Kafkis, Nick, 10, 30, 86, 171, 203, 204, 216, 218, 272, 275, 295, 338

Kagianas, Bill, 16, 29, 252, 267, 273, 285
Kakarakis, C.G., 198
Kakis, Stanley A., 36
Kalamatis, Christ, 131
Kalevas, Mrs. George, Dawn, 40
Kallas, Dessa, 117
Kalogerakis, A. Freddie, 117
Kalogeras, Chris, 108, 114, 205, 263, 313
Kalogeras, Pauline, 108, 313
Kaludis, Peter, 134
Kamberos, Frank, 224, 330
Kamberos, George, 45
Kamberos, Peter, 312
Kambilis, John, Yetta, Mrs. John, 10
Kanakaredes, Melina, 317
Kanakis, Estelle, 254
Kanellos, Helen, 294
Kanellos, Mary, 156
Kanellos, Nick, 28,156, 198
Kanellos, Theodora, 35, 60
Kanellos, Tom, 193
Kangles, Constantine, 210
Kanton, Mrs. Andrew, 11
Kapsalis, Tom, 155, 172, 230, 342
Kapsimalis, George, 328
Karafotias, Angie, 56, 97
Karafotias, Christ, 27, 198, 199, 253
Karafotias, George, 28, 253
Karafotias, Nicholas, 253
Karakas, Nicholas, 330
Karakourtis, Kay, 99
Karalis, D.N., Pauline, Elena, George, 56
Karambelas, John, Ann, 30
Karampelas, Doria, 159
Karanikas, Alexander, 144, 249, 259
Karavites, Christine, Peter, 95
Karazeris, Mrs. Michael, 74
Kariotis, Elizabeth, 41
Kariotis, Georgia, 62
Karcazes, George, 33, 62 91, 132, 235
Karcazes, Roula, Demetrius, 132
Karkazis, Anthony, 257, 267, 326, 332, 337, 338
Karkazis, Euthemia, 74, 95, 107, 210, 257, 267, 322, 327, 328, 332, 336, 340
Karkazis, Frank, 257, 276, 313, 337, 338, 340
Karkazis, George, 188
Karkazis, Georgene, 257
Karkazis, Helen, 328
Karkazis, Lambros, 74, 95, 107, 257, 267, 322, 327, 328, 332, 336, 340
Karloutsos, Rev. Alex, 142, 224
Karloutsos, Rev. Michael, 224
Karloutsos, Rev. Peter, 224
Karp, George, Denise, Danielle, 136
Karras, Marion, 98
Karras, Nicholas, 309
Karris, Mrs. George, 96

Karrys, Mrs. Effie, 25
Karup, Anna, 87
Katsenes, Karen, Nicholas, 37
Katsenes, Cynthia, 98
Katsis, Vickie, 66
Kaulentis, Dana, Jim, John, John, 136
Kavathas, Helen, 268
Kavooras, Dorothy, 152
Kazantzakis, Helen, 287
Kennedy, Hope, Robert, 329
Kerhulas, Rev. Chris, 263
Kezios, Rev. Spencer, 224
Kiotas, Theodosis, 267
Kladis, Mary, Nick, 68
Klovens, Georgia, 321
Kmieciak, Peggy, 216
Koconis, Angela, 269, 290
Koconis, George, Tula, 290
Koconis, Jim, 290, 291
Koconis, Mary, 37, 95, 130, 202, 205, 206, 290
Koconis, Pamela, 37, 45, 201
Koconis, Peter, 37, 130, 202, 205, 206, 290
Kokkinakis, Archbishop, 199
Kokoris, Charles, 304
Kokoris, Elaine, 151
Kokoshis, Dennis, 40
Kontos, Evon, Diane, 329
Kontos, Shirley, 41
Koopmans, Katherine, 298
Kopan, Alice, 50, 265
Kopan, Andrew, 50, 144, 150, 172, 205, 246, 249, 258, 265, 266, 297, 324
Kopan, Sophie, 205
Kopley, Charles, Sam, 106, 216
Koplos, Bess, 78
Kopsian, Alex, 50, 333
Korbakes, Chris, Marianthe, 272
Koretos, Dino, Dana, 97
Koretos, Helen, 43
Koretos, Vance, 48, 97
Koretzky, Danny, 48
Koretzky, Sophia, 49, 64, 105, 134, 218, 246, 264
Kornaros, Achilles, 315, 316, 322
Kornaros, Danae, 207, 322, 315, 316
Kornaros, Nicholas, Aristotle, 315
Kostantacos, Tasha, 245
Kosner, Alyssa, 275
Kotsakis, Alexandra, 40
Kotsakis, Mrs. Michael, 78
Kotsinis, Maria, 211
Kotsiopoulos, Georgia, 164, 312
Kotsos, Mary Ellen, 325
Kouchoukos, Deborah, 38, 45
Kouchoukos, James, 38
Koudounis, Chris, 13
Koudounis, Eugenia, 13, 25
Kouimelis, Annette, 36
Koukis, Mimi, Nick, 24
Koulogeorge, Mary, 109, 289
Kounanis, Mrs. James, 78
Kountouris, Emanuel, Maria, 157

Kouracos, Bill, 93
Kouracos, Jean, 67
Kouros, George, 74
Kuchuris, Frank, 137, 224, 235
Kuris, Milton, Angela, Chris, 94
Kurtides, Stephen, 191
Kurtides, Mrs. Stephen, 74
Kusulas, Elias, 195
Kutulas, Rev. John, 224, 261
Kutrumanes, Michel, 98
Kyriazopoulos, D.G., 297

L

Lambesis, Tasia, 88
Lambros, Andrew, Ted, Jeannie, 271
Lambros, Yiannis, Antigone, 249, 282, 294
Lamnatos, Athey, Christ, 205
Lamperis, Dean, Helen, 129, 158
Lamperis, Glykeria, Alex, 28, 279, 282
Lamperis, Nicholas, 129
Lampros, Constantine, Connie, 130
Lampros, Laura, Louis, Ann, 335
Lappas, Kathy, 127
Laskaris, Mrs. Denny, 40
Latto, Rev. Dennis, 71, 122
Latto, Lula, 132, 212
Latto, Stamo, Nicholas, 238
Lazarus, George, 123
Lefakinis, Bill, 336
Legaros, Christopher, Nicholas, 159
Legaros, George, Connie, 143, 159
Leibrandt, Tom, Marianne, Sara, 313
Lelon, Tom, 9, 124
Lelon, Alexis, 9, 18, 31, 38, 124, 194
Lelos, Candy, George, 202
Leonard, Jean, 71
Leroux, Charles, 248
Leventis, Angelo, 310
Leventis, Dino, Marie, 156, 216, 272, 328, 338
Leventis, Vicki, 131
Liakos, J. Dimitri, 41
Liakouras, Chris, Bill, 227
Lianos, Nick, Peggy, 93, 205, 234
Liapis, Peter, 312
Liaros, Bill, 192, 212
Liaros, Dolores, 212
Liaros, Deanne, 269
Limperis, John, 304
Limpert, Charles, Diana, 264
Linardos, Rose, 321
Lithas, Harry, 95, 291, 316
Lithas, Helen, 42, 95, 316
Litsas, Fotios, 249
Lolakes, Mrs. Paul, 25, 209
Lulias, Kurt, Helen, Curt, Jr., Cheryl, Jennifer, Allison, 261

M

Machinis, Fay, 152, 240, 328
Machinis, Peter, 240, 328
Macridis, Consul General Nicholas, 76, 86, 121, 228, 231
Macridis, Toni, 76, 86, 126, 231
Macridis, Alexander, 228
Maharis, Helen, 205
Makris, Joanna, 131
Malas, Mattina, 205
Males, Spiro, 122
Malevitis, Louis, 197, 273
Malleris, Mrs. Gus, 215
Mallis, Handa, 235
Mammas, Virginia, Steven, 38,45
Manatos, Mike, 197
Mandis, Kathryn, 41
Manhard, Don, Jean, 95, 336
Manhard, Katie, 336
Maniates, Cynthia, 247
Maniates, Eileen, 191, 247, 338
Maniates, George, 61, 129, 199, 247, 338
Mannos, George, 195
Mannos, Nicholas, 39
Mannos, Tom, 214
Manos, Kay, 18, 33, 215, 225
Manos, Mary, 110
Manos, Nicholas, 18, 29, 33, 36, 66, 68, 174, 189, 213, 215, 225
Manos, Stathia, 215, 225
Mansour, Marie, 245
Manta, Ann, Jimmy, 336
Manta, Frank, 286
Manta, Mrs. Frank, 38
Manta, Mrs. John, 10
Manta, Mrs. Stephen, 215, 245
Mantelos, Stella, 54
Mantice, Helen, 13, 213, 216
Mantice, Tina, 213
Mantice, Tom, 13, 159, 213, 216
Mantzores, Peter, 128
Manus, George, Maria, 10, 129, 142, 158, 239, 255, 306
Manus, Irene, 10, 129, 142
Maragos, Cleo, 122
Maragos, Sam, 122, 203, 239, 264, 298
Maragos, Tom, Jim, 122
Margaris, Theano, Papazoglou, 41
Margarites, Andrew, 198
Marinakis, Constance, 146
Marinakos, Leon, 10, 36, 86, 106, 145, 154, 175, 204, 249, 254, 287, 309, 317
Marinakos, Maria, Constantine, 145, 309
Markos, Nicholas, Kiki, Georgia, Socky, Christopher, 333
Markoutsas, Elaine, 37, 40, 111, 119, 134, 148, 202, 232, 247, 249, 270
Markoutsas, Mrs. George, 40
Marks, Bea, 126, 154, 219, 260
Marks, George, 154, 198, 298

Marks, John, Christopher, Andrew, Nicholas, Dean, 154
Marks, Niki, 298
Marlas, Connie, 256
Marlas, Dennis, 16, 256, 309
Marlas, Helen, 309
Marlas, Jennifer, 256, 280, 309
Maros, Alexandra, 279, 315
Maros, Bess, 240, 279, 291, 314, 316
Maros, Frances, 315, 316
Maros, Jim, 137, 206, 240, 279, 314, 316
Matis, Nicholas, 163
Mastoris, Dr. Michael, 303
Matsoukas, Anthony, 139, 257
Matsoukas, Avra, Niki, David, 159
Matsoukas, Dan, 48
Matsoukas, George, 337
Matsoukas, Mary, Euthemia, 139
Matsoukas, Nick, 34, 158
Mazarakis, Daphne, 110, 319, 264
Mazarakis, Gus, 40, 71, 101,110, 264, 312, 319, 332
Mazarakis, Thomas, 40, 101, 110, 264, 319, 338
Mazarakis, Tula, 40, 71, 101, 110, 264, 32, 338
McCormick, Hope, 127
McDowell, Dena, 130, 332
McHale, Chrisanthe, 245
Melas, Danny, Dorothy, 257, 291
Melas, Elizabeth, 337
Melas, Nick, 159, 176, 220, 234, 249, 255, 262, 274, 291, 297, 301
Melonides, Mrs. Spiro, 71
Merakou, John, Irene, 222
Mercouri, Melina, 281
Mezilson, Christ, 152
Mezilson, Dorothy, Michael, Shirley, 240
Mezilson, Jimmy, 125, 152, 240, 249, 254, 328
Michalaros, Anthony, 80, 206
Michalaros, Demetrios, Helen, 80
Michalaros, Ellie, 206
Michale, Mary, 9
Michaels, George, 194, 251
Michas, Chris, 52
Michas, Luke, Bess, 24, 48
Michas, Mariane, Anthony, 24
Michols, Stephanie, Steven, 329
Mikuzis, Constantine, 199
Mikuzis, Steven, 144
Mikuzis, Peter, 93, 104, 105, 141, 144, 199
Mikuzis, Terry, 98, 105, 141, 144, 199
Mircic, Snezena, 316
Milonas, George, Electra, 86
Mitchell, Georgia, 86, 190, 212, 268
Mitchell, Louis, 330
Mitchell, Dr. Nicholas, 36
Mitchell, Peggy, 79, 98
Mitrogos, Alexander, 301, 342

Mitrogos, Karitas, 301
Mitsakopoulos, Jack, 330
Mokas, Mrs. James, 78
Monzures, Maria, 105
Moran, Tina, 343
Moschaidis, Mrs. John, 24
Moskos, Alexander, 177
Moskos, Charlie, 177, 288, 329, 330
Moss, Jonathan, Frank, Dee, 335, 343
Moss, Geoffrey, Dr. Gregory, 343
Mouskouri, Nana, 127, 149, 189
Munger, Jim, 137
Murphy, Constantine, Daniel, 326

N

Naktos, John, 197
Nassos, Ernie, Marie, 80
Nassos, Jeanette, 12, 25, 60, 80
Neubauer, Ellen, 262
Niarchos, Charlotte, 24
Nicholaou, Nicholas, 330
Nicholas, Lou, Vickie, 252
Nichols, Anthony, 36
Nichols, James, 151, 198
Nicholson, Dr. John, 288
Nickas, Andrew, 130
Nicklas, Dr. Jim, 10, 188
Nikolaidis, Nicholas, 41
Nicolopulos, Vickie, Demetrios, 236
Nielsen, Penny, 291
Nikoloulis, Panagiotis, 116, 275
Nikoloulis, Dana, 275
Nikolopoulos, George, 198
Nikolopoulos, Paul, 159
Nixon, Mrs. Richard, 127
Noplos, Philip, 130

O

Onassis, Aristotle, Christina, 237

P

Pakis, Mrs. John, 18
Pall, Don, Katie, 36
Palmer, Elaine, 91, 122
Panagiotou, Michael, Callie, 136, 328, 338
Pandas, Connie, 40
Panos, Ernest, 249
Panos, Peter, 81
Pantelis, George, 97
Panton, Christina, Peter, Evan, Robert, 327
Panton, John, 327, 340
Panton, Mrs. John, 74, 327, 340
Panton, Lisa, 326
Papadenis, Mrs. John, 78
Papageorge, Evan, 28
Papageorge, Helen, 56, 229
Pappageorge, Chris, 36, 62, 81, 132, 217, 247, 248, 254, 283, 338

Pappageorge, Elias, Gus, Kathryn, Vicki, 247
Pappageorge, Faye, 62, 234, 338
Pappageorge, Gloria, 62, 132, 141, 248
Pappageorge, George, 247, 248, 283, 320
Papaioannou, Nicholas, 141
Papanicolaou, Dr. George, 149
Papanikolaou, Rev. Byron, 18, 142, 263, 286
Papas, Constantine J., 198
Papas, Dina, 128, 261, 318, 334
Papas, Elaine, Bradley, Curt, 318
Papas, Gregory, 129, 261, 318
Papas, Mrs. James, 38
Papas, John, 198
Papas, Mrs. John, 31
Papas, Maria, 25, 54, 78, 105
Papas, Pamela, 38, 33
Papas, Spiro, 31, 51, 145, 261
Papaspyrou, Demetrios, 141
Pappas, Bill, 41
Pappas, Chris, 35, 47, 73, 116, 190, 230, 236, 275, 291
Pappas, Cleo, 149
Pappas, Dana, 48, 116, 190, 203
Pappas, Elaine, 35, 47, 116, 190, 230, 275, 291
Pappas, Fofo, 10
Pappas, Gary, 190, 269, 275
Pappas, Gus, 110, 201, 202, 272, 91
Pappas, Helen, 240
Pappas, Joan, 110, 201, 202, 272
Pappas, Jimmy, 205, 230
Pappas, John, 190, 275
Pappas, Kathleen, 269
Pappas, Lucy, 149
Pappas, Maria, 25, 54, 78, 105
Pappas, Milt, 11, 126
Pappas, Peter, 202
Pappas, Steven, 195, 209
Patras, Harriet, 18
Patras, Jim, 130
Paulos, Mrs. Constantine, 40
Paulos, Dr. Louis, 11, 100
Pavlakos, Dino, Jean, 16, 90, 108, 263
Pavlakos, Harold, 90, 108, 263
Pecharas, Thomas, 41
Pekras, Rev. Philip, Chris, 92
Penn, Barbara, 104, 131, 226
Pepke, Daniel, 335
Ponie, Harold, 249
Peponis, Jim, 36
Percy, Senator Charles, 29, 32, 33, 94, 197, 200
Pergakes, Phyllis, 15, 62
Perivolidis, Arthur, 62, 304
Perry, Mrs. Dimitri, 159
Perry, Stanley, 11
Petas, Susan, 245
Peters, Christina, 117, 214
Petrakis, Andrew, 13
Petrakis, Harry Mark, 10, 34, 159, 178, 213, 223, 249, 278, 288
Petrakis, Rev. Mark, Stella, 9
Petris, Hon. Nicholas, 338

Petropoulos, Eugenia, 13
Petropoulos, Athanasios, 87
Phelus, Dean, 81
Philippidis, Nina, 286
Philippidis, Nick, 249, 286, 325
Philippidis, Yvonne, 94, 286, 305
Phillips, Dr. and Mrs. Theodore, 43
Phillips, Frank, 133
Phillips, George, 198
Photopulos, Bud, 55, 121, 179, 219, 262, 283, 292, 320
Photopulos, Georgia, 55, 92, 121, 136, 179, 203, 219, 262, 283, 292, 320
Photopulos, Jimmy, Kerry, 121, 262
Pichinos, Sophie, Nikki, 41
Pilafas, Eugenia, 79, 87
Platis, Dena, Iakovos, Panagioti, 263
Politis, Alexandra, Lucas, 38, 45
Polydoris, Eva, 9, 15, 63, 141, 310
Polydoris, Stuart, 141, 310
Porikos, Georgia, George, 219, 298
Porikos, Kathy, 219
Porikos, Peter, 298
Poulakidas, Aliki, 227
Poulos, Angelyn, John, Rose, Dean, Jeanne, Jim, Pete, 331
Poulos, Gus, 156, 222, 331
Poulos, Mrs. James, 9, 56, 95, 222, 227
Poulos, James, Niki, Steven, Connie, Nancy, 222
Poulos, Steve, Priscilla, 73, 156, 331
Powers, Lucille, 16
Powers, Marianne, 130
Prassas, Nicholas, 198
Presvelos, Gus, Amphie, 313
Price, Bill, Holly, Dr. Kevin, 260
Price, Debbie, 76
Principato, Nathan, 195
Prodromos, John, 78, 112
Prodromos, Althea, 100, 112
Prodromos, Debbie, 274
Psyhogios, James, 195
Pullos, Lynne, 87
Pyshos, Carol, Constantine, 67

R

Regas, Georgia, 33, 250
Regas, Jim, 249, 250, 254
Regas, Pete, 312
Regas, Suzanne, Dean, Allyson, 250
Relias, Mrs. Alexis, 43
Rexinis, Eugenia, Rev, 194
Rexinis, Theano, 36, 41, 60, 194, 214
Rigas, Lynn, 269
Rochester, Jennifer, 263
Rummel, Bill, 200
Rummel, Mrs. Zoe, 16, 200
Russis, Connie, 139, 251, 26

Russis, Euthemia, 156, 251
Russis, James, 48, 139, 158, 251, 267
Russis, Martha, 35, 139, 158, 251, 296
Russis, William, 101, 106, 139, 158, 249, 251, 296
Russis, Vasili, 251,267

S

Sacopoulos, Eugenia, 85, 112
Safrithis, Margaret, 41
Sakellarides, Dr. Achilles, 197
Sakoulas, Byron, George, Goldie, 13
Samaras, John, 13, 28
Sampalis, Cynthia, 269
Sampalis, Elaine, Nicholas, 38, 45
Sampalis, Sue, 45
Sapounakis, Mrs. Paul, 24
Sarantakis, Georgia, 87
Sarbanes, Paul, 153, 163, 197, 220
Sarlas, Chris, 130
Sarocco, Elaine, Kathie, Toni, Robert, Billy, 247
Savalas, Telly, 141
Savas, Tina, Pat, 130
Savoy, Elena, 249
Scholomiti, Mrs Nicholas, 40
Scoulas, Alexandra, 189, 192
Scoulas, Catherine, 192
Scoulas, Rev. George, 192, 210, 212, 261, 289
Scoulas, Mary, 192, 210, 289
Secaras, John, 33, 36, 181, 271
Secaras, Maria, 271
Secaras, Mary, 12, 37, 52, 79, 87, 99, 271
Sedares, Billy, 36, 116, 247, 248, 251, 286
Sedares, Louis, Katherine, 247
Seifer, Herman, 143
Selz-Cheronis, Thalia, 132
Seno, Ginie, 268
Sfondilias, Steve, Mary, 205
Shanley, Georgene, 320, 322, 327, 328, 336, 344
Shanley, Larry, 320, 322, 327, 328, 344
Shanley, Mia, 344
Siavelis, Arlene, 131
Sigalos, Lou, 210
Simmerman, Andrew, 262
Sinandinos, Jim, 130
Singh, George, 239, 255, 306, 320
Singh, Jack, 142, 239
Singh, Irene, 158, 239, 255, 306
Skan, Leon, 94, 239
Skan, Martha, 33, 94
Skan, Mary Ellen, 126
Skontos, George, 146, 230, 239
Skontos, Ioanna, 230
Skontos, John, Mary, 146
Skontos, Kathy, 215, 230
Skoules, Lillian, Steve, 329

Skountzos, Nick, 138, 296
Skuteris, Regina, 16
Smenos, Ann, 10, 192, 195, 209, 291, 296
Smenos, Brian, 204, 26
Smenos, Daria, 296
Smirles, Jim, 124
Smyrniotis, Bess, 315
Sofianopoulos, Tasia, 285
Sorokos, John, 76
Soter, Art, Tina, 13
Soter, S.D., 106, 249
Sothras, Nicholas, 77
Spheeris, Andrea, Andrew, 51
Spiropoulos, Esther, 325
Spyrrison, Pandora, 120
Spyros, Diana, 25
Stamas, Mrs. George, 15
Stamelos, Maria, 300
Stamos, Colleen, 269
Stamos, Daisy, 180
Stamos, Helen, Theo, Jana, 304
Stamos, James, 288, 304
Stamos, Judge John, 16, 180, 304
Stamos, Paul, 50, 265
Stamos, Sam, Mrs. Katherine, 16
Stassinopoulos, Arianna, 305
Stassinopoulos, Jean, 51, 146
Stassinopoulos, Margarita, Nicholas, 51
Stathas, Pericles, 27
Stathos, Michael, 29
Stavropoulos, Ernest, 324
Stavropoulos, George, 300, 305
Stefanos, Michael, Sophia, Leo, 270
Stevens, Ann, Steve, 35
Stevens, Dr. Basil, 72, 198
Stevens, Cat, 101
Stevens, George, 232
Stevens, Julia, 72, 198, 285
Stevens, Katherine, 105, 232
Stevens, Stanley, Kiki, 105
Stitzel, Stan, 133
Stratigos, George, Julia, 42
Stray, Mary Kay, 117
Stuart, Malcolm, 63
Svourakis, Mike, 36, 92

T

Tappas, Nicholas, John, Connie, 324
Tarachas, George, 24
Tarant, Christine, William, 329
Tarant, Elaine, 136
Tarsino, Dr. Louis, 86
Tasiopoulos, Dr. John, Connie, 344
Terzis, Ioannis, 190
Terzis, 41, 60, 65, 188, 190
Teska, Connie, 284, 322
Teska, Mike, Bethany, Laynie, 322
Thalassinos, Panayiota, 145, 309
Thalassinos. Rev. Theodore, 145
Theodorakis, Mikis, 231, 340
Theodore, Connie, 147

Theodore, Matina, 147, 322, 328
Theodore, Peter, 147, 284
Theodore, Theodore J., 28, 198, 199
Thodos, George, 182, 288
Timotheos, Bishop, 72, 126, 212, 216, 225
Tomaras, Dr. and Mrs. Andrew, 195
Tompary, Peter, 16
Tompary, Mrs. Gust, 44
Toscas, Pamela, 245
Trakades, Ida, 130
Trapalis, George, Helen, Mary Ann, 24, 42
Treantafeles, Tina, 329
Trigourea, Gladys, Mary, Bessie, Sam, Kiki, Esther, 313
Trilikis, George, Peter, 200
Tripodis, Alexandra, 38, 45
Tripodis, Marinos, Mr. and Mrs. 38
Trivelas, Carrie, Rev. Nick, 251
Troy, Helen, 205
Tsaoussis, Cari, 62, 202, 344
Tsaoussis, Cynthia, Julia, 344
Tsaoussis, Frances, 62, 202, 344
Tsaoussis, Solon, 344
Tsaoussis, Themis, 62, 106, 202, 344
Tschilds, Mrs. Ivan, 40
Tsenekos, Bill, 95
Tsenes, George, 41
Tsongas, Paul, 197
Tsoumas, A.T., 268
Tubekis, Alex, Phyllis, Rita, 202
Tubekis, Bessie, 285
Tubekis, Dino, 107, 189, 326
Tubekis, Elizabeth, 51
Tubekis, Susan, 326
Tzakis, Andrew, 30, 183, 193, 207, 229, 321, 327
Tzakis, Cynthia, 117, 193, 210
Tzakis, Dee, 9, 38, 40, 71, 87, 105, 117, 124, 125, 146, 166, 193, 210, 267, 269, 280, 332
Tzakis, Irene, 11, 14, 30, 56, 65, 97, 123, 183, 199, 207, 219, 229, 303, 315
Tzakis, Jeannie, Renee, 302
Tzakis, Marcia, 193, 210, 251, 269
Tzakis, Nicholas, 207, 229. 269. 288. 302
Tzakis, Nick, 193, 210
Tzakis, Sam, 87, 117, 146, 193

Valanos, Conrad, 339
Vallas, Mrs. Gust, 38
Vallas, Paul, 184, 330
Valone, Katherine, 231, 249
Valos, George, 189
Valos, Thomas K., 198
Vanides, Steve, 195
Varney, Kathy, 131
Vaselopulos, Helen, 288
Vaselopoulos, Popi, 294

Vaselopoulos, Renee, 131
Vaselopoulos, Spyros, George, 331
Vasil, Leo, 10
Vasilatos, Anastasios, 41
Vasilomanolakis, Joanne, 132
Vasils, Themi, 112, 114, 133, 185, 237, 256, 287
Vasils, Theodora, 133, 185, 237, 256, 287, 291
Vastis, Maria, 326
Vavoulis, Beverly, 124
Vavoulis, George, 75, 124
Veikos, Thomas, 331
Verveniotis, Niko, 138, 196
Vlachos, Angela, 245
Vlachos, Dimitri, 201
Voutiritsas, Fannie, 304
Vovos, Bobby, Mary, Anda, Aris, 203
Vusikas, Maria, 269

W

Wilson, Bess, 288, 328
Wrasman, Brent, 117

X

Xanthopoulos, Rev. Joseph, 313
Xenakis, Rosemary, 60, 65
Xeros, Gus, Julie, Peter, 42, 95
Xeros, Katie, 42, 95, 291

Y

Yanni, 339
Yiannas, Constance, 269
Youtsos, Athena, Gust, 343
Ypsilantis, Evan, 81

Z

Zafiratos, James, 304
Zaharis, Basil, 53
Zane, Bill, Thalia, 323, 338, 343
Zane, Billy, 276, 317, 320, 343
Zane, Lisa, 317, 320, 343
Zappas, Gust, 137
Zeppos, John, 136
Zervos, Rev. George, 313
Zettos, Fran, 10, 95
Zografopoulos, Kosta, 211, 311
Zombanakis, Minos, 127
Zoros, Ann, 95, 291, 338
Zoros, Ted, 95
Zoros, Melissa, 338
Zoumboulis, Tina, 43, 66